MEMOIRS OF A TRUMPET TEACHER

SAM BENNETT

WWW.MARTINSISTERSPUBLISHING.COM

Published by

Martin Sisters Books, a division of Martin Sisters Publishing, LLC

www.martinsisterspublishing.com

ISBN:978-1-937273-13-2
Memoir

Printed in the United States of America
Martin Sisters Publishing, LLC

DEDICATION
"To Ann, who inspired me to finally get off of my keister and put these stories into a book!"

Martin Sisters Books
An imprint of Martin Sisters Publishing, LLC

CHAPTER ONE

"Anthony! *Aaannnthony!* Come on down for your trumpet lesson!"

I had forgotten what an unbelievably nasal voice Anthony's mom has, but I am glad she called him to start his lesson. It's already 3:47, and his lesson was supposed to start at 3:40. I try to finish at Anthony's house by 4:10, because then I have to go to Teddy's house to start his lesson at 4:15. I don't want to get behind schedule after just the first lesson of the day. After a few more *"Aaannnthony's"* from his mom, he finally stumbles down the stairs. He seems as excited about his trumpet lesson as I am.

As I wait in Anthony's basement, I notice a few unusual items while I look around. When you wait in basements for students to come downstairs as often as I have to do, you start to notice things. And...Anthony's basement is full of *really bizarre* stuff. I can see three sets of brass knuckles, a mace, and several knives of assorted sizes. C'mon, Anthony, hustle! I don't really want to hear you play your trumpet, but I am dying to ask you about those brass knuckles that are on the table. I wonder if he knows what they are.

"Yeah, Mr. B, sure I know what they are. I play with them all the time. They're cool! Do *you* know what they are? I can show you how to use them. If you want, you can take some home. I've got lots of 'em.'"

Let's see, I can take some home...yeah, a set of brass knuckles on the coffee table would be a real conversation starter. I can put them right next to the cement shoes. "Uh, no thanks, Anthony."

He then tells me that his dad uses these items all the time at work, and that dear old dad brings home some of the extra ones. Well, maybe his dad just has a knife throwing act in the circus! I try not to gulp too loudly as I ask:

"What kind of work does your dad do, Anthony?"

"Oh, he works for some lawyers."

"Does your dad use the knives at work, too?"

"Yep, he says the lawyers sometimes have tough meat on their sandwiches, so first they pound on them with the brass knuckles, then they cut them with the knives. You can have some of those knives too, if you want."

Anthony proceeds to hold up some of the knives for me to touch.

Great, I'm thinking! Those sandwiches must be very tasty, if they go to that much trouble to make them. I hope Anthony's dad at least washes off the blood and any leftover DNA after he uses them. What a nice thing it is for a father to bring home souvenirs from work for his ten-year-old kid to play with! That way they can keep everything in the family, and pass down the family business from one generation to the next. Maybe I'm teaching "The Godfather's" grandson! I have visions from the movie: I can hear that kid who was practicing his trumpet scales while Brando was getting shot at the fruit stand. Can you hear him tooting his trumpet, too? I wonder if that kid's name was Anthony.

With my luck, if I touch these knives, the police will come storming in here. Then I'll be arrested for some mob murder. How am I going to explain *that* to Ann?

"No thanks, I don't really want to hold the knives." I tell Anthony.

"You sure, Mr. B? Here, look how they stick in this table when I throw them."

Wham!! Wham!! Wham---

"OK, Anthony, I can see. Thanks for the demo."

As I look around the basement some more, I can see that he does have the latest video games, a baseball glove, and some baseball cards.

"Anthony, do you ever play video games?"

"No, they're boring."

"How about baseball? I see you have a glove."

"No, I've never gotten into that. I just like the stuff my dad brings home from work. I play with those things all the time, Mr. B! Let me show you something else."

Now Anthony goes to get some of his little sister's dolls, and proceeds to punch them several times while wearing the brass knuckles. According to Anthony:

"My dad says I'm doing a good job with these, but I need to concentrate more on hitting the nose."

I'm not going to ask what his sister thinks.

Then Anthony notices something about this "toy:" "Oh yeah, this is the set of brass knuckles that has some red marks on it. I can't seem to wash the red off. Can you try, Mr. B? Please?"

"Well, I better not, Anthony. Uh...I think I'm catching a cold." Gee, for some reason I don't believe these red marks are from his sister's dolls, unless dolls bleed nowadays.

"OK, Mr. B. Thanks anyway. Maybe dad can get the red out."

Anthony also tells me that he's going to bring the brass knuckles to school soon because he is the "Star of the Week." His dad will be coming to school as part of a program where the kids learn what their parents do at work.

"Are you bringing the knives, too?" I ask.

"Oh yeah, them too." he replies.

"Can I come to your school on that day, Anthony?"

I'd love to be a fly on the wall during that discussion.

7

Speaking of flies, they never have a chance in Anthony's basement. Not flies, nor ants, nor any other kinds of bugs. I'm not sure why, but Anthony's basement seems to have lots of crawling or flying objects in it. When Anthony sees one during his lesson, he immediately puts down his trumpet and waits for the bug to land on the table. Then, showing unusual quickness for a ten-year-old, he duct tapes the bug to the table while it is still alive (yes, duct tape!), quietly picks up his trumpet, and waits for my next instruction, as if nothing had happened. During the course of the lesson, there might be five or six bugs duct taped to this table, struggling to escape and slowly expiring. I hope they like the sound of the trumpet, because that's the last thing they're going to hear! Maybe we should be playing *Taps* for each of them. It took me a while to get used to this sight, but it never seems to bother Anthony. Also, their basement doesn't seem to get cleaned very often. After a few months of lessons, I can see twenty or thirty of these duct taped flying martyrs that are stuck to the table. Anthony never says a word about it.

I've been teaching Anthony once a week, at his house, for almost three years now. He has a very nice mom and, big surprise; she always pays me in cash. So far, however, I've never met his dad. I have taught Anthony at many different times of the day and evening, and I also teach him sometimes on Saturday morning, but his dad always seems to be at work. I better continue being nice to Anthony. Otherwise, I may have to get someone to start my car for me. Just in case.

As Anthony's trumpet playing improves, he keeps asking me if he can learn this one popular song that his dad really likes. For weeks now, I've been telling him to be patient, until he becomes good enough to play it. Anthony's trumpet playing isn't quite to the point where he can play this particular song. Maybe he can in another few months, but not now.

However, today Anthony tells me that his dad *really* wants him to learn the song *soon*. He doesn't want Anthony to have to wait any longer, and he hopes that I understand. I look around at the brass knuckles and the knives, and I tell Anthony:

"Don't worry, Anthony, *I completely understand.* I'll make a recording of the song, with me playing the melody on my trumpet. That way, you can practice along with it. Don't worry if you get lost while you're playing the song. Just pretend to go on playing while my recording keeps going. Do you think that would be OK with your dad?"

"Oh yeah, Mr. B, I'll keep going. Dad will like it, or else he'll let you know about it somehow."

He'll *let me know about it* somehow! Oh man, please don't put a horse's head in my bed! I better make this recording a good one.

*

I started teaching Anthony the "Theme from The Godfather" that very day. After a few weeks of practicing it with the recording, Anthony played it for his dad. I had told Ann that I was worried about what his dad's reaction might be. "He sleeps with the fishes" keeps crossing my mind. Now I arrive for Anthony's next lesson. I start stammering, trying to ask Anthony what his dad thought of the performance. I sound like Piglet from "Winnie the Pooh:"

"Uh-uh-uh, so Anthony, d-d-did your d-d-dad like it?"

"He sure did, Mr. B! He told me that he liked it so much that he wants to do something for you."

Wow, what a relief! He wants to do something for me? Hmmm. Right away, I can think of several of my students that he might be able to rub out...nah; I still need the money I get from teaching them: out...nah; I still need the money I get from teaching them: "Well, Anthony, let me think about that for a while---"

Just then, I start to hear someone walking down the stairs, but I can only see a large shadow on the wall coming down each step. The shadow's getting closer and bigger, and it looks like it's pointing something long and skinny towards me. I think I'm about to get shot by Alfred Hitchcock! As the shadow reaches the bottom step, I hear a low, booming voice:

"You must be Mr. B! I'm Anthony's dad. I loved it when Anthony played "The Godfather" for me. Here's a nice bottle of wine for you and your wife. Thanks for helping him with the song. Anthony, get Mr. B some brass knuckles to take home, too. They're a riot to have around the house."

"Thank you, s-s-sir, my wife will be glad that I made it home safely tonight... err, I mean, with the wine."

*

After Anthony's lessons, I often go to Teddy's house, just a few blocks away.

I teach Teddy at 4:15. Teddy is also ten like Anthony, but he's not the most dynamic trumpet student. In fact, I rarely have a "normal" trumpet lesson with him. He often leaves his trumpet at school, or he can't find his music. I always bring one of my trumpets with me, so I'm able to demonstrate for the kids, and show them different kinds of brass instruments. I also carry extra music with me, so the excuse of forgetting his trumpet songs at school doesn't work too well for Teddy, either. He really doesn't want me to come over and teach him, but I show up there every week, anyway! His mother had originally contacted me, and after a few months of these frustrating lessons (for me, anyway), I finally explain to her that maybe Teddy just doesn't want trumpet lessons.

"Oh no, no," she says. "He's *very* interested...keep coming over and he'll show you." OK, show me what?

Teddy realizes that his plan of forgetting things isn't working, so he starts to not come home by 4:15...or 4:30...or 4:45, which is the end of his lesson. So, I end up sitting in his basement for a half hour, while his mom tries to find him. And, there are no brass knuckles for me to play with, either! Most often, Teddy just walks home from school *very slowly* (he should normally be home by 3:30). I've often ended up giving him a fifteen, or ten, or even a five-minute lesson. Some weeks, I only have time to tell him to practice the same music for next week as I run out the door to go to my next student's house.

If his mom is home when I get there, then she'll go and look for him. But, if she is out somewhere, I have to sit in my car for the entire time. Unfortunately, this had happened quite a lot over my seventeen years of teaching trumpet lessons. It isn't so bad in nice weather, or when it's still daylight, but in the winter, and at night, thirty minutes can seem like an eternity! I never have enough time to go to a restaurant or store and warm up, so after about fifteen minutes of waiting I just drive to my next student's house. I'll try to start their lesson early, if *they* are home. There's nothing more fun than sitting in my car, in the dark, when it's about two degrees outside. Ah, just another perk of teaching trumpet lessons!

Well, finally today, our studious young trumpeter Teddy gets home on time. He actually has his trumpet, and he has his music, too. Maybe he's ready for a quality lesson this time? Not quite. Teddy still has no interest in playing the trumpet, let alone taking private lessons. I've been finding out recently that he has one more plan to avoid having his lessons, and that is to become sick as often as possible. His illnesses the past few weeks aren't the typical ten-year-old problems, such as "my stomach hurts," or "my head hurts." When Teddy gets sick, he really gets sick. I've been hearing him say:

"Mr. B, my liver has been acting up." or:

"I think I'm having a flare-up of my pancreas today." Or, here's my favorite:

"Well, Mr. B, I'm sorry to tell you that I've been coming down with leukemia in the last hour, so I can't breathe too well. I guess we'll have to stop the lesson. Good-bye." Amazingly, he is always very calm and matter-of-fact about these life-threatening problems. I was shocked the first couple of times he did this, but then I began to look forward to his newest medical situation. After announcing his illness of the week, he would then go up to his room, leaving me in the basement. I'd go up and find his mom, and explain to her what he just told me. She would just shrug, say "Oh, that's too bad," pay me, and tell me to come back next week, at which point the whole process would start all over again. I always want to laugh when he tells me his disease-of-the-week...where *does* he come up with these wild ideas? Then, the following week, I would ask him about his big problem from the week before. He would just tell me in a very deadpan voice:

"Oh, Mr. B, that cleared up nicely." Or:

"The doctor said it was a miracle. I have no more symptoms. See?" He would then point to whatever part of his body had the phenomenon, and start pushing on it. *Eewww!*

"Great news, Teddy! I don't... err, can't believe it."

I've realized that I've been wasting too much of my time with Teddy, and I've decided that if he springs another infirmity on me today, this will be his last lesson. He's actually been playing OK so far today, but after about ten minutes of the lesson, he starts gyrating around and moaning, as if he's in pain. I can sense that he is rehearsing his illness announcement in his head. I bet I'll be informed of it soon. I can't wait...this will be the last ailment I have to hear about for poor Teddy...I sure hope it's a good one!

"Uh, Mr. B, I have some bad news. I've been told that my colon has been 'blurping' back and forth, and I have to go lie down. Good-bye."

I can't help myself:

"Oh, Teddy, I was always told that it's a good thing when your colon 'blurps' back and forth. I've actually had that, too. In fact, that happened to me when I rang your doorbell today. Let's keep playing...that should help the 'blurping' to settle down."

Teddy won't give up that easily, however:

"Oh no, Mr. B, it's OK when your colon 'blurps' up and down, but when it 'blurps' back and forth, that's very dangerous. I have to stop right now."

As Teddy starts up the stairs, he turns and says:

"And, Mr. B, I can't have a lesson next week, either. My arm's been bothering me, and I think they have to amputate it. And the *only* time they can do it is right before our lesson time."

I go up and tell his mom what he said. Once again, she barely looks up at me as I explain his latest calamity. She just shrugs, tells me "that's too bad," pays me, and says "see you next week." Uh, I don't think so, lady. I've had it with Teddy and his maladies.

"Excuse me, ma'am, but this has to be Teddy's last lesson. I'm going into the Witness Protection Program soon. They'll be setting me up as a proctologist in Spillville, Iowa. What do you think of that idea? Oh, and please don't tell anyone. So long!"

Even that didn't get a rise out of Teddy's mom. She yawned, and just said "that sounds good." Then she turned, and walked away.

I've always wondered whatever became of Teddy. Maybe I should Google him...I bet he's a surgeon now!

*

Starting at 4:50, I teach Michael and his brother David back-to-back, which makes it easier on me and on my car, especially in the winter. Their basement has every game and toy imaginable, and every week when I go to their house, there are *even more* new games and toys. Plus, they get entire new game systems, too. When I ask the brothers how they like these new gadgets, however, they say that they are boring and that they don't care about any of them. They'd rather just play their trumpets, and be in the Band at school, which is a very refreshing attitude for me.

The most unique item in the boys' basement is a photograph, about 20 x 30 inches in size. It's in a frame, hanging on the wall right in front of us. It's a picture of a woman on a beach, and it just shows her neck down to her stomach, so you can't see her face. The woman is wearing a bikini top, but the unusual thing about it is that one side of the bikini isn't on, thus exposing one of her boobs.

I haven't said anything about the picture to the boys in all the weeks I've been teaching them, even though this oversized boob is only about five feet in front of us. The brothers haven't said anything, either. It seems to me that they are about the right age to start being curious about things like this, but I guess they must be used to the picture. Finally, my curiosity gets the better of me, and I ask Michael about it. He's thirteen, and is the older brother. I would think that he has to be fascinated by something like this! That 20 x 30 boob has been staring us in the face every week...what is it doing there, and why doesn't- anyone seem to care?

"So, Michael, that's an interesting picture on the wall."

"Oh yeah, that's my mom."

What? That's your *mom!* Now, his parents are very nice, but they're not exactly Madonna and Sean Penn. They seem like a typical middle-aged couple: he's bald, and she always wears baggy sweat suits. Her figure isn't exactly like an hour-glass; it's more like a shot-glass. Now I'm going to have to make conversation with their mom every Monday, while I see her picture in my head.

"Michael, let's turn around and face the other way, OK?"

At this point, what else can I say to him? Maybe:

"Boy, Michael, your mom looks like..." Or:

"Michael, your mom's a real..."

No, maybe I better not say anything.

We turn our chairs around for the lesson, and Michael never brings up the photo again. After Michael's lesson, I decide that I'll talk to his brother, eleven-year-old David. He has a more outgoing personality than Michael, and maybe he can provide me with some insight. I have to get to the bottom of boob-gate:

"So, David, that's an interesting picture on the wall."

"Yeah, that's my mom. My dad took that picture when were in Mexico. He said he liked it and wanted to blow it up bigger. Then he took it to another store and they framed it."

"Uh, David...what did your mom think about all this?"

"Oh, at first she didn't know about it. My mom said she was adjusting her top, and didn't know dad snapped the picture. My dad surprised her with it on her birthday. She was really mad at first, but then dad showed it to everyone at mom's birthday party."

"Your dad did that?" I can feel my chin hitting the floor.

"Yeah, and all the other men at the party said it was *awesome*. They started to ask their wives if they could take a picture like that, too. All except Mr. Fahartland, our neighbor, who didn't say anything. My dad says *Mrs.* Fahartland weighs about two and a half bills. I think that means she puts her money on her bathroom scale. Anyway, Mr. Fahartland looked sad when he saw the picture."

I'm almost speechless by this point, but not quite:

"Uh, David...what did your mom say when everyone at the party was looking at the picture?"

"She got a little red, but then she started talking to Mr. Becker, and they were laughing together for a long time while he kept touching the 'picture-boob.' All of a sudden, my dad yelled at me to go to bed. The next day, dad was gone when I got up, and he didn't come back for about a week. Mom said he was on a business trip."

I have to ask:

"What kind of work does your dad do, David?"

"He's a gynecologist. Most of the neighbor ladies are his patients, including Mrs. Becker, and Mrs. Fahartland."

Now, I am speechless. I must be in the middle of the 1980's version of *Desperate Housewives*.

I'm also trying to imagine the clerks at the drug store who got to develop this picture. Remember, this is 1984, way before home computers, the Internet, etc. To get your pictures developed, you take them to the camera store or the drug store. The one-hour-photo people develop them for you, and then you pick them up a few hours later. That picture must have been the hit of the store. I wonder: did they give the family half-off for development?

Then, after seeing the picture, the dad brought it back to be blown up to 20 x 30 size, which took a few more days! And, he even brought it to yet another store to have the picture framed! I bet whenever this family drops off pictures at the store, no one calls in sick the next day when they're going to get developed. And, I always wonder, do they ever use that picture for their Christmas card? I can see it now:

"Happy holidays from Mexico. Wish you were here!"

*

It's usually about 5:50 when I finish David's lesson, and then I have ten minutes to get to Sam's house for his 6:00 appointment. Most of the time this schedule works out well, unless there is too much ice and snow, or my car door handle freezes, or if I have been plowed in during the lesson.

My last lesson of the evening finishes at 9:00 pm, so I don't get to eat dinner until I get home at about 9:30. Sometimes, however, parents seem to feel sorry for me (it must be my sympathetic Puss 'n Boots eyes), and they give me a piece of pizza, or a chicken leg, or whatever they are eating when I'm at their house. Often, I basically eat at these houses from 5:00 to 9:00, while at the same time blowing into my trumpet and teaching the lessons. What a veritable smorgasbord I have, and I get to do this while teaching three nights a week! Ah, just another thing they didn't teach me about in college.

Arriving at Sam's at 5:58, I ring the bell and am greeted by Sam's mom, Mrs. Levin. I have to walk up five or six steps to get to the front door, and the person answering the door is still two or three feet above you. Mrs. Levin is almost always the one who answers, and it can be quite interesting when she opens the door (to say the least). If the weather is cold, she wears some kind of robe, but if the weather is warm, she always has on a bikini and sunglasses. Mrs. Levin is about 5' 10'', and is quite skinny. Try and imagine the angle I now have as I look up at Mrs. Robinson...err, I mean Mrs. Levin. Remember, she is standing two or three feet above me as the door opens. Gulp:

"Hi, Mrs. Levin."

"Hi, Mr. B." she says in a rather sultry voice.

"Go on up to Sam's bedroom....he's waiting." As I brush past her on my way upstairs, she smiles again, still looking out from behind her sunglasses.

Sam and I get started with his lesson. He's a pretty good student, so I enjoy playing along with him and demonstrating new songs. He's only in fifth grade, however, so it's not a real high level of music that we're playing. After a while, I do get a little bored, and I start looking out Sam's window. It's a typical suburban area, with several backyards joining together. There are lots of trees, and fences are dividing the yards. The neighbors can't see into anyone else's area very much.

While I gaze down from Sam's second floor room into his backyard, I suddenly see Mrs. Levin laying on a chaise lounge. She's on her stomach, but, I can see that her bikini top is no longer where it should---

BLAP-BLAP-BLAP! Sam interrupts my train of thought with some wrong notes.

"Uh, hang on, Sam....that wasn't exactly right. How 'bout if you try that part again?"

Sam continues to play, and I start gazing out the window again. Wait... Mrs. Levin has turned over. She's lying on her back, putting on sun tan lotion. But, she has no top---*BRAP-BLIPPY BLIP-BROP-BLOOP!*

"Sam...Sam...go up to the top and try that one more time." Did I really say go up to the top?

Sam starts over at the top. Mrs. Levin takes the sun tan lotion and starts over at the top, too. Since she has those sunglasses on, I can't really tell which direction she's looking. I sure don't want her to see m----

"Mr. B, did I play it better that time?" Sam asks.

"Uh, yeah, great Sam, much better." I actually hadn't heard one note.

"Mr. B, you're sweating, and your face is all red. Are you OK?"

"Sure, Sam, I'm fine. It's just a little hot in here."

"Mr. B, you wanna stick your head out the window for a

17

while?"

"Well, uh...err, no, that's OK, Sam. Why don't you play that solo you started on last week?"

Sam begins playing, and I take another peek out the window. I can't believe Mrs. Levin is doing this---

Uh-oh, Mrs. Levin is smiling, and I think she's waving at....at....me. I feebly wave back, sort of a sheepish Queen of England type wave.

"Who ya' wavin' at, Mr. B? Is it my mom? Oh, she lies down out there all the time and waves at people. The other day, she was waving for a long time at the man who was fixing our antenna. He was up on the roof for hours. I guess he had trouble with the antenna, 'cause he had to bring some extra guys over to finish getting it up."

"That's a little too much information, Sam. Say, didn't you tell me that you got a new book of popular songs for trumpet? Which one did you get?"

"Oh, Mr. B, it's really cool! It's a book of Simon and Garfunkel songs. I can't wait to learn them, but isn't the lesson over now?"

"Well, Sam, this is turning out to be a really interesting lesson....I'll tell you what....I think I can stay for an extra half hour today!"

Where have you gone, Joe DiMaggio?

*

Finally, all of my lessons for the evening are finished. It's 9:00, and after teaching eight trumpet students at seven different houses, I can go home. I've been munching on different foods at several of these houses, so I'm not super hungry. Let's see....should I stop at a fast food joint and pick up a couple of milkshakes---oh, shhhugar! I forgot to leave some music at Jacob Wallace's house when I was there before. *Great*....now I'll have to make an extra stop. Fortunately, Jacob's house is right on the way home, so I can drive over there fairly quickly to deliver it. OK, here's his house now. Mrs. Wallace answers the door, and I hand her the music. We talk for a few minutes, then I head back out to the car. I've left the motor running, thinking I wouldn't there very long. But, *wait....what....oh, no! I locked the car door! WHAT A *&%$^ GENIUS!! YOU DUMB A&%@#&*LE!!* Now it's about 9:15, and I'm already exhausted. It's dark, and my locked car is running with just enough gas left in it to get home.

Remember, this is 1984. No one has a cell phone or remote key entry yet. Plus, no local gas station will come out to help me this late in the evening. Mrs. Wallace sees my predicament (I sure hope she didn't hear me swearing), and she offers to call the police station, which is luckily just up the street.

Just a few minutes have passed, and I can now see a police car coming down the block. After getting out of his squad car, the officer glimpses at me like I'm a big dope (which is appropriate, I guess).

"Hello, sir. I see we have a locked car here, that's still running?"

"Yes, Captain Obvious." Oops, I didn't just say that out loud, did I? Please tell me I said "Officer." Uh-oh, now he's glaring at me, as he starts to slip some kind of crowbar inside my car window to try and pop the lock.

"Don't worry, sir, I'll get this open soon. We do these kinds of things all the time."

After a few minutes of prying, however, the policeman seems to be getting frustrated.

"Just a couple more minutes." he groans.

Ten more minutes go by, though, and still nothing, except less gas in my tank. I feel bad since I'm the big idiot who caused this problem.

"Thanks, Officer, I appreciate you trying."

As he stops using the crowbar, he asks me "what year is this car?"

"1980," I reply.

"Oh, no wonder," he says, "This crowbar only works for 1981

cars and up. What model is it, XE or LE?"

"It's an LE." XE is the more luxurious car, and LE is the lesser expensive model. I always wondered if that's why the car company used those initials.

"Oh, this is an XE crowbar. It won't work. We don't have any LE crowbars at the station."

An XE crowbar. He's kidding, right?

"Oh…well, uh, thanks anyway." I had no idea that there are so many different types of crowbars. The policeman shrugs, says how sorry he is, then leaves in his squad car. I better ask Mrs. Wallace if I can call Ann. She'll have to drive the half an hour up the highway to unlock the door with her key. Great….just what she wants to do, drive up here at 9:30 at night after teaching all evening herself.

As I walk back towards the Wallace's front door, Mr. Wallace comes out.

"Mr. B, I have a similar model car. I know it seems crazy, but could I try my key? It might save your wife from having to drive up here."

"Sure, Mr. Wallace, go for it."

What do I have to lose? My car is running out of gas and now it's about 9:45. Ann probably expects me to be home any minute. But, I'm thinking, his key will never work…a key to a different car *should never work, right?* Don't we all think that our cars have unique keys, and that they won't open each other's doors? I don't know whether to hope that his key works or not!

Mr. Wallace tries his key in the door lock… *voila! The lock pops right open! "Wow…thanks so much, Mr. Wallace!"*

"You're welcome, Mr. B. I can't believe it worked. Have a safe trip home!"

I can't believe his key worked, either. I'm happy and relieved, of course, but I'm a little freaked out, too. Should I be worried that our car could be stolen at any time by anyone with a similar model key?

Mrs. Wallace offers to call Ann and tell her what happened, and that I'm on my way home now. I also asked Mrs. Wallace to tell Ann that I wasn't very hungry, so that she doesn't make dinner for me. I've already eaten four slices of pizza, some carrot sticks, three cookies, and an ice cream bar between all of the houses I've been to this evening. I can't wait to see what's going to be for dinner at my six student's houses tomorrow night!

Finally, at 10:00, I can drive home. I'm passing by the police station that's up the street from the Wallace's house. I should stop in and tell that officer how Mr. Wallace's key---

rrraaHHRRR, rrraaHHRRR.

"Pull over to the side, sir."

What? Me? What could I have possibly done?

The policeman gets out of his car, and walks up to my window. It's the same policeman who tried to help me get the door lock open. Maybe he just wants to know what happened.

"Hello, Officer. The owner of the house got my car door unlocked...isn't that lucky? Is there a problem now? I've just been driving for about a block, so I know I wasn't speeding."

I can tell that he isn't interested in my story, but I can't imagine that I've done anything wrong.

"No, sir, you weren't speeding. If you get out of the car, I can show you what the problem is."

"Uh, uh, yeah, OK." As tired as I am, I'm still pretty nervous. The policeman walks me around to the front of my car.

"There, sir," he says, "now you can see the problem."

As I glance at the front of the car, I can instantly tell what he means:

"Oh, no," I declare, "one of my headlights is out."

"Yes and here's your ticket, Captain Obvious."

Not exactly "The Waltons"

CHAPTER TWO

My Dad tried to warn me about days like these. He's the one who gave music lessons for all those years, going from house to house, even on Sundays. I remember him telling me about the student he had who jumped out the back window and ran down the street when Dad rang his doorbell for the lesson. That kid ended up having fifteen-minute lessons by the time his mom caught him and brought him home, but Dad always got paid the full amount for the thirty minutes, which was probably $3 at the time. Dad's the one who also told me not to schedule the students so close together. Well, here I am, stuck in traffic, late for my 1 p.m. lesson at the Wentworth's house.

It's not that I'm excited about teaching this lesson...that Wentworth kid is lazy, and the sound he gets out of his trumpet is similar to a wounded animal. Here I am, finally pulling up to his house. I better not start talking to his brothers and sisters today, or I'll never get back on schedule. How many siblings does Gary have....*eleven*? And, all of these kids look alike, except for being different heights. Their ages range from about one to twenty-one, and all of them have this kind of reddish-orange hair, just a little redder than Bozo. They constantly stare at me with big, round, blank looking eyes that look right through me. I would say that they remind me of *The Waltons*, but maybe it's closer to the Zombies in *Night of the Living Dead*.

To get into the Wentworth's part of the house, I've got to open the downstairs door and climb up the stairs to the second floor. That's where this family of fourteen lives.

I ascend these stairs every week, and Gary's eleven siblings are constantly gawking at me as I come up. Their eyes and heads move simultaneously as I climb, following me up each step. The creepy thing is that none of them ever say a word, but their mouths are all hanging wide open.

I guess Mr. and Mrs. Wentworth had the twelve kids in about twenty years. In the words of a famous comedian, "They should have gotten cable TV sooner for something else to do". I always think of Groucho Marx when I arrive at the Wentworth's house. Groucho had a contestant on his old game show that told him she had six kids in seven years, and his reply was something like:

"Lady, I like my cigar, too, but I take it out of my mouth once in a while." Being live TV, the next thing I saw on the screen was the old test pattern....they had taken Groucho off the air for a while.

OK, here's the door, let's see if all of those kids are staring at me again---

BLAAAAAMM!

Whoa! What the heck was that? Just as I grab the doorknob, an explosion of some kind knocks me right on my back. I look down at my hand, and it's been burned slightly. That blast was loud, too. I think there must have been a firecracker attached to the doorknob! What's the date today? Oh, of course, it's July 3. What a greeting I just got from Gary Wentworth....that thing could have blown my hand off! Well....I'm in no mood to teach a mediocre trumpet student now. I believe this is going to be a very short lesson for Gary today. As I get to the top of the stairs, Mrs. Wentworth is there to greet me, along with several of her "anti-Von Trapp" kids. Their eyes are transfixed on my every step, but they never move their heads or say anything.

"Oh, Mr. B, I'm sorry about that. The kids have been setting off those firecrackers all over the place. Gary probably thought one of his brothers would open that door before you did. Are you all right?" asks Mrs. Wentworth.

"Well, no, not really....and I don't think I can teach Gary, after what I just went through."

"That's OK. Gary isn't here, anyway. Would you mind teaching Bobby instead?"

Oh, no, I blew it. That's not what I meant at all. My hand hurts, and I'm still shaking. I just want to get the hell out of here, and I certainly don't want to teach Bobby. He is one of Gary's little brothers. I can never keep track of all the ages of these siblings, but I think Bobby is about nine, while Gary is eleven. If I have time in my schedule, I sometimes stay and teach Bobby after Gary's lesson. The Wentworth's have these two old trumpets that have been in their family for years. They're not worth much money, but they work just fine, considering the way Gary and Bobby play.

Bobby has just started on the trumpet, and it is nice for me to get paid for two lessons while just going to one house. However, I haven't heard Bobby play in a few months, and he was terrible the last time I taught him. Even after three or four lessons, I still don't think that Bobby knows which end of the trumpet to blow into, but I don't take that personally. Bobby's trumpet tone is even worse than Gary's is. It also sounds like a wounded animal, but Bobby somehow manages to mix in a little bit of air horn noise, too. Teaching Bobby, and hearing that awful sound come out of his horn, surely won't make up for the pyrotechnics that I just experienced.

"Uh, Mrs. Wentworth, I don't feel all that well, and I think I'll just be going home now."

"Oh, please, Mr. B. As long as you're here, can you please just teach Bobby today?"

Trying to quickly reason with myself, I know that I should stay. I've driven almost forty minutes to get to their house, and we can certainly use the money. Which brother would be more torture to teach, Bobby or Gary? At this point, I'm still more mad at Gary for planting the firecracker. I guess I'll teach Bobby, but I am curious, since Gary did have his lesson already scheduled.

"Uh, Mrs. Wentworth, where *is* Gary?"

"Oh, he ran away again, but we're used to it by now. He's run away three times this year already, but he always comes back."

Maybe he won't come back for at least another half hour, I hope.

"Bobby said he's been practicing and needs some help."

I bet. "OK, Bobby, let's get started. Open your book to the page you practiced the most."

Bobby starts to flip the pages without any idea of where to stop. I know I'm in for some disgusting trumpet noises today. He must have practiced all of thirty or forty seconds in the past few weeks. Bobby finally finds the right page, and begins groaning....I mean playing:

"BBRROOPPP....BLOOPBLOOP....AAOOOGGA!"

"Bobby, that sounds very interesting. But, I don't see any *"AAOOOGGA"* notes anywhere on that page."

"Oh yeah, Mr. B, I went ahead in the book. I learned those notes on my own."

"Great, Bobby. Keep going." Ugh. I've got to listen to twenty more minutes of this?

As Bobby continues *"AAOOOGGA-ing,"* my mind begins to wander, and I start looking around the room and down the hall. I can't help but see into several of the kids' bedrooms, and they all have bunk beds stacked up in them. There's not much privacy at all, which must be especially annoying for the older kids. I also know that they have just one bathroom, but I try my hardest not to think about the logistics of all of them sharing it! Oh well, I guess that's one more bathroom than what *The Waltons* had. No wonder Gary runs away.

I continue to look around, and all of a sudden I start seeing *them* staring at me.

There are ten big, brown sets of eyes, all accompanied by red hair, with blank faces and open mouths. This entire brood is peering at me around the corner from their bedrooms, looking into the living room. Every direction I look, they're staring, staring at this stranger....me. Four here, three over there, three more in the back, different heights, but all the same faces! They start coming into the living room, moving towards me...closer, closer. No expressions in their faces. They're going to kill me---that's what Zombies do, isn't it? Here they come, closer, clo---

"*AAOOOGA-UGA-UGA!*"

"How's that, Mr. B? Isn't that better than last time?"

Bobby has exploded with another group of chilling trumpet notes, jarring me back into the real world (such as it is).

"Yes, Bobb-"

Just then, Gary comes running up the stairs. He's carrying his trumpet case under his arm.

"Hi mom. Hi Mr. B."

"Hi Gary, have you been out making money playing your trumpet?" Little did I know.

"Gary, where have you been?!" demands Mrs. Wentworth.

"Look in here, mom. I'll show you." Gary opens up the case, but there's no trumpet in it!

"See...I traded my trumpet for some firecrackers. There's some M-80's, and three smoke bombs. I'm gonna quit playing trumpet soon anyway, and I can just use Bobby's if I want. This will be so cool tomorrow on the Fourth of July, don't you think, Mr. B? I'll be right back. I gotta go put my bike in the garage."

"But...Gary...," says Mrs. Wentworth, sadly.

"But...Gary...," says me, sadly. Is this how *Jack and the Beanstalk* got started?

"Don't be sad, Mr. B." Bobby whispers to me. "You'll feel better in a minute. Wait 'til you hear what happens to Gary when he starts to turn the handle on the garage door!"

"BLAAAAAMM!"

"You're right, Bobby. I do feel better now. Thanks!"

*

Sometimes, Ann or I teach lessons at a house where the father is totally out of touch with his family. These dads usually provide tons of money for their family, but they're only concerned with their own expensive suits, shoes, cars, or the latest skybox tickets for the upcoming game. They are clueless when it comes to what activities they're family is doing.

One such family lives in a typical ritzy suburb, the kind of place where one household is constantly trying to out-do the next. Ann teaches one sibling of this family named Mark. He's an eleven-year-old flute player. I teach the trumpet to his brother, thirteen-year-old Tom. They are both nice, respectful boys. They both practice their instruments, and are proud of playing them.

Ann and I go to their house on separate days because of our different schedules, so we're never there at the same time. The boys' dad is rarely home when either Ann or I come over, but we have each met him about three times over several months of lessons. Their mom is very nice, and she signs the checks for us. Today, after I ring the doorbell, their dad opens the door for me, but their mom isn't home.

"Yes, can I help you?" he says to me.

"Hi, Mr. Russell, I'm Mr. B, and I'm here to teach Tom."

"Oh, OK. Mark, someone's here to teach you something." That is encouraging to hear, but I don't think I'll include it on my resume. Tom knows it is time for *his* lesson, not Mark's, so he comes to the door to meet me, but his dad still isn't quite sure what's happening:

"Mark---"

"I'm Tom, dad."

"Oh, right. This man's here to teach you. What does he teach?"

"The trumpet, dad."

"Oh, you play the trumpet?"

"Yes, dad, I have since 4th grade. Don't you remember all the concerts at school that you go to?" Tom has played the trumpet for over four years now, but I guess the dad hasn't noticed. Tom has told me that his dad is always too busy trying to impress the other dads at school concerts. Tom says that his dad shows off stuff to the other dads, like the tassels on his shoes, or some new cufflinks.

"My dad never really listens when the bands are playing." Tom informs me remorsefully.

"Uh…," his dad says to Tom, "OK, Mark, have a good lesson on your, uh..."

"I'm Tom, dad. It's the *trumpet*."

"Right."

After Tom's lesson is over, he hands me the check for both Ann and I. This will cover Mark's lesson, too. The check is signed by their mom, of course. In spite of the rocky start we had with his dad, Tom and I ended up having a fun lesson. As I leave, I walk by Mr. Russell. He wants to let me know the depth of his musical acumen:

"Well, sir (he can't remember my name), did Mark have a good trombone lesson?"

"I'm Tom, dad."

"Right."

"He had a good lesson, Mr. Russell." I try to tell him about it, but he has more acumen to brag about and isn't finished yet.

"I always liked that slide on the trombone, don't you, Mark?"

"I play the *trumpet*, dad." Tom said.

"Right, the trumpet. What does that sound like, Mark?"

"I'm Tom, dad." Whenever Tom says this, he always sounds very matter-of-fact, as though he has to tell his dad ten times a day

29

who he is. I admire his patience.

Something else bothers me about this scenario, too. Mr. Russell is asking about the sound of a trumpet, even though he has just heard two trumpets being played for thirty minutes? I guess he *is* too important and busy to hear my further explanation of Tom's lesson, for he turns and starts to walk away. Not so fast, buster:

"Well, Mr. Russell, Mrs. B will be here tomorrow to teach Mark." I didn't give him any more details about how Ann teaches Mark the flute. I can't wait for this response:

"Who's that?" Mr. Russell asks.

"That's my wife, she teaches---" "Oh, she teaches Tom the clarinet!"

"I'm Tom, dad."

"Well, no," I say, "she teaches Mark---"

"She teaches Mark the clarinet!"

"Well, no, she teaches Mark the flute." I'm finally able to say. "Mrs. B says Mark is doing well, too!"

"He is? Oh, right, of course he is. Now, the flute is the curvy gold instrument, right?"

"No," I explain, "that's the saxophone."

"Of course it is." he replies. His ego is puffing out to match his rather prodigious belly: "I'll have to listen to Tom play that flute tomorrow!"

"I'm Tom, dad. I play the trumpet. Mr. B says I'm doing good."

"Right."

At this point, I think I'll wait for Abbott and Costello to show up. Maybe they can actually clear up the situation. I can't help myself, so I think I'll continue to try and confuse Mr. Russell even more:

"Why don't you have Tom and Mark play both of their instruments for you at the same time? Then they can show you what they've been working on in their lessons." This idea should really bewilder him.

"Tom and Mark together, you say, on the saxophone and the

trombone? That's a good idea, Mr. C."

"I'm Mr. B." I try to explain. "The boys play the trumpet and flute." Now *I'm* being dragged into this weirdness!

"Right," Mr. Russell answers. "Trumpet and flute, can't wait to hear that. I've never heard them together before."

"Dad," Tom pleads, "you just went to our school concert last week, remember?"

"Yeah, right. You and Tom were both in that? Were you there, too, Mr. G?"

"I'm Tom, dad."

"I'm Mr. B, Mr. Russell.

"Right."

"Hey dad, can we play our instruments for you tomorrow? That would be fun for me and Mark." Tom asks hopefully.

"Now, you guys know I'm going to the ballgame tomorrow. I have second row seats with my friends. I can't do that." Mr. Russell sounds very condescending. I feel bad for Tom, so I try to advocate for him:

"Well, Mr. Russell, if you can hear them play sometime, I think they'd really appreciate it."

"Well," this "Big Important Man" replies, "I'm playing golf on Friday, going to the club Saturday, and then I'm out of town for two weeks. I would tell you that it's for business, but really we'll just be entertaining clients in Florida; probably playing lots of golf. That'll be great, don't you think!" He has totally forgotten what we were talking about. Again, I implore him:

"Well, maybe someday you can hear them, Mr. Russell. I bet that would be a highlight of their day."

"Hear who?" he responds. Oh my, I think Mr. Russell's mind is now focused on his putter. His golfing putter, that is. I think.

"You can hear Tom and Mark. They'd love it!" I appeal.

"Hear them do what?"

"Play their instruments for you."

"Oh, yeah. Play the saxophone and clarinet, right? Sure...maybe someday, Mark!"

"I'm Tom, dad."

"Right."

I can't take any more of this. I start to leave, and I tell Tom that I'll see him next week. Tom nods his head sadly, while rolling his eyes towards his dad.

Mr. Russell chimes in:

"Do you come here every week, Mr. T?"

"Rrriight."

*

One student that I really look forward to teaching each week is George. He's thirteen, and is in eighth grade. He plays the trumpet well for a student that age, and he is also interested in the history behind famous trumpeters, other musicians, and styles of music. That's rather unusual, especially for someone only in eighth grade, and it makes the lessons a lot more fun for me.

There are several other reasons why I enjoy teaching George, and also why I enjoy going to his house for the lessons. He has a good sense of humor, and understands most of my sarcastic remarks about people and about life. If I refer to someone as a "genius," he knows I'm usually kidding. Or, if I say that someone is "the greatest" at something, whether it is playing the trumpet, teaching, or whatever, he'll know I'm being flippant about that, too. Most kids (and many adults, too) tend to take me literally, so I have to be careful about how I use my sarcasm.

Driving to George's house today, I start to think of how fun it is to talk to him about so many different subjects. He's a very "streetwise" kid. I'm also reminded of another reason I enjoy going there, and that's to talk to his mother, and to listen to her have conversations with the TV set during the lessons. Often times, George and I will be playing our trumpets in the living room, and we'll be able to hear his mother from the kitchen. She usually has an ongoing discussion with whoever is talking on TV. During *Jeopardy*, for instance, I might hear her say:

"Ha, what a dope...he's a *f*@%^& idiot!* "

Or, during a talk show, she might say:

"That's total *bulls&%#*. No way an *ass* like him would believe that!" I can tell from her tone of voice that she's not really mad. Those words are just a part of her normal speech patterns, at least when she's at home.

George just sits there during these outbursts, not paying any attention. He seems like he's used to it, but I'm thinking....did I actually hear her say those things? I didn't listen that closely for the first few weeks, but then I started realizing why George is so streetwise. His mom really is a very nice person, quite calm and relaxed, and she always has a smile on her face. After she makes these statements, she usually starts singing quietly to herself. She doesn't use words like that when she's talking to me. She just doesn't suffer fools gladly, and has little patience for phony people. Once she gets it out of her system, she just goes about the rest of her day.

On the other hand, I've also met George's dad several times, and he's been home during many of the lessons. I've never heard him swear, or say a bad word about anybody. I appreciate the fact that both of his parents are very kind to me. I'll have to check back with George when he grows up, and find out what his opinions are about people's behavior.

When I think about George's mother, and her use of the language, it takes me back to my childhood all over again with my own mother. I grew up in a house where my Mother had very little patience for a person with a big ego. My Dad was a professional musician for his entire career, starting in the 1930's during the Depression. The music business was (and is) extremely competitive, and few musicians were functioning under steady contracts when I was a kid in the 1960's. Dad was very easygoing in spite of the uncertainty of freelancing, and not having a steady paycheck. Mom, however, was the opposite, and took this competition for jobs with other musicians very seriously. Mom also had a secret weapon: she oozed with charm to help support Dad's dealings with people, whether she was talking to other musicians on the phone, or in person.

I ended up learning almost all of my swear words and acquiring my cynical attitude towards people from Mom. She might let loose with something while just watching a TV game show, or the evening news, the same way George's mother does. Here are some examples of Mom that I recollect from my childhood:

"What a *dumbass*...he should have known that answer!"

Or, "that *genius* president...who the hell voted for that *stoop!*"

I was the only one home at the time she said things like this, and I was maybe four or five when I first recall hearing these kinds of statements. I would look up from building my tower of blocks and wonder what she was saying, but I figured out quickly that she was never talking directly to me.

My Mom had been a Big Band singer in the 1930's...that's how my parents met. As a child, she had been a singing and dancing performer around the Midwest, so she grew up in this entertainment business full of inflated personalities, and developed a strong sense of self. The story goes that after one audition for the job of Band singer (one of the ones that Dad played in), the leader told Mom the usual "don't call us, we'll call you," and she replied *"you do that....and soon!"* Once my parents got married, Mom quit singing and never went back to the business.

I specifically remember one long and fascinating scene with Mom from when I was about nine. Dad was driving Mom and I home from a restaurant, and we passed by the house of another musician, a competitor of Dad's who was always trying to undermine Dad's playing ability to Band leaders. In spite of this, Dad was still friends with this guy. Dad was above all of the "office politics" of the music business, and didn't seem to care. Mom, however, hated this guy for what he was saying to other musicians, and had also found out that his wife was saying bad things to the other wives, too! But, Mom was trying her best to befriend the wife in order to make things easier for Dad.

As we drove by their house, we saw this couple standing out in their front yard. Mom was in no mood to talk to them on the spur of the moment. She needed time to psych herself up before any kind of meeting with them, so she could work up the strength to be nice. She said to Dad: "Keep going...don't slow down...I don't want them to see us." Oops...too late. They recognized our car, and Dad pulled over. This was in the mid-1960's, and the new car we had featured those new-fangled power windows. You pushed a "way-cool" chrome lever to make the windows go up or down, which I thought was the neatest thing. As Dad parked by the curb, Mom reluctantly lowered her window, and the couple came over. The husband was very friendly to us, but even as a nine-year-old I could tell that the wife was being phony, and not genuinely nice. I remembered that her voice was extremely whiny and nasal sounding. She spoke as her face and voice both slowly sagged:

"Oh...hi...so nice...to see you." Soon, the men and women were having separate conversations, and I was bored as usual in the back seat, carefully studying those shiny chrome window levers. These new car gadgets were some of the highlights of my ninth year. After a few moments, I heard Mom get up the courage to ask:

"Hey, we should get together. How about Saturday night?"

"No, we're busy." said the wife matter-of-factly.

"OK," Mom replied, "how about a week from Saturday?"

"No, we have plans that night."

Mom kept trying: "Well, what about the Sun..."

"No, that won't work, either."

I could sense Mom's blood pressure rising as her voice got more intense. She despised this woman already, and now the wife was blowing off my parents when Mom was actually making an attempt at friendship! Finally, Mom took a deep breath and made one last effort. Her voice kept rising as the anger was seeping through:

"Well...how 'bout three weeks from Saturday? That would be

the 22nd!'"

"Uh, let's see..."

The wife seemed to be stalling while thinking up an excuse. She continued: "That won't work. I'm going to have a headache that day."

Mom exploded: *"Let's go!"* she snapped at my father. Dad started to shift the car into Drive, while Mom violently pushed at her shiny power window lever. As the window went up, getting faster with a crescendo of sound *(zzzzeeeeeiiiiiiii),* Mom couldn't be nice to this woman anymore; her inner-Vesuvius erupted:

"YOU CAN SHOVE THAT HEADACHE *RIGHT UP YOUR...*"

(zzziippp...) *"ASS!"* Dad and I started laughing like crazy, but Mom was beet red. She never spoke to the wife again, yet Dad remained friends with the husband for rest of their lives.

My Dad had an extremely successful career in many phases of the music business. He performed in top-level groups for forty years, from nightclubs, to big bands, to playing on literally thousands of TV and radio commercials. He worked with all of the big name performers: Sinatra, Dean Martin, Sammy Davis, Jr., Nat 'King' Cole, and Ella Fitzgerald...just name a great star from the 1930's through the 1970's, and Dad played in a Band for them. Then, after deciding to retire from playing, he campaigned for office and was elected president of the local Musician's Union.

Dad would often say that most of these top stars were very nice to the Band members, and were easy to work with. Many would come to town for a two or three week "run" in a nightclub, or a theater. They would often buy gifts for the Band members at the end of the run as a token of appreciation. I remember hearing that Dad received a money clip from Jack Benny in the 1940's, for example (a money clip from Jack Benny...how ironic!). Dad spoke with great admiration for many of these iconic performers.

Dad would just laugh off the behavior of anyone that was not nice to him professionally. In fact, I *almost never* heard Dad say anything bad about anyone, and I *never* recall him swearing. For musicians, this is unheard of! The most he would say would be "Cheeeze…," which was an even nicer form of "Geez," and "For Cry…," which I always thought was a short version of "For Christ's sake," but Dad never would say that. I still have musicians tell me what a gentleman Dad was, and how they liked him for that reason as much as they liked him for his musical talents. When Dad would walk into a room, he thought of everyone as his friend, and other musicians still tell me that they thought of him as their friend.

Over time, I learned from Mom that people aren't really what they seem to be:

"They just pretend to be nice, but they're really *a%*&#les* the rest of the time." she might say.

But, I also learned from Dad to tolerate people as much as possible:

"Ah, just ignore them…no big deal." he would often reply.

These lessons have proven to be extremely valuable to me. After all, I'm trying to weave my way through this same competitive music business that Dad was so successful in.

It's fun thinking about my parents and my childhood as I drive to George's house. I always wonder if there will be a new "swear word" that George's mom pops out today, or what subject a Jeopardy contestant may fail at, which might elicit a venomous response from her.

I also look forward to situations involving George's dog. He's a black Spaniel who is very playful, but he usually leaves me alone once I get in the door. He likes to lie down in the corner, or walk around the kitchen looking for crumbs. He does have one interesting habit, and it's one he shares with many other dogs. He loves to drink out of the toilet! It must be the super-cold water that he enjoys so much, especially on hot days. I should ask George why they don't just put the toilet lid down to prevent this canine guzzling, but I guess boys will be boys.

During the lessons, I can hear the pooch go into the bathroom, and his drinking sounds get gradually faster and faster:

Sshhlluurrppp...shllurpp...sllurpp...slopp...slop...slop.
Sshhlluurrppp...shllurpp...sllurpp...slopp...slop...slop.

He's good for four or five drinks each session, and then George's mom will catch him:

"Oh s#%&. Get out of there, you d*@& dog."

This hound knows the routine, though, and he tries to sneak in a few last gulps:

Slopp...slurppp...slurrrrppppppp!

This is followed by:

"Huh...I told you to get the hell out of there."

The dog goes back to the corner and lies down, but I can tell from her tone that George's mom isn't really upset with him, and I think the dog knows it, too. She doesn't speak these things too loudly, or in a harsh vein. Instead, they just sound like normal conversations with the dog. And, after the dog's drinking binge is over, George's mom starts singing to herself again. George sits there during all of this, and shows no emotion. This whole scenario will then repeat itself two or three times each lesson. I can only imagine this going on all day long...what a riot! At the end of the lesson, I thank George and his mom: "Nice to see you again, and thanks for the conversation, George!"

*

I've been practicing my trumpet quite a bit lately. I'm trying to learn and memorize about one hundred songs. I get to play these tunes at gigs with the band that I'm in, and it will make things a lot easier for me if I can memorize them. That way, I can go from one song to the next without having to flip pages in this giant songbook that we use. If the director calls a tune that begins with the letter "Z," and we're currently playing a song that starts with "A," I can be ready right away. And, that's important, because being the trumpet player I get to play the melody a good deal of the time. It's tough for me to turn pages and play my horn at the same time!

Most of these songs were in movies and Broadway shows that were written from the 1930's to the 1960's. They're fabulous tunes composed by people like George Gershwin, Cole Porter, Richard Rodgers, and Irving Berlin. The band I'm in performs often at charity balls and society parties, and the guests love to dance to these tunes. And I really enjoy playing them, too! These songs have unforgettable melodies, interesting chord changes, and clever lyrics, unlike most of the popular songs of the 1980's. Tell me...who's going to remember a typical '80's tune in twenty or thirty years?

I think I also enjoy playing these great tunes because it reminds me of my Dad's career as a musician. He was playing all of these songs when they were initially popular, just when the public was hearing them for the first time. I never got to perform with my Dad, but when I'm playing these songs I can at least pretend that I'm sitting alongside of him in a band from that era. 'Swonderful...I get a kick out of that!

OK...I better get started with my practice session today. It gets really hot in our apartment since there is no central air conditioning. We just have one tiny window unit in the dining room, and that doesn't do much good. Even though I've got the AC unit turned on full blast, I'm sweating like a pig already, and I haven't even begun to practice! I think I'll open the window, in case there's a breeze---

"COUGH-cough-cough-COUUGGHH!! GGuullPP!"

UGH! Our apartment is on a very central, busy street, and an old, smelly bus just went by. These buses are constantly going past this building, and the pollution often makes it hard to breathe, even up on the second floor where we live. I guess I'll shut the wind---

"rrriiRRRiirrr...rrriiRRRiirrr...BEEP-BEEP...rrriiRRRiirrr!"

Oh, and did I mention that this building is located in between not one, but *two* fires stations? The fire trucks relentlessly travel up and down this boulevard, too. The noise gets annoying enough during the daytime, and I don't know how many times Ann and I have been woken up in the night by the---

"COUUGGHH!!"

Needless to say, we would *love* to eventually buy our own home! Maybe then we could have at least a little peace and quiet, air conditioning, and more space to live in. Ann and I have been putting away as much money as we can. We hardly ever go out to eat, except to have a pizza once in a while. And, we've only seen a few movies lately...all at the cheap theater. Plus, whenever I have a gig downtown, I drive around and around looking for a parking spot on the street, so that I can save the $15 I'd have to spend in a garage. We're trying...ah; someday, Ann, we'll get that house we want!

All right....maybe now I can actually start practicing. I've been playing regularly for about two weeks now, usually for an hour or so almost every day. I think if I can practice for a couple of more weeks, I'll have most of these "Smarvelous" tunes memorized. I'm up to the letter "N" now. Let's see..."Night and D---"

"rrRRIINNGG--rrRRIINNGG!!"

"rrRRIINNGG--rrRRIINNGG!!"

Oh, great. There's the phone. I'm coming...I'm coming---

OWWW!! Uh-oh...whoa...WHOAAA...BOOOM!!

S%*T!! Another one of these dumb parquet floor tiles is coming up, and I tripped and crashed into the wall. There are several of these pieces curling up throughout the apartment, and I didn't pay attention as I went for the phone. I'll sure have a sore shoulder and a bruised big toe tomorrow.

And, I missed the phone call, too. The answering machine is picking up:

"Beep. Hi, it's me." That's Ann. "I'm at my Mom's house. Some jerk parked in our space again. And, with that parade tomorrow, there aren't any parking spots anywhere. I'll have to park over here and walk home. *This su---Beep!"*

Ann's mom lives about six blocks from our apartment.

Since our building is on such a central street, they use it for the parade route every Fourth of July. The parade in this suburb has become so popular to watch that people steal parking spaces days in advance, so that they can have a close access to the street. It's just another annoying "perk" of living here.

OK...finally, I think I can start my practice session. *Night and Day*, right?

"Tu Tu Tuuu..."

*

It's been about a month now since I began to practice regularly. I've finished memorizing almost this whole book of songs, and today I'll work on tunes that start with the letter "W." All right...the first one I can play is *What Kind of Fool Am I?* Oh, I see that the mailman is walking out of the building. Maybe I'll go downstairs and get the mail. Nah...I'm not stalling...really! Every musician just *loves* to practice, right? All I want to do is go down to the lobby to get the mail---

"zzzZZZzzz. zzzZZZZZZ. ZZZZZZZZZ!"

Oh my...I see that our resident homeless man is sleeping down in the lobby again. I'll have to call the landlord once more, and I better tell Ann to use the back stairs when she comes home. I'll just step over him to get to my mailbox---there, got it. Hey, what's this letter? It's from some kind of law firm:

"O'Malley, Goldstein, and O'Malley, Attorneys at Law"

It must be a solicitation. Well, maybe I better open it anyway:

Dear Mr. Bennett:

The neighborhood association of your street has retained our law firm. Your entire block has signed a petition, insisting that you immediately cease and desist from making any more of your trumpet noises.

If you continue to blast your trumpet, you will be evicted from your apartment.

Have a nice day.

Sincerely,

Irving O'Malley, esq.

WHAT!! Cease and des---signed a petit---evicted!
No one has said a word to me this whole month about me practicing in the apartment! And...don't most of these people work during the day? And...how could they even hear me with the buses and fire trucks always going by? *AARRGGHH!*

Well, there go the rest of my practice sessions. Let me get this straight: because we live in this building, we're not allowed to have kids, or dogs or cats, or give lessons, or practice my trumpet. But, we do get to sweat like crazy in the summer, have a homeless man sleep in the lobby, and have our parking space taken. I *can't wait* until we can get our own place!

Anyway, what songs do I have left to memorize?
Who's Sorry Now?
Why Can't You Behave?
Young and Foolish.
Gee, do you think maybe someone is trying to tell me something?

*

Every Monday night, my last teaching stop is at Adam's house. He's a sophomore in high school, and he is fairly serious about his trumpet playing and about preparing for the lessons. I've been teaching Adam at his home for about four years, starting when he was in junior high. Even though he now goes to one of the high schools where I give lessons during the day, I've found it easier for my schedule to continue coming to his house for lessons. That way I can free up a time slot for another student at that high school.

I usually arrive at Adam's house about 8:00 p.m., and when I walk in the door the theme music from the TV show *Newhart* is almost always playing on the set in the next room. This is the show where Bob Newhart is the innkeeper in New England, and he's surrounded by all of those quirky characters. I wonder if he ever taught trumpet lessons, too. Ann and I were big fans of Bob Newhart's first TV show, the one in which he played a psychiatrist, but I've rarely been able to watch this show since I'm teaching lessons at the same time. Sometimes during Adam's lessons I can hear Bob Newhart talking to one of the other cast members, but I don't know much about the plots. When Adam and I are packing up our trumpets at the end of the lessons, I can hear the *Newhart* theme playing again to close the show.

Since I've just come from George's house, I'm in a pretty good mood again tonight. It's springtime, and it's staying lighter out later in the evening, which helps me mentally as I drive to twenty-five houses each week. Adam's lessons are a nice way to end a long day of teaching. I pull into Adam's driveway about a little before 8:00, ring the bell, and Adam's mom lets me in. There it is...I can hear it: the theme music to *Newhart*.

"Hi Mr. B," she says. "I'll get Adam."

"Thanks," I reply. "I'll get set up."

"Actually, Mr. B, tonight we'd like to invite you to watch a TV show with us, instead of giving Adam his regular lesson."

"Well, uh, I'm not sure. I wanted to help Adam learn a new solo, and then play through some jazz songs."

"We know, Mr. B, but tonight is the finale of *Newhart*. The commercials are on now, but it's going to start any minute. Adam said it's OK, and he wants to watch it, too." (You have to remember that it's 1990, there are no DVR's or TiVo, and not too many people even have a VCR).

"Well," I say, "sure, OK." I wonder whether or not I'll get paid for this lesson?

The show comes on, and I'm not exactly sure what the story is about, since I've hardly watched any of the episodes. It's funny, though, and I still like Bob Newhart a lot. During the commercials, Adam runs and gets his trumpet.

"Here, Mr. B, let me play that scale for you…I know it this week!" As opposed to last week, I hope.

"Go ahead, Adam."

He begins to play: *"Bah---bap-bap-bap-bap-bap-bap--Bah---"*

"How's that?"

"That sounds good, Adam. Try it faster now."

"OK. *Bah---bp-bp-bp-bp-bp-bp-Bah---"*

"Very good, Adam. I'll get my trumpet and play that jazz song for you quickly."

I hustle to get my horn out while the commercials are still on. Adam gets out the music to *Satin Doll*, and I play the first part of it for him.

"OK, Adam. Try playing that with your tape for next week." The jazz song book we use comes with a record and a tape for the student to play along with. (In 1990 there are no CD's yet, either. Believe it or not, many of my students still use record players, and only some have a tape player).

"OK, Mr. B, I will…*ooo, the show's starting again."*

The *Newhart* finale continues, but I still don't know the characters quite well enough to know what's happening. We're getting towards the end of the show, and Adam picks up his trumpet again.

"Hey Mr. B, play that solo for me so I know how to practice it."

I ask Adam's mom if it's all right that I play while the show is going on, and she says yes. I begin to play, and make it through the first sixteen measures or so. Adam nods a few times…I can tell that he understands the rhythm of the piece, and also the tempo. I'm sure he'll practice it for next week. I continue playing the next section, while I glance over at the TV screen. Wait…what's happening? I stop playing and look more closely. There's Bob Newhart, but he's in his bedroom from his first TV series. What's going on? Adam would be too young to remember that show, but the rest of us are watching very intently.

"Come on, Mr. B, keep playing."

"*Shhh*...quiet Adam," says his mom. "We'd like to watch this."

All of a sudden, we see Bob Newhart's wife from his first TV show, Suzanne Pleshette. She sits up in the bed, and Newhart begins to explain to her about this crazy dream he's had where he's an innkeeper in Vermont. Adam's mom and I are really surprised...what a great way to end an entire TV series! And, the best part is that I got to watch it while I also "sort of" taught a trumpet lesson! I sure hope I get paid, though. I'll find out soon.

Adam looks over at his mom. He's totally confused by the show's ending.

"I'll explain it to you later, Adam." his mom says.

As we hear the Newhart theme music playing for the last time on the TV, she tells me:

"Mr. B, how about if you finish playing that song for Adam next week? I know it's late and you'd like to go home. We're glad you got to watch the show. Wasn't that ending something else? I'm sure it will be talked about for years! Oh, and one more thing. You were probably wondering...don't worry, here's your check for the lesson, and thanks for coming!"

Mr. Ruuctum and other stories

CHAPTER THREE

"Joey, how many flats are there in the 'Ab' Scale?"

"Uh..."

"You're close. Now, think about it, Joey, we went over this last week, and it was part of your assignment. How many flats do you think there are?"

"Two, Mr. B."

"Well..."

"Three."

"Closer."

"Four."

"Right!"

Now that Joey and I have climbed this first giant step in the study of music, we are ready to jump over the next hurdle.

"All right, Joey, which four flats are in the 'Ab' Scale?"

"B, E, A, and..."

"Right so far. What's the fourth one?"

"G."

"No..."

47

"F."

"No."

"Uh…"

"Remember, the four letters are going to spell a word: B-E-A-…"

"BEAF."

"What?"

"BEAN."

"BEAN! Joey, are there any musical notes named N? Try again."

"BARF."

"I will soon, Joey, but that's not quite the right answer."

By this point, I'm ready to join the French Foreign Legion.

"Come on, Joey, think! B-E-A-…"

"BEAD."

"YES! You got it! Now, how about doing something to help lower my blood pressure?"

Since Joey finally knows what notes are in the scale, he can now attempt to play the scale. Yes, learning the trumpet actually does involve playing the trumpet, although sometimes as infrequently as possible.

"OK, Joey, go ahead and play the scale, but go very slowly."

Joey begins to play each note of the scale. Good…good…OK…*ouch!*

"Try it again, Joey."

Good…yes…yes…*oooh!*

"One more time, please."

Yes…yes…that's it…*UGH!*

"Joey, what's the name of the fourth note?"

"Uh…"

To give him a hint, I ask:

"What letter comes after C in the alphabet?"

"Uh…"

Believe it or not, Joey is a sophomore in high school and has been playing the trumpet for five years. I say playing, not really practicing or studying the trumpet.

For Joey, just looking at his trumpet case, with his trumpet still inside of it, seems to qualify as practicing. I assigned him this scale two months ago, but each week he plays it worse and worse.

"OK, try it again, Joey. Think of the alphabet. A-B-C......"

"D."

"All right! Now, go ahead and play it again."

Joey gives it another try. Right...right...yes...*AARGH!* I wonder what color combination my face and my shorts are at the moment.

"Joey, I can't believe you made that same mistake again. And, that's the fourth time today you've made the same mistake. When I was taking lessons, I never would have made the same mistake four times in a row, right in front of the teacher.

"Joey," I ask, "what do you have to say?"

"Well, Mr. B, maybe you had a better teacher."

*

The long process is finally over for Alex. He has practiced hard and prepared his trumpet solo very well. Three months of listening to *Carnival of Venice* is enough for him and for me. He has finally learned which fingers to push down to play an 'Eb,' and also how many counts are in a two-count rest (yes, the answer is two). I can't believe that Alex is finally performing this piece at the Solo Contest. And, he is sounding very good so far. If he can just make it through the final part of the solo, he might get a "1st" rating from the judge. There...that's it...he did it! *PHEW!* I sometimes think it's harder for me being the teacher, and having to sit and listen to my students play these solos, than it would be for me to play them myself.

Now that Alex has finished his performance, and the judge has added up the score, we're waiting for it to be posted in the hallway of the school. Being in these hallways is always similar to watching an old western battle scene in a movie...being run backwards on the projector. We're standing in a school building that was built to hold 600 people at a time, and today there are 1,500 frantic people running around. Plus, since it's still wintertime in the Midwest, everyone is wearing thick coats and boots. Sardines have an easier time moving around inside their can.

"Here Alex, I think they'll put the score up over—*OUCH!*" I was just jabbed by something.

"Excuse me." I turn around and see six junior high girls charging towards me, brandishing their violin bows.

"We *have* to get in that room...*NOW!*"

"That room" is an oversized closet which already has thirty-eight people in it.

"Can you 'pleeease' move?" I am asked, and not very nicely at that. As I turn once again, I can see someone else lumbering towards me. It's either William "The Fridge" Perry of the 1985 Bears in drag, or it's an extremely large woman with a fur coat on. Sensing an impending collision, I duck through the nearest door. Uh-oh...I'm now in the girls' bathroom!

From inside the ladies room, I shout in my best squeaky falsetto:

"Alex, I'll be right there!" I hope my mustache doesn't give me away to any girls that are in here. After a few more seconds of fright, I finally get back out into the hall again. Everyone is so panicky at these music contests that no one even cared I was in the girls' bathroom.

Sometime later, I'm still waiting with Alex for his score to be posted on the wall. Oh great, here comes his school band director.

Now, you should be aware that some band directors are a curious breed (I know, because I've been one for many years myself). Some are fairly far down the food chain of human behavior, and are capable of quite a few misdemeanors. Many are more interested in having power over their students than they are in actually teaching or motivating kids to have a love of music. Alex's band director fits most of these descriptions, and I was really hoping to not run into him today. Oh well, there's no avoiding him now.

"Hi Alex. Well, hello *mister* trumpet teacher Sam B."

"Hello, John." I reply grudgingly.

"How did you play, Alex?"

"Well, Mr. B said I did pretty good. We're still waiting for the score."

"That's good, Alex. What's the matter with those *idiots* in the contest office? They can't get anything---"

"Uh...John." I try and stop him before he goes off on his colleagues right in front of Alex. I continue:

"Alex and I are trying to be patient. By the way, John, do you remember when you were the contest host last year, and somehow most of the scores got mixed up?"

"Yeah, I remember that! I had to wait a week to get my score last year!" recalls Alex.

"Oh, shi---you're right. Son of a bbb...gun." John replies, in his usual Neanderthal fashion. I can sense that John is mad at me for bringing that up. He always needs to pretend that he's the boss of me in front of Alex (even though he's not), so I'm guessing that I'm in for a quick lecture from him. John turns towards me:

"Say Sam, don't you think you should start teaching Alex his solo sooner next year? Also, I think he should switch to a different mouthpiece. You should be helping him with that. Make sure he holds his head up more, and, by the way Alex...tell your sister to wear that same skirt to band practice next week."

WHAT! Did he really just say that? Yes, I'm afraid so. Once again, John is showing what a classy role model and mentor he is for his students. I've heard him say things like that before, but usually it's just in front of other adults.

I also *love* being lectured at by a band director right in front of my student! I should have expected it...many, many band directors have an ego the size of the Grand Canyon. I wonder if I should tell Alex's parents the interesting remark that John just made about

Alex's sister.

Maybe now that John has finished lecturing me, he can try to figure out some way to keep so many of his students from quitting band. From talking to my own students who play in John's school band, I know that none of them are excited about being there. They just like to play their trumpets, so a few do stay in the band. But, they say they're all really scared of John, and they think he's a big bully.

I can recall hearing about an incident from a few years ago, when John's 4th grade trumpet class was finishing their lesson. Our hero John the band director had just been yelling at them for thirty minutes straight. The kids were now supposed to go eat lunch, but John wouldn't let them out. He wasn't quite finished hollering at them yet. Don't forget, these are nine-year-olds with short attention spans and big appetites. The kids were squirming and talking, and John was screaming. Finally, one of the kids came right out and asked:

"Can we go eat lunch now?"

"F%#K lunch!!!"

That's tellin' 'em, John!

Well, enough about him. I have to get away from this guy. In the meantime, Alex and I are *still* standing in this hallway, waiting for the contest people to post the score for his solo performance.

"Alex, wait here, I'll be right back. John, after seeing you, I suddenly have to go to the bathroom."

I think I'll try the men's room this time. Maybe John will go away and bother someone else. He probably wants to check out the ladies room, anyway.

As I leave the bathroom, I can see that John has gone. Alex looks relieved, too. Ten more minutes go by, but still no score. Alex and I can see his dad, Mr. Ruuctum, rushing down the hall to meet us. He's a kind man, and they've been a nice family for me to deal with over the past four years of Alex's trumpet lessons.

"Sorry I'm late, Mr. B. I had to work longer than I thought. How did Alex do?"

"He played well." I replied. "You should be proud of him. We're still waiting for them to post his score."

It's been about two hours now since Alex finished playing. Finally, the contest runner comes over to the trumpet scores that are on the wall, and puts up the latest results. Wow...Alex *did* get a 1st rating, which is also called "Superior."

"That's terrific, Alex!" I exclaim. "You worked hard and deserve it!"

"Thanks, Mr. B." Alex replies.

"Oh yes, thanks so much for all of your help," Mr. Ruuctum says. "You know, Mr. B, I've been thinking. Alex is playing so well now, and he practices a lot. In fact, he's been doing so much better that I think I'll get him a better teacher to take lessons with from now on! Come on, Alex, let's go celebrate."

*

Summer is fast approaching, and school is coming to an end. For many years, Ann and I have been teaching lessons at several suburban high schools, and this year I've been at three high schools spread over four days each week. I give lessons during the day to the trumpet players, either when they have a free period in their schedule, or sometimes during Band practice. Some days I can get seven or eight lessons in.

After school, I then stay in the building and give more lessons, either to the kids who couldn't be scheduled during the day, or to students from the feeder schools who can come over after school. I have many days when I stay at the high school, and teach after school from 3:30 until 9:00. This is a good way to get the younger kids started, since they'll be attending that high school eventually, when I can then hopefully teach them during the day.

However, there can be many frustrating situations that arise when you're at these schools that late in the evening. This is the

1980's, so there are no cell phones or laptop computers. And, the offices with phones are all locked up. Students often have to cancel at the last minute, so what do they do? Call my house, of course. Ann can't call me to tell me, however. I can't call the students, either. One of these high schools is literally fifty miles from my apartment, so I can't run home if I have a cancellation. I might have four out of the eight students cancel, especially if there is a team or religious activity happening, and (of course) it's rare when any of them bother to tell me about it ahead of time.

Oh yeah, I definitely love driving a hundred miles round trip just for four students. And, I don't get paid if they cancel at the last minute like that. Not very often, anyway. You can try to pry the money out of them, but that creates bad feelings, and the idea is to keep teaching them for many years, not to make them mad. So, I sit there, all alone in the Music Wing of this big high school, with my newspaper and my Mountain Dew, and wait for the next student to hopefully show up. When I get home about 10:30 that evening, I'll find out if any of my students have called, but it's too late to call them back.

And, *all alone* is exactly right! Imagine yourself in a big band room that can hold around two hundred students. This is part of an even bigger Music Wing, which is stuck on to the school either at the end of the building, or in the basement (almost all Music Wings are placed that way). Or, sometimes the band room is locked, and I'm stuck teaching in a tiny practice room in the music wing, which is usually the size of a glorified closet. There's just enough room for me, my student, one of my butt cheeks (while the other sticks out the door), and some broken acoustical tiles with the phone numbers of the last four homecoming queens scratched into them.

On a side note, one of the best students I have ever taught started his trumpet playing career with several lessons in one of these minuscule practice rooms. He was about nine-years-old at the time, and I think he might have been a little nervous, or claustrophobic (I know I was). He kept wiggling around in his chair, and ultimately fell off of it onto the floor, while still holding his trumpet. And...this happened several times over the first few months. I thought he had some kind of problem, but didn't want to ask. A few years later, I found out that he was fine, but just a little nervous and squirmy. It was quite interesting when I'd look around and see that he had fallen on the floor. Eventually, he became a terrific student and trumpet player!

Now, back to this spooky music wing. Remember, no one is around. And, it's *very* quiet. There are only a few windows to look out, and they are about twenty feet up off the floor. There may be other activities that are happening in the gym, but I can't hear it or see anyone from my end of the building. The band teachers usually leave as soon as possible after school, and they *might* tell the daytime custodian that I'll be staying late, and then he *might* tell the night custodian, but often there is something lost in this chain of command.

The outside doors of the school may or may not be locked, so I don't dare go out to my car or go get something to eat...I may not get back in. Besides, if I'm waiting for a late student, and I decide to leave for a while, my student can then show up at any moment. I won't know if that student has actually canceled until I arrive home at 10:30 that night. My students usually have enough trouble getting into the building...I have to keep an ear out for them when they bang on the door, then I run down the hall every thirty minutes to let them in. I'm all alone, with no communication from the outside world. I'm Gilligan with a trumpet. But, even Gilligan had Ginger, Maryann, the Skipper, and "the rest."

I make friends with the school custodians all the time, and they're always very helpful. Most of the time, though, they don't know that I'm there giving lessons. They're always busy, and I'm only there one or two days a week. If I don't find them to say hi, they'll forget about me. Three times this year, the custodian has finished cleaning an area, and then he's turned off *all the lights in the entire Music Wing!* Now I'm stuck sitting there, either in the Band room or in one of the sardine cans…*err*, practice rooms, and it's *pitch black*! There are no windows to try and find some light. I may be alone, or I may be with my student. What's worse? I'm not sure. Often times, I'm sitting on the top row of four risers, surrounded by drums, tubas, and music stands.

When the lights are turned off like this, I launch into a routine that any self-respecting clown or gymnast would be proud of. After calling out for help, I blast my trumpet, and "gingerly" (with apologies to "Maryann") try to creep down these risers. Here I go--

"CRRAAASSHHH!!!" Oops…I just knocked over some music stands. Oh well---

"BOOIIINNGG!! Boing, boing, boing, boing." There goes the big bass drum down the risers. Good… that means I'm still on the third riser, so at least I know where I am! Keep going, you dope---

"OUCH!!" I think that was the bell of a tuba which just swatted me in the nose. I continue to slink along…almost down to the bottom now…two more row---

"YEeeooOOW!!!" What was *that?* Something impaled me just to the south of several important body parts! I can't see what it was, but now it feels like my foot is standing on something moving, like a bunch of drum stick---

*"Trriippp, and trip, and trip, and trip…*THOSE F%$*ING DRUMMERS LEFT THEIR STICKS RIGHT IN THE MIDDLE OF THE FLOOOOOOR…*BOOOOMM!!"*

Ugh…now I know where the bass drum ended up…on the floor, with my face buried in it. Even though I've made it to the band room door, there are no light switches…these lights only turn on by using a custodian's key. Of course, in the winter, it gets dark at about 4:30, and it's about ten degrees anyway. So, even if I do find an outside door, it doesn't help my gloomy situation.

In the meantime, while I've been doing my Fred Astaire imitation, I wonder what has been happening to my student. I told him to just sit there, but after all, he's only ten-years-old. Is he hiding in the timpani? Or another tuba? Worse yet...did he knock over my Mountain Dew?

After a few more minutes of stumbling around in the hall, I finally find the custodian. He apologizes, but he didn't even know I was here tonight, and I tell him that it's certainly not his fault. He turns his key to put the lights back on. The problem now is that it takes ten minutes for them to gradually get brighter! As more light steadily appears, I wobble back up to the top of the risers, trip, bump, yell, blast my trumpet, trip, repeat, etc. My student is just sitting there, as if nothing had happened. He looks totally bored, and I'm sweating like a pig.

"Where'd you go, Mr. B?" he asks innocently.

"Well, Bobby, I had to find the custo---"

"Mr. B, did you know the lights went out?"

"Why, uh, yes, Bobb---"

"Hey, you're bleeding on your leg."

Thanks Bobby. Glad you pointed that out!

It's finally bright enough to start the lesson again...should I charge his mom the full price? After all, the lights going out is not my fault, right? Or, should I not say anything to his mom?

Oh...now I can see what speared me through the leg: it was the drum major's four foot long baton. At least, it *was* four feet long. Is any of it still stuck in my leg? Thank goodness, I have my Mountain Dew to calm me down!

A similar situation occurred a couple of weeks ago, except at that time I was in the bathroom when the custodian turned off all the lights. This quickly became quite exciting. I couldn't even find the door to my stall, let alone the bathroom door, the hall, the band room, or the custodian. While stumbling around in the bathroom, I slipped and fell on something I could only hope was an old burrito. Maybe it was a good thing that I couldn't see it. By the time I found the custodian, I had dragged this big-old burrito around most of the school. When the lights came back on, I tried to clean it off my shoes, and socks, and pants, and the back of my shirt. My student (a different one) asked the mandatory question:

"Hey Mr. B, did you know the lights went out?"

This was followed by:

"You have something on your back." Once again, a student of mine is super observant.

"Thanks, Jimmy, that's a big help."

And later, I had to put my winter coat on over my stained shirt. I tried hard to convince myself that it really was a burrito. Where's that Mountain Dew when I need it?

*

Now, back to my original problem of trying to schedule my students for the summer. Some students will take a break over the summer, and others will be gone just for a few weeks here and there. Making the new schedule can take me a couple of weeks, since families are figuring out their summer plans and it takes a while for all of them to get back to me. You wouldn't believe some of the ridiculous excuses that I hear from parents about why their kids are *so* busy. Their priorities are astonishing, and their kids become so overscheduled that they can barely function from day to day. I'm just starting to call all of the parents now to try and forge a plan. Let's see what the next mom has to say about her son taking summer trumpet lessons:

"Mr. B, we'll be gone on the 16th and the 23rd, and I only want one lesson for him this summer, on July 7."

Aargh! She just wants him to have *one* lesson for the entire summer? He won't make any progress that way. Plus, that's the third parent to tell me that they'll be gone during those weeks. That means I'll have a hole in my schedule from 10 a.m. until 1:30 during those weeks, unless I want to drive the fifty miles home, eat lunch in five minutes, then drive the fifty miles back. No thanks.

With the big emphasis on sports these days and with the kids playing on these traveling teams five or six days a week, all year round, scheduling my lessons can present a huge problem. Here are some samples of what parents have told me in the past:

"My son has travel soccer every day until 11:30 p.m."

"Oh, really?" Is the only response I can choke out. "Is the team good?"

"No, they never win. But, Mr. B, they do practice until 11:30 at night, unless the coach makes them run some more laps. The coach says that the team is almost ready to score now. Anyway, can my son come to his trumpet lesson after 11:30?"

And another situation I encountered with a parent:

"My daughter made the travel 'tiddly-winks' team. They have tournaments in five states, and she's one of the top 'winkers' in the area."

"Oh, really?" there's my classic reply again. "I thought she was a 'tiddly-er.'"

"*No*, Mr. B. The coach said my daughter is a bodacious 'winker.' Isn't that just great, Mr. B? We're *so* proud of her! So...can she come for a trumpet lesson every other Saturday at 9 p.m.?"

Here's yet another one of my favorite examples of an outrageous excuse:

"The travel curling team is all that my son talks about, Mr. B. We feel that this is a really important activity, and will help him later in life. The coach said that he's not allowed to miss any practices, or else he won't be a starter broom pusher, and he really has to start, or else he'll quit, you know, Mr. B. Also, the coach said that my son's curling will only go to the left unless he practices six hours a day, and he really has to curl to the right, too, you know. Other kids can curl to the right, you know, Mr. B. The coach said that the teams from the other suburbs practice six hours a day, so we really have to do that too, you know. My son is really proud of his broom, Mr. B. You should see his broom, it says 'Travel' on it, and the letters all curl."

"Did you say hurl?" I ask innocently.

"*No, no! Curl*, Mr. B. The letters c-u-r-l...get it? Well, because of this commitment, my son will have to quit every other activity in or out of school until he's eighteen in order to really concentrate on his curling. I know you understand. Thanks, Mr. B."

Oh, really? I understand?

Last week, I was talking with another student, George Blorniak. He's a nice boy who is in 5th grade, and his dad was picking him up after his lesson.

"George, do you have any fun plans for the summer?" I asked.

"No, Mr. B." George looked very sad.

"Oh, you're not going on a vacation?"

"No, my dad says that Blorniak's don't believe in vacations."

Oh, that's too bad, George. How come?"

"Ah, dad says that the only things you get from vacations are memories."

OH, REALLY!

*

Trumpet players often use accessories to alter the sound of a trumpet. These small pieces of equipment are called mutes. There are several kinds of mutes, including ones that you place inside the bell of the trumpet, and others that you hold over the bell with one hand, while working the valves with your other hand. Some mutes just make the sound come out softer, like a cup mute or a straight mute. Others can change the trumpet tone into a more comical sound, like a Harmon or "wah-wah" mute. To operate these mutes, you put them in the bell, then cover and uncover the hole in the end of the mute with your hand while blowing. This creates the "wah-wah" or baby crying-like sound. And, still another type that can make an amusing noise with a trumpet is a plunger mute.

Yes, that's correct...a plunger! This type of sound was popular in the 1940's Big Band era. You might remember hearing the trumpet players using a plunger in the song *Tuxedo Junction*, made famous by the Glenn Miller Band. That group featured plungers on several of their tunes, to get that "doo-wah" sound effect.

To use a plunger on a trumpet, you simply hold it over the bell, and move it back and forth to create the "doo" (closed bell) and "wah" (opened bell). If you move it quickly, it can sound like you're trying to talk underwater. The more slowly you move it, the more it can also sound like a baby crying. Trumpeters have used this effect over the years to imitate everything from a train horn, to a growling type of noise, to the sounds of the grownups talking in the *Peanuts* TV specials. Do you recall those cartoons? You would never actually see the adults, but you could hear the plunging trumpet yelling at the kids about something from off camera.

In addition to the trumpet, just about all of the other brass instruments can use a plunger, especially the trombone, which uses a bigger size. I've even seen them for the big tuba. This requires two people: one who holds and maneuvers the plunger, while the other person plays the tuba. Some musical instrument companies do make these plungers. They might have special designs, or be painted different colors. But, you don't have to purchase a plunger that's made by an instrument company.

Instead, you can just use a toilet plunger. That's right...a plain, old-fashioned toilet plunger. Of course, you don't need to use the stick that's attached to the plunger when applying it to a trumpet.

Occasionally, I bring my plunger to a lesson, especially if I'm on my way to a performing gig and I need to have all of my equipment with me. Let's see what happens today when I present my plunger at Alec's lesson. He's just finished the fourth grade, which means he's played the trumpet for one school year. He's only nine years old, and I've just given him about five or six lessons. He has a fun, go-getter type of personality, and he is always eager to learn and try new things. We're coming to the end of Alec's lesson now, and I reach into my "gig bag" for the plunger:

"All right, Alec. I've got a new trumpet toy to play for you. It's a kind of a mute. Mutes change the sound of a trumpet. This kind is called a plunger."

Alec starts laughing, then his eyes get real wide as he looks at the plunger.

"Eewww, Mr. B, that's a plunger for a...a...*toilet*!"

"That's right, Alec."

"But, Mr. B, did you ever use it in a toilet? I don't want to touch *that!*"

"No, Alec, I never used it in a toilet. I just use it with my trumpet."

"Oh, phew! That's good. But...where's the stick that goes into it?"

"Well, I just unscrewed the stick and took it off, and then I leave the stick at home. Let me play some sounds with it."

I proceed to perform a few growling noises, some crying baby sounds, and then I demonstrate how they make the voices of Charlie Brown's parents. Alec is laughing hysterically:

"Wow, Mr. B, that is *way* cool!"

"Here Alec, you can try it now." As often happens with the younger students, Alec's arms are too short to reach the end of the trumpet bell and still hold onto the plunger. "I'll hold the plunger for you, Alec. Just play a steady, long note. Let's see what happens."

As Alec plays his long tone, I move the plunger to cover and uncover the trumpet bell:

"Waaa...waaa...waaa...waaa...waaaaaaa!" He sounds like a hungry baby. Alec loves it:

"Mr. B, do some more!" OK, Alec. This time, play the same note as many times as you can, and play them all short and fast:

"Wa. Wa. Wa. Wa. Waaa!" Now, he sounds a little like *The Penguin* when that character sarcastically laughs in *Batman*.

Alec stops because he's laughing too hard to play:

"Ha! That's great! Can we play more, Mr. B?"

"Sure. How about if you play one more long note, and move your valves up and down as fast as you can:

"Whoa-woa-woa-woa-woa-woa-woahhh!" Ah yes, it's the familiar underwater yelling sound that the plunger can produce. Alec is sold, and, as often happens with my students, he

wants to get a plunger for himself:

"Where can I get one, Mr. B?"

"Well Alec, let's talk to your mom first, OK?" Alec goes and gets her from the other room, and he starts to explain about this new essential piece of equipment that he *absolutely* has to have for his trumpet. Unfortunately, Alec's mom is not quite as enthusiastic about the idea:

"Uh, OK, Alec. I guess we can get one. Where do you go for it?" she asks me.

"You can just go to the hardware store. They're inexpensive. Ask the hardware man for a small size plunger, and tell him that you don't need the stick. Sometimes they come without the stick, and it might be a little cheaper that way."

Uh-oh...did I just say what I think I said about not using the plunger stick?

"COOL!" exclaims Alec. "Wow, I can't wait to see the look on the man's face when I tell him that we don't even use the stick! Eewww...he'll think we're crazy!"

"Yeah, that's right, Alec." I start to add more fuel to the fire.

"Tell him how tough you are, and that you just use the plunger part without the stick. But, don't say anything about using it for a trumpet. Let me know what the hardware man says then. And, tell your mom how your arms aren't quite long enough to hold the plunger and play your trumpet at the same time. Your mom or dad will have to hold it for you."

I glance towards Alec's mom, and she looks slightly sick to her stomach.

"Well, Alec, you'll have to get your *father* to hold *that*. I'm not touching it!"

"That's OK, mom. Can we go and get it right now? Can we?"

"All right, Alec. *Thanks a lot,* Mr. B. See you next week."

A week has now gone by, and Alec answers the door to begin his next lesson:

"Mr. B, we got the plunger! My dad's been holding it for me while I play, and my mom's *totally* disgusted. You should see!"

"That's neat, Alec. I can't wait to hear it. I'll hold it for you today. What did the hardware man say?"

"His name is Bob. He has it written on his shirt. I told him that we're so tough that we don't even need the stick. We just use the plunger part. I didn't talk about the trumpet, just like you said, Mr. B. The hardware man's eyes got *so* big, and he asked if we're sure about that. I said 'Yes, sir! Just the plunger part is all we need to do the job.' He looked at us like we're crazy. It was fun! I've been telling all my trumpet friends from school to go there and get plungers, too. You know them, Mr. B, because you teach them, too. They're all going to tell the man that they only use the rubber plunger part, so they don't want to buy the stick. I told them to ask for Bob. We'll see what he does when they all go to buy one."

Gulp. What kind of plunging monster have I created?

"Uh, that's cool, Alec. Let's start your lesson."

*

Now that Ann and I are thinking more seriously about buying our own house, we will eventually be in need of...you guessed it...a plunger. And, coincidentally, the plunger I use for trumpet playing is wearing out, too. I'm on my way right now to the same local hardware store that Alec and his friends have been frequenting. I've already been to this store a couple of times, but that was before I started Alec and his buddies on their plunger quest. This place is a really neat, old-fashioned type of hardware store. It's got wooden floors, and the whole place smells like rubber. There are a million aisles, and all the signs are hand-written. Every clerk is a hardware expert, especially compared to me. My home improvement skills are slightly below those of *The Marx Brothers*. I need to get two plungers, but I only want one stick. I'm praying that Bob is off today.

What aisle are those plungers in, I wonder? Maybe I can find them on my own. C'mon, hurry up, before I run into Bob---

"Hello, sir, can I help you? My name is Bob."

"Uh, yes, hi. I'm looking for toilet plungers. I'm going to need two of them, but---"

"Oh, right over here, aisle 7. Let's see...it seems as though the shelf is empty. Let me go to the back and bring out some more. I'll be right back."

"Thanks."

OK, genius, do I tell him that I need two plungers, but only want one stick, just to save a little money? Or, should I just go ahead and buy the stick, too? Maybe I'll try and---

"Here you are, sir." Bob dumps (sorry for the pun) a bunch of plungers on the shelf, and hands me two of them. Each of them has a stick attached.

"Oh, thanks. Actually, I only need one of them to have the stick. I just need the rubber plunger part for the other one."

Bob looks confused. "Really, sir?"

"That's right. I won't be using the stick with the other one, so I'd rather not buy it."

Now Bob smiles, and asks me a question:

"Excuse me, sir. You wouldn't happen to be a trumpet teacher here in town, would you? I've had a series of little boys coming in lately to buy plungers, which is strange enough. Then, they all say that they are 'really tough, and they don't use the stick.' Finally, after about the sixth or seventh one of these boys told me this, I asked him what he *was* going to use the plunger for. He told me it was for making funny sounds on a trumpet, and that his teacher told him not to say anything about it to me. Are you all these boys' trumpet teacher?"

"Uh, yes, sorry about that, Bob. The boys were having fun, but I should have had them tell you that they were only using it to play their trumpets."

"Oh, that's OK, sir. We all got a good laugh out of it afterwards, and it was amusing just to see their moms seem so awkward talking about plungers."

Bob looks around on the shelf, and hands me a plunger without a stick, but it's a much larger size than what I need.

"Thanks, Bob. But...this one's for a trombone."

*

I got a call the other day from a mom who wants trumpet lessons for her son, Benny. She had gotten my name from a friend of mine, the band director at a private high school where I teach. Benny is going to be a freshman there in the fall. She wants him to have a few lessons now in August to get back in shape for playing trumpet in the school band. That should work out perfectly for me. I'll go to his house a few times in August for lessons, and get him started on a practice routine. Then, after school starts, I can try and plug him into a time slot during the day right at the high school.

The mom wouldn't stop going on and on about how good this kid plays:

"He's the *best* trumpeter at his junior high, and everyone says he could become a professional right now. They all tell me they've never heard anyone play like him at his age (well, I *guess* that's a compliment). He can play jazz and classical music, and he's great at everything! Wait until you hear him, Mr. B. I know he'll already be the best one at the high school, too."

That's great, but I'll believe it after I listen to him play. I hear this all the time from parents; their kid is always the best trumpeter anyone has ever heard. There have been many times when I go to listen to the latest phenom, and the kid can barely blow his nose, let alone a trumpet. I said to her:

"I'm glad he's so into playing the trumpet. Did he play a solo at the music contest last year?"

"Yes," she replied, "and he played *so well!* But, he only got a Second Rating (First is the best). He had a bad judge. The judge didn't like the shoes my son was wearing, and marked him down a *whole grade!* Can you believe that? We were going to sue the judge and the contest organizers, but our lawyer said not to bother.

To top it all off, the judge said that Benny was the best trumpeter he heard all day!"

Well, first of all, I've judged at dozens of these contests myself. If the judge doesn't like the student's shoes, or jeans, or whatever, a *point* is taken off, not a *whole grade*. Only deducting one point would usually not change the entire rating, so there's a problem with this lady's information. And, secondly, I believe I know who the judge was at this specific contest: *me!* I did adjudicate the contest for Benny's school last spring, but since I probably heard about fifty trumpet solos that day, I don't remember Benny or his shoes in particular, and I'm sure I wouldn't have said: "You are the best trumpeter I've heard all day!" But...I'm not telling Benny's mom, though!

I'm on my way to Benny's house now. I had given his mom the list of trumpet books that I want him to use, and I told him to make sure his trumpet valves went up and down, like they're supposed to. Sometimes in the summer, students don't touch their instrument, and the valves tend to freeze. If Benny is the next Louis Armstrong, however, he probably oils his valves regularly. When I called to confirm everything yesterday, Benny said that they got the books, and that his horn was working fine.

Benny's house is not far from my apartment, and it's only taken me about ten minutes to get here. Here's his driveway, now...*wow...what a mansion!* It looks like a brand new, three-story house, with a design like a castle. I can see all of these spires and overhangs, just like medieval England. I wonder if they have any gargoyles, or maybe a moat and a dragon? It's so big that they must have torn down two smaller houses, and built this one across two lots. Attached to the side of the house is one of those nineteen-car garages. I can't even imagine what the inside looks like.

Benny opens the door:

"Hi Benny, I'm Mr. B. I'm looking forward to hearing you play! Is your mom home? She said she'd be here to meet me." I almost said:

"Hi Mr. Benny, I'm B..." like Dennis Day used to say to Jack Benny, but I caught myself.

"Hi Mr. B. No, my mom's not home. She might be back later."

Oh well, I thought, no big deal.

"Benny, this is quite a house. Do you have any brothers or sisters?"

"No, just me."

I glance around at the inside of the house, and the first floor alone has several giant rooms. Benny leads me through this huge foyer, which reminds me of the inside of *The Beverly Hillbillies* exquisite front hall. We start to turn a corner, and as I'm looking upward at the skylight, I bump into someone.

"Oh, pardon me." I exclaim. Maybe that's Benny's mom? Or is it *Uncle Jed*? "Hello, I'm Mr...*ow—ooo—wwoaahhh!"...zziippp-ffffft—boioioioing-"ow!"-crash-boom-"woahh! dingdingdingdingdinggg...*

Benny is laughing his butt off. What just happened? I must have tripped over Benny's mom, and now I'm entangled in some enormous metal and wire contraption. But, what went flying by my nose as I was falling? My trumpet case is still in my hand, so at least I didn't fall right on top of it and smash the trumpet, thank goodness. Slowly taking the wires off my head, I stagger to my feet and apologize:

"Excuse me, Mrs..." Benny's starts laughing even louder. I can now see that the person I just introduced myself to is really a seven-foot-high suit of armor, holding a crossbow over my head.

"Benny, *what was that*?"

"Well, when you bumped into the armor, the crossbow shot off the arrow. It almost hit you, too...that was *way* cool! Then, you fell right into our wind chimes. That was one of the funniest things I've ever seen!" He continues to laugh very loudly.

"Thanks, Benny. I appreciate the support." I reply. "Do you have the Holy Grail in here, too?"

We begin to progress farther into this fortress...I'm getting a little winded. I see some stairs off in the distance. Perhaps the dragon of the realm lives under them, like in *The Munsters* TV show?

"Are we having the lesson in the basement?" I ask breathlessly.

"No. We have a big basement, too, but we can just go in here…"

He points towards some kind of a living room that looks slightly smaller than the *Rose Bowl*.

"We also have five bedrooms upstairs." Benny adds.

Now I'm wondering if Rochester and Don Wilson from the old *Jack Benny* program live here, too?

"Oh, five bedrooms…that's great, Benny. Do your grandparents live here, too?"

"No, just me. My dad travels a lot, too."

Hmmm. Let's see if I've got all my facts straight so far. This family lives in a house that's way bigger than what they need, the dad's gone all the time, and the parents will be paying several thousand dollars a year in tuition to send Benny to a private high school, even though they already live in a wealthy suburb with perfectly fine schools. I think I've landed smack in the middle of the American dream! Maybe I should raise my rates for this family?

"All right, Benny, let's get started. I've heard you're a fine player. Get your horn out."

"Well, uh, Mr. B, I don't have my trumpet."

"Really? When I called you yesterday, you told me that your trumpet was here. Well, is it in the repair shop?" I ask.

"Well, uh, maybe. I'm not sure. I really haven't seen it all summer. I'm not sure where it is. I told you that my trumpet is working fine, but I didn't say I know where it is."

What? He's supposedly the new Dizzy Gillespie, and he hasn't even seen his trumpet in almost three months, let alone played it? The worst part of all of this is that Benny is telling me this news without really seeming to care, either. The whole time, he's been staring at a *huge* TV set at one end of this *Rose Bowl* room, and he's watching the Cubs game. He hasn't looked at me once. I'm starting to feel my blood boil, but I try and keep my cool.

"Well, Benny, I know some people at the music store near here. How about if I call and see if your trumpet's there? Maybe your mom took it in at the end of the school year. Can I use your phone?"

"I dunno. If you want to, I guess."

Man, such enthusiasm from this future musical star. I call the music store, but they haven't seen his trumpet, either.

"Benny, does your mom know that you don't have your instrument?"

"I dunno."

"Did she leave me a note someplace about the trumpet?"

"I dunno."

He's still hasn't looked at me, but instead keeps watching the Cub game.

"And...Benny, do you know when she'll be home?" I ask, without much hope.

"I dunno."

OK, this is going nowhere. I better switch to Plan B.

"Benny, I'll get my trumpet out. I can demonstrate all of the songs that I want you to practice for next week, if you can find your instrument. Your mom said she got all the books that you'll need...can you get them out, and I'll play my trumpet for you?"

He's still staring at the TV, and doesn't respond.

"BENNY, GET OUT YOUR NEW TRUMPET BOOKS, AND I'LL PLAY THE SONGS!"

"Uh, uh, OK." He finally turns towards me. "But, uh, Mr. B, uh, I don't have any, uh, trumpet books."

"What? Your mom told me on the phone that she got the books the other day."

"Uh, I dunno. She never told me."

"Well, Benny, can you look around your room, maybe? Or, try

checking your mom's desk? Maybe they're around somewhere?"

"I guess so."

Ugh...more enthusiasm from this young wunderkind. I'm getting more and more pissed off, but I may be able to teach this kid for four years, so I better try and keep being nice. Benny walks from the *Rose Bowl* into the next room, which looks like a replica of the Roman Coliseum. After that, he ventures into another gigantic space that has absolutely nothing in it. Huh...maybe *this* is the new Chicago Bulls practice facility that I read about in the paper. Benny turns and shrugs at me. No luck finding any trumpet books yet.

"Benny, are there any lions in that one room?"

"What, Mr. B?"

"Never mind. Do you want to go upstairs and check your room?"

"No, I never practice upstairs."

"Oh, that helps narrow it down, Benny. Tell me, then, where *do* you practice?"

"I dunno. I haven't in a long time."

I can't hold my anger in much longer:

"Benny, I've heard that you're one of the top trumpeters for your age. How *do* you like playing the trumpet, and being in the band?"

"I dunno."

"Well, Benny, now you'll be in a new band at the high school and the director is really cool. You'll have lots of fun."

"I guess so."

There's a grandfather clock over by that titanic TV, and I think it's the size of Rhode Island. I can't help but notice that nine whole minutes of Benny's tutorial have gone by. What a fabulous first lesson we're having! Maybe it's time for Plan C.

"OK, Benny. I'll write down the names of the books, in case your mom didn't get them at the store. And...I'll play a little bit of each of the pieces that I want you to practice, so you can hear what they sound like."

I've had several of these songs memorized for years, so it's not a big deal for me to play parts of them now. As I start my demonstration, I notice that Benny is still watching the Cubs game on TV. Ah, what the hell, I should watch the game, too, while I play my trumpet. He won't notice, or care. Yeah, I'm glad I thought of that...at least I'll accomplish something during this lesson. Look...there's Harry Caray, singing *Take Me Out To The Ballgame*. Benny never even looks over at me, and at the end of my performance I ask him how he liked it.

"OK, I guess."

"Benny, I'm glad I practiced so hard all those years just so I could play for you today!"

"Yeah...I dunno."

Fifteen minutes have now passed since I arrived. There's no sign of the mom, the trumpet, the books, or Benny's personality, if he even has one. If he left his persona in another room, it might take years to find it. We both continue to watch the game for a while, in silence, and he seems perfectly content doing that. About twenty-five minutes have now gone by, and I decide to leave Xanadu.

"Benny, I've left you the list of books, and played the songs for you. I think I'll be going now. Your mom said to come at the same time next week....did she leave me a check for today?"

"Uh, I dunno."

No check...I bet it was lost next to his personality.

"OK, I'll call your mom. Tell her that I came over, and I'll see you next week. Bye, Mr. Benny."

A few hours later, I call the mom:

"I've been waiting for your call, Mr. B, and I must say that I'm quite perturbed. Benny said you never showed up for his lesson!"

The phone drops off of my hand, and my jaw drops off of my face.

"Excuse me...I was there, but Benny did not have his trumpet, or the books. He said he didn't even know where his trumpet was. I played the songs for him, and I left him another list of the book titles to get at the store."

"Oh, Mr. B, *are you kidding*? The trumpet and the books are right here by the front door. That's where I left them when I went to my daily spa facial treatment. I've been going for fifteen years, Mr. B, and I have to go every day. And, I had left the check on top of the trumpet case. *I don't know what you're talking about, Mr. B!* There is no list of books here. Benny is really upset that you didn't come...he's been practicing all the time, and he sounds marvelous! We'll give you one more chance next week, but if you don't show up, we'll be looking for another trumpet teacher."

BANG! She hangs up the phone angrily. Wait a minute...she goes to the spa *every day?* For *fifteen years?* That must be quite a face she has on her. It didn't even take that long for them to carve out Mount Rushmore! I'm disappointed, too. I never got to tell her how I was almost decapitated by Sir Lancelot!

*

As I wake up the next day, I've decided that I'm not going back to Mr. Benny's house for any more abuse, either from him, his knight, or his mom. I did like watching the ballgame on that giant TV, though. Having an experience like this really makes me wish that I could teach lessons at my own place, instead of getting insulted and beheaded at some moron's house. Of course, I can't have trumpet students coming over to our apartment for their lessons. The landlord wouldn't allow that.

I've decided to call Benny's mom again, but instead of arguing with her about our phantom lesson, or asking her for the money again, I'll tell her I'm just too busy for any more August lessons. It's really not worth fighting over. If Benny wants to study with me when school starts, at the high school, his mom can call me to set that up.

I think I have the courage to dial the phone now. Here goes......*ah, did I get lucky!* Her answering machine picked up, so I don't have to talk to her. I hurry and leave my message quickly, in case she's just walking in the door from the spa. I don't want her to pick up the phone during my message. I can't wait to see if she calls me back, but I think I'll let *my* machine answer it.

*

Now, a few weeks later, school has begun. I haven't heard a peep from Benny's mom. I'm setting up my teaching schedule at the high school, and I notice Benny's name isn't listed on the band roster. I start to ask the other kids if they know a freshman named Benny, who was going to play trumpet in the band? I told my other students that this kid was supposed to be such a terrific trumpeter, so they should find out about him. As for me, I've never even heard him play one note. One of my students comes back later and tells me some Benny news:

"Oh yeah, Mr. B, he's in my gym class. I asked him about band. He said he hasn't played his trumpet in four years, and he never signed up for band. I told him you were asking about him, and he said that he never heard of you!"

What? Was I hallucinating during this entire episode? Will the world never get to hear this all-star trumpet sensation? More importantly, is his mom still *UGGG---LY*? You never know, but if they ever add a fifth face on Mount Rushmore, we just might know who it is...

Good-bye, Mr. Benny!

*

Ann and I have been looking at houses for a couple of months now. After saving for many years, we think that we're about ready to buy our own home. Living in our apartment for the past six years has been all right, but it is also very frustrating for us. We would really like to start a family, but the landlord has always told us that the apartment complex doesn't permit children. What's become more annoying, however, is that another couple in the building *did* have a baby, and they still continue to live here. We're not sure why that is being allowed, and we don't really know that couple well enough to ask them about it. The most maddening part about the whole thing is that we have to share the laundry area with them, and Ann is constantly finding cloth diapers that have been left in the washer and dryer!

Besides the diaper sightings, there are other reasons why it's also become wearisome for us to keep being "apartment dwellers." As we look out of our second story window, the first thing we always see is a very nice house that's right next to our building. It's a medium size house, with a backyard big enough to have kids play in it. The house was just sold, but it was too expensive for us to afford. I can see from our window that the moving van is in the driveway now. They're unloading a swing set and taking it into the yard. *OH, MAN...SOMEDAY THAT WILL BE US! WE'RE GETTING CLOSER!*

As I gaze out the window, I wonder if the couple that bought the house is about our age. Wait...I can see a car pulling up. This must be them...there is a man and a woman, and they are helping two little kids to get out of the car. I'll check out the husband to guess how old he might be---wow, this guy is *tall*! And, he's got a big, black beard. He seems like he's about my age. I can hear him talking...what a deep voice this guy's got! He reminds me of someone, but I can't quite put my finger on who---*I know!*

He looks and sounds like Bluto, the villain from *Popeye*! You remember him, right? Bluto is the guy that was always trying to steal Popeye's girlfriend, Olive Oyl. And, Bluto would constantly bully Popeye, until Popeye finally would eat his spinach towards the end of each cartoon, and then proceed to beat the crap out of Bluto. Yeah, that's it...I think my new neighbor was the inspiration for Bluto! *THAT'S JUST GREAT!* Now, every time I look out this window, I'll be reminded of Bluto and his family, getting to live in this neat house. I'm starting to feel depressed, like Popeye must have felt *before* he ate his spinach. *DON'T WORRY, ANN! WE'LL BE IN OUR OWN HOME SOON, I HOPE!*

For the most part, Ann and I have been looking at houses in six or seven of the different suburbs where we travel to give lessons. We've been finding that some of these neighborhoods are way out of our price range, and that other areas have their own idiosyncrasies about them.

For instance, there's one suburb where it seems like several of the parents don't really want to know what their kids are doing, or even what they're like. We've noticed this in so many families in this particular town that it doesn't seem like a coincidence! These parents have lots of money, and that's why Ann and I have had so many students in this suburb. But, the parents take no interest in the lessons, and they barely say hello to us. Just think back to my story about Benny and the *Rose Bowl* house, or the one about Tom and Mark, the brothers that Ann and I teach. They are the siblings whose dad couldn't even remember his kids' names. I don't think we'll be buying a house there!

At this point, we've now narrowed our choice down to just one suburb. There are plenty of homes in this area that we can afford. We may have to buy a "fixer-upper," but that's OK. And, the schools are close enough so that, someday, our own children can walk to them. There are still lots of trees left in this town, and it's fairly close to some of the major highways. That's important, since Ann and I often have to drive downtown to play our instruments at professional performances.

We've had lots of students in this suburb over the years, and for the most part the parents have been really cooperative with us, as well as very interactive with their kids. Let me emphasize the word *most*. Because we see these parents every week, we've been able to develop more of a personal relationship with them. Most want to know how Ann and I are doing, and they're appreciative of our skills in teaching their kids. They regularly ask about the performances that we've had in the past week, and they explain to their kids how cool it is to be called to play at these "gigs." I have four lessons to give today in this suburb, and three more later in the week.

All of my students today live in the same neighborhood, and they all go to school together. They're in the fifth grade, and they've played in the same band for almost two years now. I actually teach seven boys from this school and band. I'm guessing they're all about ten years old, and they've known each other for a while.

My first student is Elliot. His family is one of the exceptions to the rest of all of these supportive, grateful family units that Ann and I have found in this suburb. Elliot is ok at the trumpet, and does practice some, but he isn't very serious about his music. He's usually respectful towards me, but he has some annoying habits, which makes it uncomfortable for me to be around him. He also seems to have a good rapport with his parents, but they're often not home until just before the end of his lessons. I must say, however, that the other students simply *can't stand Elliot!* Every week, when I go to each of the other six kid's houses from this school group, I get lots of remarks about Elliot. Here's just a sample:

"Mr. B, did Elliot pick his nose today? You should have seen him pick a winner in school!"

"Hey Mr. B, did you teach Elliot yet? What a dork!"

"How many times did Elliot fart today during his lesson? I bet Tommy that he would only do it two times. Mr. B, did you know that Elliot can fart the beginning of Beethoven's 5th? Tell me the answer, Mr. B, so I can win the bet!" Elliot actually farted four times that day, so Tommy won the bet.

"Mr. B, did the other guys tell you what Elliot did in school today? He pushed Jordan into the water fountain, and Jordan broke his tooth! But, the teacher didn't see it, so Elliot blamed it on Joe. The teacher started to yell at Joe, and Joe got mad and punched Elliot. Joe had to go to the principal's office, and nothing happened to Elliot. That's one reason why none of us like him. How was his trumpet lesson?"

And, those are just *a few* of the examples. I've heard many more stories about Elliot's public behavior, both in and out of school. The other boys have told me about Elliot starting several fights, and emitting loads of bodily functions. He always blames the other kids for everything that he does, too. He's rather small for his age, so I know he can't be winning very many of his fights. It just seems that he knows exactly how to get under other kids' skins, and he enjoys doing that all day. I'm sure the teachers are on to him, and the principal probably has his parent's phone number at the top of his speed dial list.

I pull into Elliot's driveway, and he opens the door.

"Hi Elliot, how 'ya doing?"

Uh-oh, Elliot has let loose from the backside again. I'll hold my breath and hope it dissipates quickly.

"Been eating beans again, Elliot?" I ask sarcastically, but my question goes right over his head (unlike the smell, unfortunately).

"Why?"

I can't take a breath to answer, however. Elliot's launched another projectile into the room.

"Elliot, would you like to go to the bathroom?"

"Why?"

"Oh, no reason. Are your parents home?"

"Why?" I think this means no. His parents wouldn't put up with these proctologic utterances.

"OK, Elliot, let's get the lesson started."

"Huh?"

We go along fine for about twenty minutes, at which time I begin to notice some of his annoying habits starting up.

"Let's play number 37, Elliot. One-two-ready---"

Oops, there goes his left hand into his pants. At some lessons, he does this quite often, and at others, he doesn't do it at all. I'll see what happens today.

"Elliot, put your left hand back on your trumpet."

He moves his hand back, and I count off the song again:

"One-two-read---"

Whoops, now his right pointer finger is up his nose.

"Elliot, put your right hand on the trumpet valves."

After an awkward pause, he puts his fingers on the valves. I ain't touchin' those valves!

"OK, here we go. One-two---"

Uh-oh, his left hand's down the pants again. And...two right hand fingers are together in his nose. The trumpet is on his lap.

"Elliot, let's start over. Put both of your hands on your trumpet now."

"Why?"

"You know why, Elliot. That's the way we hold a trumpet."

"Huh?"

You do need both hands to hold a trumpet properly. The left hand basically grips it, and holds it up. This is especially important for a young student to do. The right hand fingers then move the three valves up and down. Elliot finally removes his hands from his different extremities, and complies with my instructions.

"Great, Elliot! Here's number 37, one-two-ready---"

Oop...left hand's down the pants again.

Then back on the trumpet.

Right hand's up the nose.

"Elliot!"

"Huh?"

Then it's back on the trumpet.

But, his left hand's down his pants.

Then back.

Now *three* right fingers are up the nose.

"Elliot!"

"Huh?"

Then back.

Oh my, now both his hands are down the pants, and his trumpet is on the floor.

"Elliot, how about if I play a couple of new songs for you? You can just listen."

"Why?"

Once again, however, I'm unable to breathe too deeply. Elliot's let go with an SBD, and it's filled up the room. I wonder if this is how Beethoven started when he composed his 5th *Symphony*. Nah, it can't be…this one was silent. Even though I've just thrown up in my mouth a little bit, I bravely soldier on and play the songs for him. My trumpet mouthpiece isn't tasting too great at the moment, and I'm sure not going to look and see where Elliot's hands might be!

After finishing my demonstration, my first thought is "let's get out of here!" I don't think four of my five senses will ever be the same again. Time is up, anyway.

"Elliot, I'll see you next week. Try and go to the bathroom once in a while, OK?"

"Why?"

"Did your parents leave you the money to give to me?"

"Why?"

"Good-bye, Elliot."

"Huh?"

*

I'm off to Tommy's house now. He lives just around the corner from Elliot. I can see Tommy waiting outside for me.

"Hi Mr. B! Oh, you don't look so good. Did you come from Elliot's house? I bet he picked and farted! Ooo…I'm gonna call Joe and tell him. Do you want to lie down? You look all green."

"No thanks, Tommy. Let's go play our trumpets."

"OK, Mr. B, but your face looks like the green beans my mom made last night. They looked terrible, too.

*

After Tommy's lesson, I drive over to Joe's house, and I hear the same story there:

"Mr. B, Tommy called and said Elliot ficked and parted! I mean…are you gonna throw up? Tommy said you were all green. That's cool! Now you're kinda white looking, like toothpaste. Do you want to lie down? Then maybe you can throw up for me? "

"No, Joe, I'm OK."

*

Next, I go to Jordan's house. He's my last student of the day. At last, I'm feeling less queasy. It's amazing that these kids have noticed how colorful I've looked today. I bet Elliot has that effect on everyone, not just me.

Jordan is the boy who lost a tooth on the school water fountain, thanks to Elliot pushing him.

"Mither B, wook what Ewiot did to my mouf! Are you gonna turn gween again? Joe said you might thwow up. Can he come ovah and watch?"

"Uh, Jordan, I can tell you're having some trouble talking. Your mouth looks very swollen and red. Do you think you can play your trumpet today?

"Thure, Mither B. I can pway my twumpet. How was Ewiot's wesson?"

"Well, when I was at Elliot's house, all of my senses were going wild, Jordan. *Wild.*"

*

After the long, nauseous day I had yesterday, I think I've recovered now since I've gotten some sleep. Ann and I are on our way to this same suburb to check out some houses. I've told her all about Elliot, Tommy, and my other little guys in this group of students. In fact, she knows *a lot* about Elliot, even though she's never even seen him. She has several of her own students up here, and she gets to hear plenty about Elliot's bodily functions from those girls. I can think of some examples now:

"Mrs. B, do you have to go to Elliot's house with Mr. B? I hope not...I heard he just sits around all day picking his nose and, well, you know, making sounds and smells come from his other end. Does Mr. B tell you about Elliot's other end?"

"Mrs. B, Jane said Mr. B teaches Elliot. *ICK...!* He's got cooties. Does Mr. B have cooties now, too?"

"How can Mr. B stand Elliot? He's *SSSO ooogy*...his cooties have their own cooties!"

"Elliot budged me in line today, and I can't stop washing my arm where he touched me...*YUK!*"

We're in the neighborhood now where our prospective homes are located. Aaah, rats...we're stuck behind a school bus letting off some kids after school. Oh, well...it shouldn't be too long. *Wait*...suddenly, all the kids are surrounding one little boy. We're too far away to see exactly what's happening, but it seems like they're all taking turns pushing and hitting this one guy.

"That's terrible." Ann says. "Look what they're doing to that kid."

"Oh, don't worry." I reply jokingly. "It's probably Elliot, and I bet he had it coming."

As we drive by the scrum, Ann says:

"There, look...the boy's getting up now."

I turn my head to try and see, and *it is Elliot!* Many of the kids recognize Ann and me in our car, since they see one of us driving it every week. They all start laughing and shouting:

"Hi Mrs. B! Hi Mr. B!"

I can see Elliot standing there, brushing off the dirt and grass from his pants. He looks at me, smiles, and waves with one hand. His other hand is alternating furiously between his pants and his nose.

"Don't tell me." Ann nods knowingly. "*That* is Elliot. *Eeewww!*"

*

Ann and I have now looked at several houses since leaving Elliot and his pals, but none seemed to be a good fit for us. We're starting to feel a little like Goldilocks...the homes are either:

"Too small." Or

"Too expensive." Or

"Too big." Or...well, you get the idea. Nothing's been "just right" for us yet.

Now we're on our way to the last house of the day, and the neighborhood appears nice as we pull into the driveway. It's a pretty area, with tons of trees all up and down the block. All of the homes around here appear to be about the size and price that we're interested in, so hopefully the people won't be snobby types like Benny's mother. This particular house is exactly in the middle of a rather quiet street. I don't think much traffic would be coming past here, and that's *great* news after what we've been putting up with in the apartment. And, we drove by a school just around the corner. That would be really convenient for our future kids.

However, even from the outside, Ann and I have noticed some drawbacks to the house:

"Ann...there's no garage."

"Oh well, we've never had a garage before, Sam. And look...the driveway...it's not concrete or blacktop. I think it's made out of road gravel!"

"Oh boy, I see it. OK...well, at least it would be *our* road gravel. But check out those rusty gutters and the beat-up siding. It all looks like it may fall off the house at any minute!"

"Yeah, I see that, Sam. All right...at least the price of the house matches our budget, so let's take a look inside anyway."

As we enter the house, we can tell right away that the inside is also quite a "fixer-upper." The house was built 35 years ago, and the décor still looks like, well...

"Sam, this is straight out of the early "Leave it to Beaver" period."

"Yeah, a lot of things look pretty rundown. A lot of this stuff may need replacing, maybe even all of the windows. And that stove has more grease on it than Fonzie's hair."

Oh well...this is a shame. After all, the house *is* in a good location. And, I'm guessing that this is about the biggest house we'll see that's in our price range. It's easy to get on the highway from here when we have to go downtown for gigs. Plus, besides the school, it's also just a short walk to several stores and restaurants.

"Sam, I'm not sure what to think."

"Yeah, I agree. But, wouldn't you just hate to buy this place, and then on top of paying for it have to spend a lot more money to replace everything in it? OK, I guess as long as we're here, let's keep going through the place. How about if we check out the backyard---*WOW, would you look at that!* What a great yard, and...what's that behind it?"

"The realtor said that's a private golf course back there. There's no road, or houses, and no neighbors behind us either!"

"Fantastic! No neighbors...that sounds good to me!"

"And, look here, Sam!"

Ann peels up a corner of the old rug in the living room.

"Hardwood floors are underneath this carpet...the realtor said we should check it out!"

"That's cool---oh, hello."

"Hello, I'm Mrs. Baker."

"Hi, I'm Sam, and this is my wife, Ann. The realtor said you are the owner, and that you might be here today."

"That's right. My late husband and I are the original owners of the house. We moved in 35 years ago when it was built. We raised our family here, and we've loved this place, especially the quiet neighborhood. But, now that my husband is gone, I have to sell it. Here...let me show you something..."

Mrs. Baker opens a closet door, and inside are pencil markings with some inches and feet listed next to several dates.

"This is where we measured our kids as they grew up...see the marks? They spent their entire childhood in this house---"

Mrs. Baker begins to cry.

"That's so wonderful!" Ann exclaims. "Would you like some water, Mrs. Baker?"

"Yes, thank you. You look like a nice young couple. I think you're about the same age that my husband and I were when we moved in. I believe you'd be happy here, too."

"Oh, thank you, Mrs. Baker," replies Ann. "We'll definitely think seriously about the house, and we'll talk to the realtor right away---oh my...look out the window, Sam...in the tree!"

As I gaze out, I can see what Ann is noticing. There is a robin's nest in one of the trees in the front yard...that's got to be a good sign! Ann and I nod at each other, and then I turn back to declare:

"You know, Mrs. Baker, we *really* want this house! Our realtor will be contacting you *very* soon. Thanks again!"

Cars, driving and policemen

CHAPTER FOUR

Driving a hundred miles round trip to teach some trumpet lessons is not exactly what I had mind for my career. And, now I'm driving that distance twice a week, too. But, this high school was one of the few looking for a trumpet teacher when I started searching for students. The band director is easy to get along with (what a surprise!), and he tries to encourage more kids to take lessons. Most of the students are very nice and work hard, and I've now been able to build it up to about twenty to twenty-five students a week over the two days.

There is one student, however, who cancels his lesson almost *every week.* His lessons are on Wednesdays, which means I get a phone call from him at exactly 9:58 p.m. every Tuesday night. It's become a running joke in our house when the phone rings...that *must* be Steve! There's really no way to tell who it is (no Caller ID in 1983), but Ann and I know it's him. He's a sophomore in high school, but his voice sounds eerily close to Peter Lorre, with the same heavy breathing included. Just like that famous actor from all of those great movies such as *Casablanca,* Steve ends almost every sentence with a sickly laugh:

"Hi, Mr. B, (heh, heh) this is Steve. I can't make my lesson tomorrow (heh, heh)."

"Why, not, Steve?" I ask.

This is where Steve has to be creative, since he can't use the same excuse every week. Steve doesn't have medical issues, like my student Teddy, but he does use academics for excuses. Sometimes it sounds legitimate, such as:

"I have to make up a test tomorrow during our lesson period (heh)." Or:

"I have to see a teacher during our lesson period tomorrow (heh, heh)."

He's got the "during our lesson period tomorrow" part memorized, but it sounds like he's reading the rest of it. Other times I've heard him say things like:

"Just our class is having a fire drill during our lesson period tomorrow (heh). Nobody else is." Or, he might tell me: "Just our class is having an assembly during our lesson period tomorrow. No other class is (heh, heh)."

He has the "just our class" part memorized, too, and his Peter Lorre voice always starts to creep me out. Now, how can I possibly check and see if that's really going to happen, especially at 10:00 at night, from fifty miles away? I have to go to this school to teach the other students anyway, so I usually end up reading the paper during Steve's lesson time. Of course, he never pays me for cancelling at the last minute.

When Steve actually does have a lesson, and starts talking to me in that breathy voice, I can't help myself. I begin to reply using a bad Bogart imitation, telling him at the end of the lesson that:

"We'll play it again next week, Steve."

And, when he has trouble getting a nice sound out of his trumpet, I'll say:

"You know how to whistle, don't you Steve? Just put your lips together...."

I always manage to stop myself from finishing *that* sentence. I hope Lauren Bacall never has to hear my lousy Bogart voice.

Since I do have to drive fifty miles to get to this school, I always check the school calendar each week to make sure they're having a regular school day when I'm coming. Maybe they are they having an institute day, with no students attending? Or, there might be some kind of an assembly, or possibly a half day of school? Or, maybe even a late start to the school day, with all the rest of the periods shortened that day? This schedule is particularly bad for me, since there isn't enough time for a full trumpet lesson during these shortened periods. I always ask my students and the band director to call me the night before if the school schedule will be changed, and usually someone does.

There was one time, however, when I drove all the way out there, and *no one* was there...they had cancelled school, and I didn't know! There's nothing like that sinking feeling of approaching the school and seeing an empty parking lot. The power had gone out at the school, so they had to cancel at the last minute. Several of my students said they called me when they found out, but by then I had already left home the usual ninety minutes ahead of my first lesson. When I got to the vacant school, I had to find a phone booth to call one of the students in order to hear what had happened. Then, I got back in the car, turned around, and drove the fifty miles back home. No lessons that day. No money, either. Just another hundred miles added on to the car. I know that was no one's fault...just bad luck.

I'm driving there again now, and traffic has been light. I've been able to make the fifty miles in about an hour, which is very good. I'm approaching the school, but...wait...now the traffic is all backed up. Great...I'll be late for my first student. I'm only two blocks away, but I can't even see the parking lot. There are hundreds of kids milling around all over the school grounds, and no cars are moving at all. I can faintly hear some music being played, too. It's only about 10:00 in the morning...what could possibly be happening now? Maybe it's just a fire drill, and the schedule hasn't been changed. Please tell me that's what it is! I'll have to park over here on this side street, and try and walk the last two blocks over to the school.

After parking, I begin to worm my way through the crowds of kids. This seems way too long to be a fire drill. Plus, these students aren't in any type of organized and quiet lines. I'm starting to get a bad feeling about teaching my lessons today. The music is getting louder as I get closer to the school. It sounds like the band from the high school, and they're playing....I can barely make it out...it's the theme from the TV show *Dallas.* I can see the band marching down the street in front of the school. It looks like they're being followed by a pickup truck, with dozens of students walking behind the truck. No wonder the traffic was completely stopped when I drove up. I ask the next student I see:

"Excuse me. What's going on?"

He points up to the pickup truck:

"Oh, it's some dumb parade for that lady up there."

That lady is standing in the truck, wearing long white gloves and waving to the crowd like the queen. With all the noise of the cheering and the band music, I can barely hear myself swearing. I try and shout:

"Who is that?"

"I dunno. All they said was that she's famous, and that they're calling off school today. Isn't that cool!"

WHAT! They're calling off school!

"When did they tell you that?"

"Oh, just a little while ago. They said to stick around for the parade and ceremony, but, are you kidding...I'm outta here!"

I slither my way closer to the band. As they march by, my students wave at me in between playing their notes. The Band director sees me, too. He can't stop and talk to me, but he just smiles, shakes his head, and shrugs his shoulders. It's too loud for me yell at them over the music, so I point toward the school, then toward myself. I'll meet them back in the band room after this is over. They nod their heads as they stride in the direction of the school entrance.

The parade seems to be slowing down, but there are so many students walking around that I can't make my way over to the school door. This might take me a while. There are still ten minutes before my first lesson is supposed to begin; maybe I can make it. Naturally, Steve is my first student, and believe it or not he didn't cancel last night! I can see the band standing at attention by the door, and they're putting a microphone up in the pickup truck by "that lady." Everyone continues to cheer. *Now what!*

I'm really stuck now. The crowd is so thick in this school parking lot that I can't move in any direction. I can see "that lady" talking into to the microphone, but I'm too far away to hear her. I ask the students next to me:

"Do you know who that is?"

"No...nobody knows."

"Then why is everyone cheering?"

"We're just glad to be out of school...isn't that cool!"

I sadly reply:

"Yes, I've heard that already."

"See ya...we're outta here, mister!"

Now I have five minutes to go before Steve's lesson. After one final wave to the audience, "that lady" has stopped speaking, and the Band has disappeared back inside. I'm still stuck in the crowd. The students are all leaving, and since I'm trying to get *into* the school, I feel like a salmon swimming upstream. I sure hope Steve and my other students wait for me inside. Even if they've canceled school, I can still teach them today as long as I can get in the building. Carrying my trumpet, lunch, and music bag, I can't maneuver very quickly through this throng. This is taking forever...now I'm already five minutes into Steve's lesson.

There are still more kids bumping by me as they leave the school, but I'm finally getting close to the door. Just another thirty yards or so to go...hang on, Steve, I'll be there!

Okay, I can see a clearer path...here's the door. I'm ten minutes late. My Canadian bacon sandwich has been squished into a ball from squeezing through the crowd, and my banana has shrunk, but at least my can of Mountain Dew hasn't exploded. Maybe Steve can stay late---*OH, SH*&! The door's locked!* I start pounding on the door, but no one seems to be around---

"Hi, Mr. B (heh, heh)."

I look over, and I see Steve standing there.

"Steve, you're...you're outside."

"Yeah, they made everyone leave, and then they locked all the doors (heh)."

"So...do you have your trumpet with you?"

"No, Mr. B. All of us left our trumpets in the band room, 'cause we have marching band tonight at 7:00. Everyone else is going home. I just thought I'd stay and tell you (heh, heh)."

My heart sinks. No lessons today. No money, either.

"Uh, thanks, Steve. By the way, what was all this about? I mean, the parade, and letting school out? And, who *is* that lady?"

"Oh, she graduated from school here a few years ago, and now she's an actress in Hollywood. She made a surprise visit to the school this morning, and the principal decided to have a parade for her. That's why we were marching (heh)."

"Yeah, I saw you, Steve."

"Yeah, and then our band director said that when the principal saw how wild everybody got out in the parking lot, he called off school for the rest of the day (heh, heh)."

"Uh, OK, Steve. Is that lady in a TV show, or a movie?"

"Well (heh), she started to get famous by winning a beauty contest when she was still here. She was named *Miss Corn-Fed Beef* of 1977. That's a pretty big deal around here, you know, Mr. B. Now she's in a soap opera called *All My Lawyers* (heh, heh)."

"Oh yeah, I've heard of that show, Steve. But, why was the band playing the theme from *Dallas*? Is she in that, too?"

"Oh, no. She tried out, but she didn't make it. That was the only song we had ready to play (heh)."

"Uh, thanks, Steve, I guess I'll see you next week."

"No, Mr. B. Remember, there's an institute day next week. No school for *any* of the students, not just our class (heh, heh)."

I had forgotten about that.

"Right. Two weeks then, Steve. Thanks...bye."

I trudge back to the car. Another wasted day, except for adding another hundred miles onto the car. There's a park bench near my car...I think I'll eat lunch now. Even though it looks like my banana has contracted further, that smashed ball of Canadian bacon smells good. I'll open that Mountain Dew now--- *CRRAACK---PIIISHHH!*

SON OF A--- all that jostling through the crowd made the can blow up, and now I have Mountain Dew all over my shirt and pants. That will make it a fun drive home for fifty miles. All right, just get in the car, you idiot---

WHAT! I got a ticket! You're kidding, right? For what?

"NO PARKING ON SCHOOL DAYS."

BUT THERE IS NO SCHOOL TODAY!

*

Of course, since I have to drive this many miles twice a week, I'm eventually going to have some other problems, too. Today, I'm worried about our car. It's getting older, and the hood won't quite shut all the way. The hood latch is barely holding, but it's not really closed and sealed. I have to drive these hundred miles again today, and it's mostly on two Interstate highways. If I cancel the lessons to get the hood fixed, I not only have to pay for the car repair, but I will also lose all of the money from today's students...that's just another perk of being self-employed. I tell Ann "don't worry, the hood will be fine."

So far today, I'm driving along with no sign of a problem, and I only have about twenty miles to go. I'm going about 60 mph, staying in the center lane of a three lane highway. This is a toll way, where there are very few exits, and I'm nowhere near one. I have my change ready to put in the tollbooth when I do exit (remember, this is twenty years before toll way transponders, so I always have to have lots of change with me).

Uh-oh...something's happening...ohhh—nooo...I can start to see the hood slowly lifting up. I reach for my change, trying to place the correct amount in my hand. There's no one working at these tollbooths to change a dollar. This is all happening like one of those slow-motion scenes from the shootout of a Western movie. My mind starts racing, and I start asking myself all of these dumb questions faster and faster:

"Do I have the right change?"

"Can I get off the road soon?"

The latch comes apart *another* notch.

"Can I get to a gas station?"

"Where's my Mountain Dew?"

"Can they fix it temporarily so I can make it home?"

"What rhymes with orange?"

"Can I get to a phone booth to call the Motor Club?"

And now the hood slips one more notch...there are only two notches left that are holding it together!

"Do I have enough change for both the tollbooth and the phone booth?"

"What *is* the name of that seventh dwarf?"

"Why am I still in the middle lane?"

"I see my Mountain Dew...its fallen in-between the seats!"

Whhooaaa!!! Yet another notch gives way, and I'm trying to get over to the right lane. One notch left to hold, and I'm still three miles from an exit. What's left of my brain is in panic mode, but it still seems like slow-motion:

"I think I can get into the right lane!"

"Who died in that duel, Alexander Hamilton or Aaron Burr?"

"Did I put on clean underpants?"

"I got it...the dwarf's name is *Bashful*!"

"Try to pull onto the shoulder, stupid----"

Whoooaaaa!!! The final notch is breaking! I'm still going 60, and I think I have my signal on (but who cares at this point). Come on, slow down! There...55...50...45. The wind catches the hood, and starts to lift it up, slowly at first. Pull over...there, right lane...now...the shoulder. I'm slowing down more. I *think* I'm on the shoulder, but I can't see anything. The hood starts rising faster and faster, and I'm still going about 40. I know it's going to go right through the windshield and impale me. My mind continues to race:

"Don't worry, Ann, it'll be fine....those will be the last words I ever say to her!"

"She'll put 'yeah, right' on my tombstone!"

"I think Hamilton died in that duel."

"Duck, you dope!"

35...30...25...as I gradually get the car to stop, the hood keeps coming towards me; closer, closer, and still seemingly in slow-motion. The hood swings up and over, getting near the windshield, and starts to break off its back moorings. I hear it creaking...the back latches are trying to hold. I still have the change for the tollbooth in my hand; Washington's nose has made a huge impression in my palm. *The hood gets just a few inches away from the windshield, but wait---I think those back latches may hold!* I grab my Mountain Dew...*I'm not gonna die thirsty!* The hood creaks a little more, but the back latches hang on. The hood stops moving, just before smashing into the windshield! I've finally stopped the car, and I guess that I'm on the shoulder of the highway.

I can't see a thing out of the windshield. The hood is blocking my view, and the wind is making the hood gently creak back and forth, but don't worry, genius, "it'll be fine." Yeah, right, just like I said to Ann! I'm frozen in my seat for a moment, and then my nose "gets a load" of something that's taken place in my shorts.

I slowly climb across the bucket seats to try and get out on the passenger side. Naturally, the gearshift is in the middle. I can't get out on the driver's side, since the cars are zooming by me at about 70 mph. Hey, do you think I should put my hood up so the other cars know I'm in trouble? No, wait...that's been done for me already! I finally get out, and wobble around next to the car, like one of those bobble heads. After about fifteen minutes, a state trooper drives up:

"Sir, are you all right?"

"Well, I'm not sure, officer. Just a little shaken up, I guess."

"OK, then. You're pretty pale, and your sweat is dripping on my shoes. Well, look at that hood. Last time I saw something like that, the hood flew off and took the driver's scalp with it."

"Thanks for sharing."

The trooper kindly pulls the hood back down, tying it shut with some rope.

"Sir, you can follow me off of the toll way, and I'll lead you to a gas station that I know about near here. They'll be able to help you to at least drive ho---say, did you step in some dog poop?"

Uh-oh. I think he's noticed my emanating "Eau du Barnyard" scent, but I'm not saying a word about it.

"No, officer, I don't think so."

"Oh, great. *Shheeesh!* I probably stepped in it myself. Do you think you can drive?"

Thanks to the trooper's description, I still have visions of my scalp flying around like a hairy *Frisbee*, but I reply:

"Yeah, I guess so."

He has me climb back into my car (no easy task with the current state of my shorts), and then I follow him to the gas station. I pull the car over to the side of the garage, and I can see the trooper explaining my situation to the station attendants. After they stop laughing, they begin bolting down the hood a little more securely.

"I can't thank you enough, officer. I really appreciate the help."

"Your welc---*WOW*, that smell is *something else! Damn dogs!* Good-bye, sir."

After they finish with the hood, the gas station guys say that it's OK for me to drive the car home. Before I get back in the car, however, I'd like to clean up a little.

"Hey, guys, do you have a bathroom I could use?"

They all burst out laughing:

"Sure, buddy. Right around the corner. It ain't the greatest, but you're floppin' in sweat like a pig. Here's the key."

Well, I can't be too choosy right now. I open the bathroom door, and---*OOO-EEE!* I think Noah's Ark smelled better than this bathroom, even on the 40th day of that voyage. Thank goodness I play the trumpet...I'm used to holding my breath for a long time. And, to think that they keep this bathroom locked...who would want to use it? At least they have some paper towels in here. After drying off my floppy-pig sweat, I wrap up those underpants in more paper towels and throw them away. This actually *improves* the smell of the bathroom. *PHEW*, that's much better. As I come out, the gas station attendants ask:

"How far do you have to drive, sir?"

"Oh, about fifty miles."

"Would you like something to eat? We'll give it to you for free because of your trouble."

"Thanks, guys. I'll just take *two* cans of Mountain Dew, if that's OK?"

"Sure...here you go, sir."

Good. Now I can begin to drive home. I hope Ann doesn't count the pairs of underwear in the laundry this week; it will be one pair short.

*

I teach trumpet lessons at another suburban high school on Saturday mornings. I have four students, from 10:00 a.m. until noon. Usually, I'm there with a trombone teacher and a tuba teacher. The band director comes over and unlocks the door for us, since he says that he has work he wants to get done anyway.

Many times, I have a gig on Friday nights, playing my trumpet in a dance band for a wedding, charity ball, or some other kind of a party. A lot of these gigs are downtown, and that means I'll usually get home about 1 or 2 o'clock early Saturday morning. That can make it a little tough to get up and go teach lessons, but as my Dad always says, you have to go when and where the job is if you're a musician.

I have gigs on Saturday afternoons quite often, too. After the lessons I usually have to hurry to get downtown, or to a suburban country club, and be there by 1:00 to make the start of the gig. These afternoon gigs are usually followed by a Saturday evening job, and I rarely have time to go home in between.

Since I'm running around so much on Saturdays, with little time to spare, I almost always wear my tuxedo all day long, starting with the lessons at 10 o'clock in the morning. This is the same tuxedo that I've just worn Friday night, and I've only taken it off about seven hours before (but I do put on a clean shirt). Wearing my tux can lead to some awkward moments when I do errands on Saturday morning on the way to the lessons. I'm usually a big hit at the gas station, post office, or grocery store. I get the typical lame remarks from people:

"When's the wedding?" or: "Who died?"

When people ask "who died?" most of the time I reply: "It was me, so if you'll excuse me, I'm late for my funeral."

My students also enjoy it when I have my tux on for their lessons. Kids don't see too many people wearing a tuxedo, and they think it's really cool that I'm an actual working, performing musician. I guess I think it's kind of cool, too. As long as I get my tux cleaned often enough, it's all right. Otherwise, it can get a little gamey in one of the lesson room/sardine can combinations. The funny thing is, the trombone teacher and the tuba teacher sometimes wear their tuxedos too. We're giving the most formal lessons in town!

When I arrive at the school today about 9:45 a.m., all the doors are still locked. This isn't too unusual; sometimes the band director is a little late. A few minutes after I pull up, the trombone teacher arrives, followed by the tuba teacher. We're all wearing our tuxedos. Soon, all of our students come for their lessons, but the band director still isn't there to unlock the door. It's about 10:10 now, and we need to get started...remember, no lesson, no money for any of us. There's no way to call the band director, but fortunately all of the students have their instruments and music with them.

We wait a few more minutes, but there's no one in sight. All of a sudden, the trombone teacher gets the bright idea for us to give the lessons in our *cars!* It's a good thing that it's a nice day out....we'll have to leave the windows open in our cars with all of that noise coming out. Normally, we give lessons in separate practice rooms inside the school music wing. We can hear some of the sounds that are coming through the walls from each other's students, but not very loudly. I can't wait to hear what all of this clatter produces outside!

Try to imagine this picture: our three cars are parked about thirty feet away from each other, in an otherwise empty school parking lot. We're all sitting behind our steering wheels, dressed in tuxedos. I'm about to play a trumpet duet with my student, but our trumpets are too long to face the windshield, so we have to stick them out the side windows. My trumpet bell is going out the driver's window, and my student's bell is pointing out the passenger window. Obviously, we can't really see each other, and we will barely be able to hear each other, since we're facing opposite directions.

I begin to count off our jazz duet, and we start playing:
"1--2--3--4!
Bop-pa-dop-pa-dop, Bop, Bop, Boo-eee...
Wait, wait, Tommy. We're not togeth---*OWWW!*
Oh...my tooth...*WOW!"*

I try to stop my student, but as I turn, I almost knock some of my teeth out as I bang my trumpet on the car mirror. He can't hear me anyway, so he keeps playing:

"Broop, Blip-Blop, Bip-Bip-Buuurrrp."

"Tommy...Tommy...stop!"

I finally get his attention, and then we start over and repeat this process several times. I try to be more careful about my teeth, however.

While this is going on, the trombone teacher and his student are practicing slide technique. They're moving their slides back and forth, in and out of his car's side windows, and the sound is getting lower and higher as the slides go slowly out and in:

"Beeee---aaaaah---rrrrrr---oh---rrrrr---aaaaah---eeeee" then faster:

"Bee—aah—rr—oh—rr—aah—ee" and still faster and louder:

"Be-ah-r-oh-r-ah-e."

Meanwhile, the tuba teacher's car has a sun-roof, which he has opened. I look over and see two tuba bells sticking out the top of his car. They start playing the famous tuba melody from the classical song *In the Hall of the Mountain King:* *"Bomp-Bomp-Bomp-Bomp-Bomp-Bomp-Bah, Bomp-Bomp-Bah, Bomp-Bomp-Bah."* Gradually they play faster and faster.

How much longer can I stand this cacophony of instrument sounds? This is like being in a *Dali* painting with music!

I can see and hear Tommy playing his trumpet:

"Bop-pa-Broop, Braaap, Baaap"

And the trombones, sliding out and in through the open car windows:

"Bearohrae, Bearohrae"

And finally the tubas, sticking out of the sun-roof:

"Bomp-Bomp-Brolmp, Brulmp, Broh...woa...woa...wwooaa"
MAKE IT STOP!

The six of us continue this weird musical journey for the remainder of the lesson. Our next students arrive for their 10:30

a.m. lessons, followed then by our 11 o'clock appointments. We keep going through this surreal process over and over again. Trumpets are blaring, trombones are sliding, and tuba bells are bouncing up and down. The noise is blasting all over the parking lot, yet there's still no sign of the band director to unlock the door.

At about 11:15, I see a policeman drive into the lot towards us. Uh-oh, how are we going to explain this to him? I can just hear us trying to enlighten the policeman now:

"Yes, officer, we're just three adults, dressed in tuxedos, playing musical instruments in our cars with three teenage boys. And, we're charging them money for the privilege. So...is there anything wrong with that, officer?"

This is all perfectly normal behavior, right? While we have the band director's phone number, there's no way for any of us to call him so that he can vouch for us, unless the policeman wants to call. I'm starting to sweat right through my tux, which was already in bad shape from my Friday night gig. How am I possibly going to explain to Ann that I got arrested in the parking lot? And...on what charge? Oh my, don't even think about that! And, I'll be late for my 1 o'clock gig! Still, I wonder...can we charge these students for a full lesson?

The policeman pulls up near us.

"All right. Everyone get out of your car. Let me see your driver's licenses."

He gazes at us with a puzzled look for a few minutes, glances over at the tuba bells that are sticking out of the car, stares at our tuxedos, then looks back again at the tubas. He's not saying anything, and the tension is unbearable. I'm so nervous, I can barely stand up. This seems like it is taking an hour, but I know it's only been about five minutes. The tuba teacher begins to try and explain our plight:

"Uh, you see, officer, we jus---"

The policeman holds up his hand to get the tuba teacher to stop, and then the officer finally speaks:

"You kids go to school here?"

"Yes, sir."

"Do your parents know you're here?"

"Yes, sir."

Then he turns to us:

"You guys work here?"

"Yes, sir."

A *very* long and silent pause ensues, and I feel like I'm going to faint, or throw up, or maybe both.

"*Ahh*...just get back in your cars...I don't have time for this *baloney!* But...don't let me catch you doing this again!"

"Yes, sir...uh...we mean…no, sir, uh...*YES, SIR!"*

The policeman then gets in his squad car, and he zooms off in a hurry.

WOW...I can't believe it...was that lucky! At this point, my tux is soaked in sweat. We all get back in our cars, and start up our lessons again. However, it's about 11:30, and these lessons are over now.

"Sorry, John. Short lesson today, I guess."

"That's OK, Mr. B, that was still *way* cool!"

"And, uh, you don't need to tell your parents about any of this. By the way, did you bring a check for the lesson today? I'll take it now, if that's all right."

"Sure. Here you go."

All of our 11:30 students have arrived, and we continue more of this musical nonsense until noon, when I have to leave for my gig. On my way out of the parking lot, I start to feel a little guilty about taking the money from that one student. I ask the other two teachers:

"Hey, guys, did you charge the student you were teaching when the policeman came?"

"Oh yeah, man." says the trombone teacher. "I need the bread."

"Sure thing." replies the tuba teacher. "Hey, how about you, man?"

"Yeah, I did too." I say. "OK, see you guys next week."

I feel a lot less guilty now.

The following Saturday, all three of us arrive at the school for our lessons, and once again we are all wearing our tuxedos. The band director drives up a minute later:

"Hello, gentlemen. How are you today? Anything new with the three of you?"

Hmmm...he's acting like he doesn't even know that he forgot to show up last Saturday. The tuba teacher asks him:

"Hey man, where were you last week? We all waited for you, and then we ended up having to teach the lessons in our cars! A cop came by, and we---"

"Oh, yeah?" the band director interrupts, rather flippantly. He starts staring nervously at the parking lot, like he's looking for someone.

"Well, let's get started, shall we? Enough talk...no time to lose! You don't want to take any time away from the kids, do you? I'll be back next Saturday to open the door. See ya!"

He turns and starts running towards his car. I call out after him:

"What's your hurry, ma---?"

Two police cars suddenly race into the parking lot, with sirens blaring. They surround the band director:

"PUT YOUR HANDS UP!"

As the other teachers and I run over to see what's going on, the policemen grab the band director and start handcuffing him.

"Officer, what's happening?" the tuba teacher asks breathlessly (it's tough running while carrying a tuba).

"Well, sir, this man is wanted for indecent exposure to a minor. We've had several complaints against him, and now we've finally caught hi---hey, wait a minute, aren't you the three bozos I saw last week! Didn't I tell you three never to--"

"Forget it, Charlie." says the other policeman. He points to the band director:

"This is the guy we want. I got his picture right here."

They put the band director into one of the squad cars. As their sirens wail and they start to pull away, the band director shouts out the window to us:

"Be sure and lock the door on your way out! And, guys, I might not be here next Saturday to open it!"

*

Well, I'm running late once again. I'm in the middle of another one of those teaching days where I have to drive to seven different houses. I've just finished my most recent lesson at 4:20 (five minutes late), and now I'm rushing in the car to my 4:30 student, who lives in another suburb. It takes me at least fifteen minutes to drive there, however, so I'll be behind in my timetable for the rest of the evening. I've scheduled these lessons as close together as possible for time and distance, but I still have to go to five different suburbs between 3:45 and 8:30. I sure didn't want to turn down any of these students when they originally called to take lessons. This was the best schedule I could come up with and still be able to put them all on one day.

Oh well, let's hope I can make some green lights. My car has been making a slight rattling noise lately, but I'm trying not to pay any attention to it. Before I left today, I told Ann that everything will be fine...hasn't she heard that before? Without saying any brand names, my vehicle is the type that the Army uses a lot. It's supposed to have a strong engine...*That's why we bought it!* As I pull up to my 4:30 student's house (at 4:40), the engine noise is getting worse. It sounds like something is loose and moving around inside of it:

"Bing...Bding...Bdli%*&ng...Bonk."

I don't have time to look inside the engine to try and figure out the problem. But, even if I did, I know as much about cars as the Cubs do about winning the World Series in 1987...in other words, nothing. Hopefully, the engine will be fine after resting for thirty minutes. If I ignore the problem, it will go away, right?

I go in and teach Billy, and when I finish it is 5:10 (I'm ten minutes behind). I have to go to the next suburb north for a 5:15 student, but it always takes me twenty minutes to get there. I'm getting farther behind schedule. However, there's no way for me to call ahead and tell him that I'm running late. Oh, well, I'll just do the best I can. Uh-oh...as I pull out of the driveway, I start hearing that noise again. Something is really banging around inside of the engine:

"Bonk...Bi#@*nk...Bududeee-Bududeee-Bududeee."

Hmmm...either Mel Blanc is in my engine, or something's very wrong (and, if Mel Blanc's in there, something *is* definitely wrong). As I drive, I'm starting to imagine my car as a combustible pinball machine. My wallet is the pinball, and it sure seems like the pinball is about to go down the hole. I can almost hear the bells and whistles of the machine saying *"game over."*

I don't really have any good choices at this point: if I stop the car now, and take it in to the repair shop, I'll lose all the money for the rest of my lessons today, plus I'll have to pay to get the car fixed. But, if I can just make it through tonight's lessons, I can then try and take it in to the repair shop tomorrow morning. My first student tomorrow isn't until three o'clock. Maybe the mechanic can fix it by then. At least I wouldn't lose any income that way.

I continue driving. Come on; let's go...I *have* to make some of these lights. I'll turn on the radio...that should help me to ignore the noise. Good...a new song's coming on, it's, it's..."Pinball Wizard!" *JUST GREAT!* I start to accelerate down this busy two lane street, and my rolling pinball machine now sounds even louder than the actual song playing on my radio. Come on...almost there...just a little farth----

"Bink—Bo*&^#nk--Craaack—Bdli@%nk--BANG-- CRAAACK—BAAA*&$%^ANG!!!"

And then, slower and quieter:

"B...i...n...k—B....o....n....k—B....l....u....r...r...r....p."

"He's a Pinball Wizzzarrrd..."

Phew...the noises have finally stopped, along with the radio. *WOW!* But, guess what...so has my motor. Now I'm blocking the right lane of this street, and I'm constantly being honked at by passing vehicles. My car won't start again. Neither will the rest of my lessons today, I'm afraid.

S%*T!! I'm only stalled a few houses from my next student's driveway. I get out of the car and try to prop open the hood, but the latches are stuck...how ironic is that, after my previous car hood escapade?! I start to run down to Jimmy's house. Along the way, I'm showered with kindly advice from the other motorists. They're gradually making their way around my car, and they can't wait to talk to me:

"BEEP-BEEP! Move that car, buddy!"

"Hey, as%&*^e...get that car out of the way!"

"Hey, you moron...move that piece of sh--"

"OK, genius!" I reply. *"I'd move it if I could! Shove it up your---"*

"BEEP!"

Maybe Jimmy's mom will let me call the motor club, and then they can tow the car in to the repair shop. I arrive at his house, slightly out of breath, and carrying my trumpet. I sure didn't want to leave it sitting in the car! Now it's about 5:40, and Jimmy's lesson is supposed to *end* at 5:45. He knows that I'm late, but he doesn't seem to notice that I don't have a car.

"Hi Mr. B. Come on in. I want to play that scale for you today!"

"Uh...sorry, Jimmy, but my car broke down just up the street. Can I use your phone?"

"Sure, Mr. B. I really practiced hard this week. Can we start the lesson now?"

"Well, maybe, Jimmy. I'm not sure. Can you get your mom?"

"OK, Mr. B, but I want you to hear that scale *right now!* Listen:

Baah-brp-brp-brp-splaaat! Oh no, I'll try it again:
Baah-brp-brp-brp-brp-splaaat! Almost! I'll get it! Just one more time, Mr.---"

"*Jimmy*...I'll listen soon. But...can you go get your mom first?"

"Oh, OK, Mr. B. *MOHHMMM!*"

Jimmy's mom comes down the stairs, and I explain my predicament to her. She lets me use her phone. I call the motor club, but they put me on hold. Jimmy is getting impatient, and then I begin to enter into a 6-way conversation between the Motor Club, me, Jimmy, his mom, his trumpet, and the car horns that are blaring as they go by:

"OK, Mr. B. I'll try that scale again---

Baah-brp-brp-splaaat! Oh shoot!
Baah-brp-brp-splaaat! Oh---"

"Jimmy...the fourth note is a flat."

"Hello, this is the Motor Club. Did you say you have a flat?"

"*BEEP-BEEP!*"

"Uh, no, no. My motor has blown u---"

"*I'll blow it, Mr. B! Baah-brp-brp-splaaat!*"

"*Jimmy!*"

"Sir...my name is Rick, not Jimmy. Did you say that your tire has blown a hole?"

"No, no. My motor has a flat...no, I mean my---"

"*A flat...I got it, Mr. B! The fourth note is A flat. Baah-brp-brp---"*

"*Jimmy!*"

"It's Rick, sir. Your fourth note is flat?"

"*MOVE THIS CAR, JERK!*"

"No, no. My fourth tire is...no, I mean my motor won't *start.* Can you come out an---"

"*You want me to start, Mr. B? OK...Baah-brp-brp-"*
"*Jimmy!*"

"Hello, this is Rod from the Motor Club. Did you say your car is shimmying?"

"No, no, that was Jimmy. Uh, what happened to Rick?"

"Rick went to tune up another engine."

"He went to tune anoth---"

"You want me to tune my trumpet, Mr. B? OK...Baaaaaah! Baaa---"

"Jimmy!"

"It's Rod, not Jimmy, sir."

"Yes...that's it! I think that a rod has broken off inside my motor. I can't get it to---"

"I broke off inside your motor, sir?"

"BEEP-BEEP!"

"No, no, not you. A rod...a rod. And I tried to jimmy the hood open, but it wouldn't---"

"Did you call me, Mr. B? OK...Baaah-brp-brp-"

"Jimmy!"

"This is Rod, sir, not Jimmy. I'm going to get my supervisor."

"No, wait. You can't do---"

"Oh, yes I can, Mr. B. Listen...Baaah-brp-brp---"

"Jimmy!"

"No, sir, this is Dee from the motor club. You're shimmying?"

"Dee? No, no, you see, a rod broke off in my---"

"No, sir. Rod is not here."

"I know. My car won't start. Can you come out and tow it to my repair shop?"

"Well, we can't be there for at least an hour."

"OK. Thanks, Dee."

"D, Mr. B? Sure, I'll play it...Baaaah!"

"Jimmy!"

"Shimmy?"

"BEEEEEP!"

Thank goodness...that *Twilight Zone* conversation is finally over! But, what should I do now? What kind of choices do I have? My car is sitting in the middle of the street, blocking traffic. I can go back there and sit, and get honked at for an hour. Or, I can go ahead and teach Jimmy. Or...?

"Mr. B, would you like a chicken leg and an ice cream cone?" Jimmy's mom asks.

I start to think it over for a few seconds. Let's see...I can get honked at, or have ice cream, or yelled at, or eat a chicken leg, or honking, or eating, or sitting in the car, or getting paid to teach Jimmy's lesson, or honking, or chicken, or....

"Yes, thank you, I would like that chicken leg, please. Jimmy, go on downstairs. We can start your lesson....I'll be right there after I grab a---"

"BEEEEEP!"

The motor club tow truck arrives soon after Jimmy's lesson. They let me ride in the truck while they tow me to the repair shop. I can just walk home from here.

*

It's the next day now, and the shop calls me at about noon. *Great!* Maybe the car is fixed, and I can still make my lessons this afternoon! I begin to listen to the diagnosis of the mechanic:

"Well, sir, a rod broke off inside the engine, and banged around inside there like a pinball (I *knew* it was a pinball!). It caused so much damage, that now your entire motor has to be replaced."

My entire what? The whole motor! Who ever heard of that? This car is only five years old, and it only has about 50,000 miles on it. Replace the entire motor now!

"Well," I ask, "how much would that cost?"

"Oh, several thousand dollars," the mechanic replies. "And it would take us two-to-three weeks to get the parts and do the work."

"Well...tell me...what if," I start to beg, "I tried to sell the car, without replacing the motor? Would you guys buy it?"

"Well, you can't really sell a car without a motor. But, if you have us replace the motor, then we might buy it."

Terrific! What choice do I have now? I'll either have to rent a car for three weeks, or just cancel all of my lessons. Plus, I have to pay for the new motor, and then...maybe buy a new car, too?

"OK. Go ahead," I tell the repair shop, "order the new motor. Give me an estimate when you can."

Great...just great. No car. No lessons. No money. As I sit in our apartment, I start to hear more noises:

"BINK—BDINK—BLURP."

What could *that* be? Am I in *The Twilight Zone* again? No...when I look I down, I see that I'm just crying in my Mountain Dew.

*

Hopefully, Ann and I will be able to afford our own home in the not too distant future. In the meantime, I have to keep traipsing to all of these student's houses each week for their lessons. Besides the wear and tear on my car, the weather is obviously a big factor for me in wanting to teach at least some of the kids at my own house. When I arrived home from my lessons a few nights ago at around 10 p.m., a car that was stuck in the snow blocked the alley behind our apartment. This is where our parking space is located, and naturally I couldn't get to it. Every resident of the building gets one uncovered space back here. When it snows, the alley often doesn't get plowed, at least not for a long time. It's common for snow and ice to build up, and then the garbage truck creates ruts when it goes through. Consequently, cars get stuck back here a lot. Fortunately, the neighbors from the many different apartments and houses that share the alley all help to dig and push each other out.

As I pulled into the alley that evening, I could see Ann standing there with a shovel. She was talking to our elderly neighbor, whose car was stuck in grooves of ice and snow. I rolled down my window:

"Hi. I'll take over now. You can go back inside."

"OK," replied Ann. "I've been out here for a half hour, but we haven't seen any other neighbors so far."

I shoveled and pushed our neighbor's car for a while, but had no luck. I see a light on in the corner house...that's Mr. and Mrs. Bluto's house! He's a big, strong dude (with that long black beard). Maybe he could come out and help. Ann and I have never actually met the Blutos, but we sure do hear them arguing a lot, even in the winter with the windows closed. Bluto's voice resonates very deeply, and his wife (I wonder if her name *is* Olive Oyl) sounds really squeaky. We can't hear what they are quarreling about, but their bickering does sound comical. Hmmm...I can't move this car myself, so I think I'll ring the bell and ask if the big galoot can give me a hand. As the front door opens, I see Mrs. Bluto holding one of their kids:

"Hi Oliv---I mean Mrs. Blut---uh, I mean, excuse me, a car is stuck back here, and I wondered if anyone might be able to come out and help?"

"NO! Can't you see I'm busy? And my husband isn't home yet...where could he be? If he's out again with that floo---, that bast---WHAM!"

She slams the door in my face. OK...*Thanks a lot, Olive!*

As I turn around, I see a car pulling up. *It's Bluto!* His garage shares the same alley with my apartment building. When I walk towards his car, he opens his window, and I'm hit with the scent of way too much musk perfume:

"Hey, Blut----uh, oh, hi...one of our neighbors' cars is stuck right over here. Would you be able to help? I bet between the two of us we could get it moving soon."

"NO, I can't help!" Bluto rumbles. "I had to work all day, and I'm tired, you know. Have a nice night."

He zooms past me into the garage, and the door automatically closes behind him.

What? Have a nice night? You too, you drone! You know, Bluto, I may be the weak Popeye right now...the one who hasn't eaten his spinach yet. And you may be the strong person now, with your house and your kids. But, one of these days I'll have my spinach, and my own house, and my own kids, *and I'll come over and kick your---*

"BEEEP! Sam...Sam...!"

"Oh, hi, Rick." Another one of my neighbors had just driven into the alley...he can't get to his parking spot, either.

"Let's get this car pushed out!"

"OK...sure, Rick."

As we dig the wedged car out, Rick asks me:

"Hey Sam, who were you yelling at just now?"

"Oh, nobody...only some cartoon charac---"

"Wee-yee-yee-yee-wee!"

"Roar-ro-ro-ro-roar!"

"Wee...Wee...yeeyeeyee!"

"Roar-ro-ro...ROAARR!"

"SLAAAM!"

Uh-oh, it's the Blutos going at it again, screaming with their two distinct voices. Maybe that musk was too much for Olive Oyl, too. Could it be that she thinks Bluto might be canoodleing with that floozy? Rick and I can't hear what they're saying, but are they ever vociferous.

All of a sudden, Bluto's garage door opens, and he starts to back his car out. He's going much too fast, and the car begins slipping and sliding, right into a huge snowban---

"KABOOOM!"

"rrrRRR...rrrRRR...rrrRRR!"

Well, now poor Bluto has gotten his poor (yet expensive) car stuck, and his wheels are just spinning around in the frozen ruts. He opens his window and yells towards us in his cavernous tone:

"HEY GUYS...COULD YOU GIVE ME A HAND?"

Rick and I have just finished getting the original car out, and we are about to go inside. Boy, this reply is gonna make me feel *awfully* good:

"Uh, no, we can't. We're done over here, and we're heading inside. We're tired, you know. Have a nice night."

"ROAR-ro-ro-ROAARR!"
"rrrRRR...rrrRRR...rrrRRR!"
Rick and I enter our building:
"Hey Sam, why are you whistling the theme from *Popeye*?"

Dogs and other pets

CHAPTER FIVE

If you're going to go from house to house and teach trumpet lessons, you better like dogs, or at least learn to get along with them. I really do like most dogs, and since I usually go to twenty-five houses each week, I'm lucky in that I enjoy being around them. I've taught some of my students at their home for five or six years, so I've really developed a close relationship with many of their dogs. In my mind, I often identify the family by the dog, not by the student. In fact, there are a few houses that I teach in where I'd much rather see the dog, than to have to endure more of my student's lousy trumpet playing!

When Ann and I were growing up, we each had a great dog for a pet. However, the apartment building that we live in now doesn't allow dogs or cats, and that's just another reason why we're so anxious to move out of our apartment and into our own home. We're becoming more and more frustrated every month that goes by, since we've already lived in this building for several years. But, we're continuing to save as much money as we can, and---hopefully---in a couple of more years, we can buy our own place.

Then, we can finally start thinking about having a family, and also about owning a cat or dog. I'm getting awfully tired of seeing all of my animal buddies once a week at my student's houses, and then not being able to have a dog or cat at home!

The dog I had as a child was *Suzi*, a Schnauzer. Suzi was already five when we got her, and she was very mature and calm all of the time. Whenever I would practice my trumpet, she would almost always get up and quietly go into another room. She wouldn't even bother to look at me on the way out, either. I tried not to take it personally. My Dad would practice his flute almost every night in those days, too. Suzi seemed a little more interested in the higher sounds of Dad's flute than she did of my trumpet noises, and she would lie down outside the door of the room that Dad was practicing in (Dad would keep the door closed). I've always guessed that Suzi liked the flute better just because Dad was a better musician than me...at least he was at that time. I was just a kid back then, so I don't know for sure...Suzi never let on. All I know is that whenever she would see me open my trumpet case, she'd get up and leave.

Suzi rarely exhibited any unusual behavior. She had her routines, including a funny one where she would rub her chin on the kitchen wall to wipe off her mouth after eating. This, of course, would make my Mom very upset. Suzi also had her favorite places to take naps, especially the corner of the couch, where she eventually left a stain of her outline from the oil on her skin. After a while, you could watch as she jumped on the couch and settled right back into her "silhouette." Being a Schnauzer, she couldn't jump very high, and she didn't bother to try. She hardly ever barked, either. When we'd let her out into the backyard to do her business, she'd just let out one quick "Yipe" when she was ready to come back in. No wasted energy with Suzi.

There was one time, however, when Suzi really surprised us, and I think she surprised herself, too. My Mom always had a giant glass vase up on a rather high counter, and she kept it filled with those little, individually wrapped, Hershey's Kisses. I used to believe that these candies were a reward for me being such a perfect son, but I think Mom snuck a few, too. Suzi never showed any interest in it. In fact, she never ate any "people food," either from the table or anywhere else. She left us alone when we would eat, and didn't even seem to like "people food."

This one night, though, my parents and I had gone out for dinner, and when we returned home, we saw that the glass vase had fallen onto our brick floor. It had shattered into a thousand little pieces. *OMG!* We figured that the vase must have been placed too close to the edge, and it had just slipped off.

"Suzi, are you hurt? Were you scared? Did anything hit you? How did this happen?" my Mom exclaimed.

Suzi didn't seem to be hurt, and she wasn't bleeding from any broken glass. She was just lying there a few feet from the broken vase, but it did look like she was having trouble getting up. I went over to check on her, and I started picking up the tiny pieces of glass.

"DON'T TOUCH THAT GLASS, YOU STOOP!" yelled Mom.

Wait a minute, I thought. Something else doesn't seem quite right. If the vase had shattered, where had all the Hershey's Kisses gone? I started looking around, and I could see more and more of the tiny wrappers, but there was no candy was inside of any of them. The wrappers were all wadded-up, nice and neat. They had been made into tidy little balls, and were in piles of four or five throughout the room. The more I looked around, the more wrapper piles I saw, but I never found any candy, and there had been at least fifty Kisses in the vase when we left.

"Uh, Mom, is anything else missing from the house?" I asked.

I thought we might have a chocolate thief on the loose, and I wondered about any other, less important items (to me, anyway), that may have also been stolen.

"What do you mean anything *else*? Nothing's missing, genius." she replied.

"Well," I continued, "all of the Hershey Kisses are gone. See, look..."

As Mom looked, we both realized that it must have been *Suzi* who had eaten the candies. *ALL OF THEM!* But, this would be *very* unusual behavior for her, and also almost physically impossible for a Schnauzer of her size to accomplish. How did she climb up on the counter? How did she knock the vase off the shelf? How did she unwrap the candies, and then proceed to wad them up again? And...all in really neat piles? She never cared about the candy before. Hmmm...she must be a secret "chocoholic." And...how did she eat fifty of those things at one time? I looked at her.

"Suzi, do you have a tummy-ache?"

Suzi just stared at me, with a big "Puss-n-Boots eyes" look, and she let out a giant sigh-groan combination. She didn't want to admit to anything, but she also didn't want to move from her spot. She was *extremely* full, and it seemed like she went outside to do her business quite often that evening. A couple of days went by before Suzi would even look at me again. I think she was mad that I had figured out she was the chocolate thief, but she never told me how she did it!

The terrific dog that Ann had as a kid was a Golden Retriever named Tanya. Ann's family got Tanya when she was a puppy, and she was super-friendly with lots of energy. *LOTS!* I got to see Tanya a lot when Ann and I were dating, and Tanya and I became good friends. To Tanya, I was a buddy coming over to play!

I used to wear a belt with a metal buckle (a teenage boy's wardrobe usually consists of just one belt, no matter how many pairs of pants are in the clothes rotation). Tanya would not only sniff the buckle (like all dogs would do), she would start licking the buckle, and we always had trouble getting her to stop! I could never figure out her fascination with this metal belt buckle. I hadn't sprinkled salt on it, and I don't think I had ever spilled any food on it, either. For some reason, Tanya just loved licking that buckle. Ann's Mom said it was probably because the buckle was nice and cold, especially when I first walked into the house during the winter. Tanya loved it!

Whenever Ann would practice her flute at home (which was a lot more often than I would practice my trumpet), Tanya would lie down at Ann's feet and listen. Ann's practice sessions would include several kinds of music, and many different types of exercises. No matter what she was playing, Tanya would lay there quietly. It could be a fast or slow song, or high or low, or classical or swing, and Tanya would sleep.

However, anytime Ann would hold one certain note for a few seconds, Tanya would get up, rare her head back, and let out a long holler:

"AAHHOOOOOOO!" Then three more fast yells:

"AHOO-AHOO-AHOO!" And, finally, one more long one:

"AAHHOOOOOOOO....!" with her chin pointing towards the sky.

She loved the note "D." But, not the real high D that a flute can play. Tanya loved the sound of the middle range D, the one that's written on the 4th staff line of the treble clef for you music aficionados. There must have been something about the frequency and range of that note that piqued her interest. Or, maybe she liked the reverberation that the pitch made as it echoed through the room.

After Tanya finished hollering, she would get really excited, start panting quickly, and look at Ann as if to say:

"Please play some more D's!"

So, Ann would oblige, and Tanya would start again:

"AHOOO-AHOOO-AAHHHOOOOOOOOOO!"

This could go on for quite a while, and looking at Tanya's head pointing up while "singing" was really fun. On the other hand, Ann would often be practicing some of the most complicated passages in the entire literature of the flute, but Tanya was never impressed. She only cared about hearing her favorite note: "D."

*

I often think about Tanya when I'm driving to the Morton's house. They have a very sweet Golden Retriever named Silky. I teach the two Morton brothers back-to-back, so I have an hour to "play" with Silky. He greets me at the door, follows me over to my chair, and lays down there during the two lessons. I've known Silky for over two years now, and unfortunately, he is getting up there in age. He doesn't have the energy he once had, but he's still really happy when I come over. He also doesn't seem to care about the sound of the trumpets playing, or even about the two Morton brothers. He just lies there, and occasionally lets out a loud yawn and sigh. That's OK, Silky, I'm bored with some of these trumpet lessons, too.

Besides a lack of energy, another problem Silky is starting to encounter has to do with his bodily functions. As the months of lessons have gone by, I've noticed more and more stains on the carpet from Silky "doing his business" in the house. I guess he just can't hold it long enough to wait for someone to let him outside. This is causing the house to smell more and more, but I think the family must be used to the smell. No one has ever said anything to me about it, but they have to be aware of the problem. Almost every time I'm there, I can hear a family member start yelling at Silky in a panicky voice:

"Come on, Silky, hurry...let's go out!"

I gather that Silky is having trouble controlling both number one and number two, and that they're trying to rush him outside before there is another accident. Silky is starting to smell now, too, and I know that the smell rubs off on my clothes over the course of an hour. I seem to get used to it, but when I get home, Ann notices the aroma and asks me if I've been visiting the zoo. I've been trying not to pet Silky quite so much lately because of the odor, and I encourage him to lie down a little farther away from me, but he likes me, so he's usually right by my feet most of the time.

Good boy, Silky, I'm still your buddy. It's just that...well...you don't smell so good!

I go to the Morton's house on Saturday mornings, and the first brother I teach is Joe. He's fifteen, and attends that same high school where I taught the lessons in my car. I used to meet Joe there for his lessons, too (but Joe's lessons weren't in my car). Then, a couple of years ago, his mom asked me to start teaching both Joe and his younger brother Robert, who is now in 8th grade. Robert and Joe will both be going to the same school next year. However, Robert is busy for part of Saturday morning, so he can't meet me at the school with Joe. When their mom asked, I decided it was worth it for me to drive to their house to teach both of them in a row. Then next year, I can teach them both at the school (or teach them both in my car if that Band director doesn't show up!).

They're both nice boys, they both practice their trumpet fairly often, and they're both interested in having lessons with me. They've grown up with Silky, but you can tell that they're getting tired of Silky's problems. They usually ignore him, or yell at him about going outside, or yell at each other about cleaning up after a Silky accident. I often get to hear both parents and both brothers yelling at each other about Silky. Even the brother that I'm trying to teach will join in these loud discussions, right during his lesson. These conversations often sound like this:

"Good job, Joe, but watch out for that note in the---"

"MOM, Silky went again!"

"Well, clean it up, Joe!"

"I'm having my lesson!"

"Robert, clean it up!"

"I can't...*you* do it!"

"MOMMMM!"

I try to break in:

"Joe, let's play that song---"

"Dad, can you do it?"

"Son of a b^#@*, again with that g^% d&%* dog...oh, hi Mr.

B!"

   "Robert!"

   "MOMMMM!"

   "Dad!"

   "Sh--! Damn dog! I'm busy! What's new, Mr. B?"

   "Quiet...Joe's having his lesson. *Don't bother him!"*

Once more, I try to get back to the lesson:

   "OK, Joe, how about starting at measure---"

   "MOM, Silky went *AGAIN!"*

   "ROBERT!"

   "MOMMMMM!"

A version of this discussion might take place three or four times during the hour that I'm there. And Silky, who by now doesn't have to go anymore, simply lies down at my feet, smelling a little worse.

I arrive at the Morton's house this morning, and here's my pal Silky to greet me, follow me, and lie down by me.

   "Good boy, Silky, how ya doin'!" I ask.

I notice that he smells a little worse today, and he's not quite so silky anymore. It seems like it's been months since his last bath.

   "Can you lie down a little farther over there, boy?"

No such luck; Silky plops down right at my feet. My clothes are going to stink for sure, and luckily I'm not in my tux for performing yet. I don't have a gig until tonight, and I have time to go home and change.

Joe and I begin his lesson. He's playing his trumpet pretty well, and I'm teaching him a fairly high-level trumpet solo for a high school student. Learning this solo is taking up most of the lesson time, but it's worth it. Once in a while, I can feel that Silky has gotten up to change positions, and then he lies back down by my feet. I'm not paying much attention to Silky today, though, since I'm concentrating on Joe's solo. About twenty minutes into the lesson, Joe completes the first part of the piece.

   "Sounds nice, Joe. Here, let me play the next section for you, starting at measure 145."

I begin to take a really deep breath to get ready to play, but my senses are interrupted by a terrible scent. I figure that it's Silky, and there's nothing I can do about that. After coughing a few times, I try again to take a deep breath---*WHOA!* What *is* that smell? My eyes roll back in my head, and my body swerves around in my chair. I can't breathe at all, let alone play my trumpet. This is much worse than the normally pungent Silky odor.

"Joe, do you think Silky's OK?"

We both look down at him. Silky is just lying there like he always does, half asleep.

"Seems OK to me." Joe replies.

As my eyes start to drift back up into their sockets, I glance down at my shoe, and thoughts of Dr. Seuss race through my mind:

I have news to share with you.

There is something on my shoe.

It is not made out of goo.

Silky has gone number two!

I try and look a little closer, but my nose wrinkles up and my eyes are watering. You should know that Silky is a rather large male Retriever.

Large dog.

Large poo.

Large poo, number two, on my shoe!

I'm still in the middle of a bad Dr. Seuss rhyme! I feel nauseous, too. My eyes continue to roll around, and I haven't breathed much in a while. I instinctively start to move my foot--- NO, DON'T MOVE IT, YOU DOPE!

Number two poo is new on my shoe.

Silky just lies there. He is oblivious to all of this. He feels fine now.

"Uh, Joe, can you call your parents and get me some paper towels?"

Now my foot is cramping because I've made it so rigid, but I dare not move it. *OWW!* I grit my teeth, and begin to take a deep breath to fight the pain in my foot, but—

WHOA, the smell—

OW, my foot—

OOO, my stomach!

"Uh, Joe, how 'bout right now with those towels, OK?"

Joe's dad hears the commotion and comes in:

"Oh, sorry, Mr. B. I guess we've got a *shi&#* dog!*"

After several towels are sacrificed, Joe's dad and I finally get all of the "shoe poo" off, and then he takes my shoe into the bathroom to wash it off. The cramp in my foot is still killing me, but at least now I can finally move it without fear of stepping in more "poo." Oh, that's better! I start to sigh— Cough...Cough...Cough...the smell is still there, however. Silky has been sleeping this whole time. Whatever was in his stomach is no longer his problem, so what does he care anymore?

Joe's lesson is just about over by now, and Robert's coming in. Great...I have to sit here for another half-hour and breathe in that stench. Silky must be making these contributions often, since the whole family seems rather nonchalant about everything.

"Hey, Robert." I ask. "Do you want to switch chairs with me?"

At least I can move a little. I now have one shoe on, and one shoe in the Morton's sink. I still have to be careful of where I'm stepping, though; Silky may have made a deposit on this---*OH, NO! I've just stepped in something over here with my sock.* Silky had a number one by this chair, and I couldn't see it with the dark carpet. Now my sock is all wet, and it's starting to smell, too.

"Uh, Robert, can you get me—"

"MOMMMM!"

"Do it yourself, Robert!"

"Joe!"

"I'm busy!"

"Quiet, Joe. Robert's having his lesson!"

"MOMMMM!"

Robert's dad comes in again:

"OK, Mr. B, your shoe is drying. Should be done soon, except I couldn't find anything to get the smell out. Is that OK?"

What am I going to say? Yes, that's OK? No, it's not?

"Uh, Mr. Morton, now my sock is wet from the carpet. Can I go wash it in the sink?"

"Oh sorry...that *da%& dog* again. Go ahead and wash it. You're just getting it from both ends, aren't you, Mr. B?"

"Yeah...right...thanks." I try and smile.

I now have one foot with a sock and a shoe, and the other is barefoot. As I walk towards the bathroom, I realize that I better watch out for more "Silky-isms" on the rug, so I start hopping. Let's see what's been accomplished so far today: Robert hasn't played a note yet, Joe's lesson was only twenty minutes long, yet Silky is still sleeping in that same spot. I keep hopping towards the bathroom, and as I avoid all of Silky's boo-boos it looks like I'm playing Hopscotch. I finally make it into the bathroom, then slip and barely grab onto the sink without falling. Neither Silky nor Robert has shown any expression during all of this.

After I rinse out my sock, I journey back to my chair, still playing pretend Hopscotch. Robert's lesson has about ten minutes left in it. My wet sock is now draped over the music stand, dripping on the floor, and I'm afraid to put my foot on the carpet for fear of stepping in something. As I dangle my bare foot in the air while playing my trumpet, a thought occurs to me: maybe Robert's dad can take my picture in this position. Then I can use it in my teaching brochure to try and recruit new trumpet students. *Yeah...that's a good idea! Just another typical lesson with Mr. B.*

Robert still hasn't said a word to me, and Silky is back asleep. We mercifully finish the lesson, and then I gingerly put my wet sock and shoe back on and squish over to the door. Silky wakes up and follows me to say good-bye. I reach down to pet him:

"Good boy...see you next week, Silky. But...*no more* surprises, OK?"

*

After the Silky experience, my next stop is Danny's house. Danny is nine, and he is *all* "little boy." He seems like he would belong more with Tom Sawyer, out playing by a river, than he does living in this fancy suburb. Today, I get to drive there with a stinky shoe and a soaked sock. Danny might think that's cool! My car is now starting to smell like Silky's "deliveries," but don't worry...I'll be home later to finally wash off my shoe...that's just *great* that I have to put up with this smell for three more hours!

Danny has a mixed breed dog, which is mostly terrier. "Sport" is his name, and he's a tiny white dog who is also *very* hyper. Sport likes me, and he goes wild when I ring the bell and come into the house. I like him, too, up to a point. Sport always jumps on my leg and stands there on his back legs, scratching my pants until I sit down. I don't wear nice dress pants to Sport's house, since I've had a few holes scratched in them by the little guy. And, besides jumping and scratching, Sport also barks like crazy until Danny and I get settled and start the lesson. All I can hear for about the first five minutes of the lesson is a very fast and loud:

"Yipe-yipe-yipe-yipe-...!!!"

Danny and I begin his lesson in his room, and Sport is lying in his usual spot in the hallway. He's finally quieted down. Danny puts up a baby-gate in his doorway, so Sport can see us, but he can't get in to bug us. He almost always stays still, unless one of us looks over at him, at which point he'll start his full throttle:

"Yipe-yipe-yipe-yipe...!!!"

Then he starts scratching at the baby-gate. I have to be careful not to look in his direction.

Besides Sport, Danny has several other pets, including lizards, toads, crickets, and several more "bug" type creatures. They all live in an aquarium in his room, but the tank has no water in it. I'm not exactly sure what all of these creatures are. Danny loves these guys---he calls them "the guys"---and he can't wait to show me his newest guy every week. I'm not really that excited about these guys, but I listen as Danny enlightens me on his newest addition:

"Mr. B, *look at this guy!* I just got him. He's green and gray...and look at his *orange eyes!* He's a kind of a salafoofer. I named him Grimy!"

"He's a sala*whatz*er?" I ask incredulously.

"A sala*foof*er, Mr. B. From the foofer family."

"The foofer family?"

"Yeah...listen to this...I've got the definition of a salafoofer memorized: 'Salafoofers are four-footed furry fellas with freckles, that may display flashes of flatulence when frightened.' See how Grimy looks like he's in the foofer family, Mr. B?"

My "salafoofer" knowledge is quite limited, and all I see is something slimy staring at me. He is a furry fella with freckles and four feet, however.

"Wow, Danny, I am impressed. Now, let's get back to your trumpet lesson. How about if we start with some mouthpiece buzzes and then we'll play our---"

"Here, Mr. B. I'll take Grimy out so *you* can hold him!"

Danny takes him out of the aquarium and shoves him towards my face.

"Uh, that's OK, Danny. I just washed my hands at the last house" (and I washed my sock, and my shoe, and...well, you remember).

"OK, Mr. B, maybe later."

Danny begins to put him back, but Grimy slips out of his hands onto the floor. I used to be scared when this would occur with Danny's creatures, but something like this seems to happen almost every lesson. Either one of the "guys" will slip out of Danny's hands as he's showing them to me, or they somehow escape from their tank. We also get to hear the sound of chirping crickets constantly throughout each lesson.

I've often asked Danny how he knows if these guys will eat each other or not. Danny says he doesn't know for sure, but he thinks "they know not to." I'm sure that's comforting to the smallest "guy" in the tank; he's probably the one who is escaping.

Danny begins to frantically search for Grimy, who has slithered away someplace. Danny's on his hands and knees, crawling around his room.

"Grimy! Here, Grimy! Come on, Mr. B, help me look."

I look around the room, but I don't see Grimy. In the meantime, Danny had accidentally left the top of the tank ajar when he took out Grimy. Here comes the mass exodus of the tank creatures...I can see them crawling up the sides and out the top---*eeewww*...my spine starts tingling and *my skin is crawling!*

"Danny! Close the top!"

"Right...got it, Mr. B! Grab that 'marmalubin', will ya?"

"Grab that *marmalade*, Danny?"

"No, the marmalubin. He's the one hopping onto your...your nose. Here, I got him, Mr. B!"

"Thanks, Danny. *YECHHH!"*

I begin to rub my nose furiously.

"Mr. B, no time to pick your nose now! Keep grabbing guys, will ya?"

"Sure thing, Danny."

I capture a few more creatures, and put them back into the tank.

"Thanks, Mr. B! Oh, there go my toads...got 'em! OK, I think only a few guys escaped. Now I *have* to find Grimy."

Only a *few* guys escaped, Danny says. I'm not sure if I feel better or not. Uh oh, now Sport has noticed all the commotion, and he wants to help. He's jumping on the baby-gate:

"Yipe-yipe-yipe-yipe..."

"Quiet, Sport." Danny says. "We have to find Grimy."

Sport settles down after a short while, and I think it's because he may have had a crunchy critter snack. Danny crawls around for a few more minutes. No luck finding Grimy. I didn't dare mention Sport's possible snack to Danny. Danny gets despondent:

"Oh, Mr. B, I'm worried about Grimy. He's new here, and doesn't know his way around. I don't really feel like playing my trumpet."

Well, now, let's see: it's already been twenty-three minutes since his lesson started, and he hasn't played one note yet. That means he hasn't made one mistake yet, either! Why ruin a perfect lesson?

"OK, Danny, how 'bout if you get your mom?"

"OK, Mr. B. Sorry."

As I get up and leave Danny's room, Sport is right there to start jumping, scratching, and yipping. He hangs onto my leg like a cast, and I drag him all the way to the door.

I have to shout above Sport's yipping:

"I BET YOU'LL FIND GRIMY SOON, DANNY. HE COULDN'T HAVE GONE VERY FAR."

As Danny opens the door, I can see some crickets moving as I peel Sport off of my leg. I can't tell if they're coming in or going out, but I get the feeling that Sport might be having a real smorgasbord soon.

*

After Danny's perfect lesson, I have to drive to the Johnson's house to teach another pair of brothers, Noah and Jeremy. It's become pretty common for Ann and me to teach siblings. In fact, we must have had at least twenty families like that over the years. Many times Ann and I each taught one child in the family, or one of us gave lessons to two siblings. There have even been two families where, between the two of us, we taught *three* siblings. In the case of one of those families, I went to their house to give lessons for thirteen years, since their kids were far apart in age.

Sometimes, these relatives didn't care for each other all that much. I can recall a conversation I once had with one of my trumpet students, whose sister took flute lessons from Ann.

"Hey, Mr. B, my sister got a job as a soda-jerk!"

"Really? Where is that?"

"At the ice cream store."

"Oh, you mean she dishes up the ice cream to the customers?"

"No. She's just a jerk!"

Now, to get back to my current students. Noah and Jeremy are nice boys, and they're almost always prepared for their lessons. They're interested in different kinds of music, so we're able to play jazz and classical pieces during their lessons. While the boys are musically fun for me to teach, however, their sessions are torture to sit through in other ways.

The Johnsons live about thirty minutes away from Danny, in one of the wealthiest suburbs in the country, on a street right across from the lake. As I drive along this street that parallels the lake, it seems that each home is more opulent than the previous one. However, the Johnson's house doesn't look like it fits into this neighborhood at all. It's very small, the rooms are tiny on the inside, and it's only one story high. I'm guessing that at one point it belonged to a caretaker's family; a caretaker of one the giant homes that surround this smaller house.

The Johnson's home also sticks out in this neighborhood because it isn't very well taken care of. On the outside, the grass is always overgrown, there is paint peeling all over the place, and one of the front windows has a crack in it. Inside, part of the flooring is coming up, there's a door that's missing a hinge and is tilting, and the carpet is very dirty. *Very dirty,* not just from the usual wear, but also from the family pets.

Ah...their pets. How can I best describe them? They have two dogs and two cats. That's the easy part. They interact with the family, like most pets, but there's not a lot of attention being paid to them. It looks like the dogs haven't been brushed or had a bath since the Nixon administration, and all four animals *smell profusely* every time they walk by me. And...not just the typical dog and cat smell, but more like a "monkey house at the zoo" smell. You know the type of odor I'm talking about. It's like one of those hot, rainy days when all the monkeys and the visitors are inside the monkey house, with the humidity and the steam (and the stench) coming up.

I learned very quickly not to pet any of their animals, since their stink and greasy ooze stays on my hands, my trumpet, my steering wheel, etc. for hours.

Unbelievably, no one in the family even seems to detect it. On top of this, however, there's a much bigger problem with these pets, and I've noticed it since the very first time I came to their house. Let me try to describe the scene of that day:

By the middle of Noah's first lesson, I was already overwhelmed by the smell. I had made the mistake of petting the dogs, and my hand was pretty gooey as I held my trumpet. About every six or seven minutes, I heard one of the cats begin to barf up a hairball in the next room. They always start with their mouths closed, and then these feline hurling sounds get faster and louder:

"MMM, MMM, MMM, *GLUCK, GLUCK, BLAAAHHHW! MMM, MMM, GLUCK, BLAAAHHHW!*" This happens randomly throughout almost all of our lessons.

We're in their living room, and there's a fireplace next to me on my right. As I look around, I see what looks like two neat piles of doggy-doo-doo, just sitting there on the hearth of the fireplace! And I mean *piles* of it, not just a little bit. Are they real? Are they like those fake vomit toys? No, I do think these are real.

"Play that piece again, Noah." I say.

I look again, and sure enough, that's what it is...you've got to be kidding me! That explains at least some of the smell in this house.

Even though it's fifteen degrees outside, I have to ask:

"Hey Noah, can you open a window?"

"No, Mr. B, my mom doesn't like to open any windows."

"Well, in that case, Noah, can you scoot over to your left a little bit? Thanks." Scooting over doesn't help to avoid the smell. Oops, time for another cat barf: "MMM, MMM, *GLUCK, BLAAAHHHW!"*

No one in the family pays any attention to the cats barfing, and they don't seem to care about the dog piles, either. What a house!

When I came back the next week, I was sure that the doggy-doo would be gone. To my amazement, though, there were now *three* piles on the hearth instead of two! Then, the week after, there were five piles! Sometimes when I arrive they look *very* fresh! I guess the dogs knew that I was coming, and they just wanted to greet me. Finally, after several weeks, the piles were gone. This pattern repeated itself over the next few months. At first there might be one or two deposits, then three or four, the next week maybe up to five or six, and then at last they'd be cleaned up. And, the family never says anything about it to me, or to each other. Do they clean it up themselves? Or, do they hire maids to come in? How'd *you* like to be those maids? My stomach stills turns a little every time I have to come to this house.

By the time I arrive at the Johnson's today, my shoe stinks and my sock is still wet from my Silky adventure. Also, my hands are full of "marmalubin" oil from rubbing my nose at Danny's house. This has become a day of high-level musical experiences, and I'm ready for another one:

"Hi, Noah, let's get started."

As I open my trumpet case, I can smell a flash of flatulence. I'm reaching in, and I feel something unusual. It's slimy and furry....there are four feet moving in my hand....wait a minute...it's...it's GRIMY! He must have crawled right into my soft, dark trumpet case, maybe to hide from the other "guys." What do I do with him now? I'm going to be here for an hour. Should I then drive all the way back to Danny's house, which is thirty minutes out of the way from my next lesson? Or, maybe I shouldn't even say anything to Danny? That sounds like a better idea. After all, Danny's probably already back at the pet store, purchasing a new member of the "foofer" family. He'll soon forget all about Grimy. But, what do I do with him now?

That question becomes moot when Grimy slithers out of my hand, and heads straight towards the dog piles on the hearth. I can't quite reach him, and I'm sure not going to put my hands anywhere near *that* fireplace. Good...Noah hasn't noticed anything. I look over at Grimy, and he seems perfectly contented in his new surroundings of "number two."

"Let's play number 2...I mean, number 37, Noah."

As Noah plays, I begin to sneak some peeks at Grimy. At first, I see him happily oozing between the piles, but when I look again a few minutes later, I can't see him at all. I continue to look later during the lesson, but Grimy's not there. Maybe he's found a new adventure, and in this house, I bet that would be easy for him to do. Oh, well, Grimy's found a new home, I guess. And, it must be like heaven for him!

"OK, Noah, let me demonstrate number 39 in the book for you."

I start to play, when I hear a familiar sound, getting faster and louder:

"MMM, MMM, *MMM, GLUCK, GLUCK, BLAAAHHHW!*"

Just one of the cats again barfing up another hairb---or, wait, there's that familiar flash of flatulence. Could it be---was that...Grimy? Uh-oh. Too late to do anything about it now.

Ah, don't you just love the Circle of Life!

*

My stomach churns and turns through Noah and Jeremy's lessons, and there's no more sign of Grimy. I'm now heading for Josh's house, which is my last stop of the day. Josh lives about fifteen minutes away from Noah and Jeremy, and his house is right on my way home. He's a junior in high school, and is one of my best students. I really enjoy ending the day teaching Josh, and he's so interested in studying the trumpet that he takes forty-five minute lessons. I have many students that do this, as well as some that even take hour-long lessons. Josh is always well prepared, is interested in many kinds of music, and is culturally sophisticated. He also has a neat brown and white Beagle named Samantha, that everyone calls Sam.

Sam's about six years old, and she is way past the stage of jumping on me when I come into the house. Sam does have one big problem with me coming over, however, and that is getting used to all the different dog smells that I've picked up throughout my day. She'll sniff my leg and shoes, and shake her head back and forth a few times in disgust.

"Where the heck have *you* been?" Sam seems to be asking.

Between Silky, Sport, and the two dogs at Noah and Jeremy's house, Sam can't believe what her "schnozz" is telling her:

"How *dare* you bring *those* smells into *my* house!"

Sam tries to bark, but instead just coughs and snorts a few times, follows me into the lesson room, and lies down in the corner. She must really be enjoying the smell of my shoe today, thanks to Silky's deposit on it a couple of hours ago.

As Josh and I play through several different songs, Sam just lies there; occasionally coughing...I guess she still can't get those other dog's smells out of her head. Josh and I practice some trumpet exercises, and then we perform a very difficult solo. We're playing some pretty loud and fast material, which takes about a half hour to finish. Sam shows no emotion during any of these songs, still just lying there in the corner.

Finally, toward the end of the lesson, Josh and I start to play a jazz style duet. We always save these fun jazz pieces for the end of the lessons; they're kind of a dessert for trumpet players. This is where the fun begins for Sam, and for me, too. After hearing just a few notes of this jazz song, Sam immediately waddles over to us, sits down, and begins to holler in a deep, low voice:

"ohrrr-OHRRR-OHRRRRRRRR!!!"

She just loves jazz duets! We can be playing any other type of song, or I can play something by myself, or have Josh play by himself, and Sam will continue to lie down quietly in the corner. But, the moment she hears us start a jazz duet, Sam gets totally into it, and she keeps booming out her baritone voice for the entire duet. Her head begins to bob up and down, as if she's keeping time with the beat. Josh stops playing, and calls out to her:

"Sam! Be qui---"

"OHRRRRRRR!!"

"SAM! SAMANTH---"

"OHRRrrrrr."

There. Sam finally stops her singing. It almost sounds like a vacuum cleaner is being turned off. But, she clearly doesn't want to quit...she often keeps singing for a few seconds after Josh and I have stopped, with her entire upper body twisting and her tail wagging in the opposite direction.

"Josh, let's start again." I say. "One-two-ready-go!"

"Bop-be-dop. Bop-be---"

"ohrrr-OHRRR-OHRRRRRRR!!!"

Josh and I start laughing. The deep canine voice is booming once more.

"SaMANtha!" Josh yells, but he's not angry with her, and he is still smiling.

"OHRRR!"

"SAM!"

"ROHRRR!"

"C'mon, SAM!"

"OHRRrrrrr."

There goes the vacuum again.

Sam seems mad, and she keeps staring at us, as if to say:

"Come on, guys, why did you stop! I'm a cool cat!"

Or, rather a cool dog...sorry, Sam.

Josh's whole family starts to come into the room. They've heard Sam howling, and they want to listen to her some more. They do this every week when she sings.

"OK, Josh. Now that we're all here, how about if we play it one more time.

You ready, Josh?" I ask.

Josh nods, trying not to giggle any more.

"Sam, are you ready?" I inquire.

Sam's staring at me while her behind is swaying to and fro. She's ready, too!

"OK, everyone. One-two-ready-go!"

"Bop-be-dop. Bop-be---"

"ohrrr-OHRRR-OHRRRRRRR!"

Somehow, we manage to finish the duet. The entire group showers Sam with shouts and applause when the song is over. At least, I think that the cheering is for her, and not for Josh and me. Certainly, Sam's tone was the loudest of the three of us, and I think she crooned the most notes. Sam's whole bottom half continues to wiggle ferociously. She thought it was an outstanding performance, too!

Since Josh's lesson is my last one of the day, I get to see and hear Sam do her diva routine every week right before I drive home. And, especially after the day I've had today, I can't begin to tell her how much I appreciate it.

Thanks, Sam!

*

As Susie opens the door, I can see Sparky sitting on her shoulder. Sparky is a turquoise parakeet, and he seems to love sitting there. He's almost always on Susie's shoulder when I come over for the lessons. Susie is a fifth grader, and she has told me that Sparky is almost as old as she is, and that she doesn't remember not having Sparky for her pet parakeet.

When I first started teaching Susie, I thought that Sparky was going to present an annoying situation. I mean, wouldn't it be just slightly distracting to try and play a trumpet with a bird on your shoulder? And, I wondered if Susie would even be listening to me trying to teach her while this parakeet was sitting up there!

Alas, I had nothing to worry about. Susie said that Sparky always sits on her shoulder when she practices her trumpet, and I know she practices regularly. In fact, these two are so used to each other that Sparky often falls asleep while he's sitting up there, even when she's blasting away on her trumpet! I didn't believe this at first, but as the weeks went by, and I got to know Sparky more closely, I could see that Susie was right. The sounds of the trumpet don't seem to upset him at all, and he's very contented the entire time I'm at Susie's house for her lessons. I enter Susie's home today:

"Hi Susie. Hi Sparky."

"Hi Mr. B."

When Sparky hears his name, his head perks up towards me. I think he knows me by now, or at least he knows the sound of my voice. Ann and I also have a pet bird at home, and his name is Larry (yes, I know it's an obvious name, but I'm a big basketball fan). Can birds detect the scent of other birds? Maybe Sparky can sense Larry's presence through me. At home, Larry sits on my shoulder a lot, too. I don't know about the scent detection, but I do enjoy being around pet birds. As we all walk into Susie's living room, I try to start my weekly conversation with Sparky:

"Hey Sparky, how are you?"

He launches right into his routine:

"Spar---ky Bird! Pret---ty Bird! *Sparr---ky Bird!*"

This is always followed by a couple of wolf whistles. Can a bird make a wolf whistle? Depends on the wolf!

I guess a bird can make a wolf whistle sound...what else would you call it? Susie and I begin her lesson, and Sparky gradually falls asleep on her shoulder, even with two blaring trumpets being very close to him. Once in a while, I can see Sparky burying his head under his wing. He's quiet most of the time, but sometimes, when we're playing loudly, he starts to whistle along with us. I can hear him slightly above our trumpet noises, and I can also see his head bobbing up and down while we play. Susie doesn't really notice.

She keeps right on playing while this happy bird is nodding and singing, just a couple of inches from Susie's ear.

Sparky's been whistling and bobbing quite a bit during today's lesson. He must have practiced a lot this week, too, because he sounds good! The only times he seems to get mad are when Susie and I stop playing. When that happens, he often keeps whistling and dancing for a few seconds, until he realizes that we've stopped. When Sparky is still whistling, I have to wait before I can give any instructions to Susie...Sparky hasn't finished his solo yet! Then, he'll start to nibble on Susie's ear, as if to try and get her to start playing again. Susie brushes him away, but Sparky doesn't always take no for an answer. He usually tries nibbling a few more times, and then he finally gives up when he figures out that we're not going to play anymore.

Susie and I are now playing our final song of the lesson, and our trumpets are getting louder and louder. Sparky has joined in, too. He's whistling, and he's also moving his head around in a circle. All of a sudden, Sparky flies up into the air...he *never* does this when I'm here! We keep playing the song while Sparky flies around above our heads. Susie is oblivious to all of this. She must really be used to it. Finally, Sparky lands on *my* shoulder, just as Susie and I start playing the long, last note of the song. We hold out the tone for a few seconds, as Sparky blasts a shrieking, steady whistle right in my ear. Susie and I stop playing, but Sparky isn't done just yet. I look over at him, and while Sparky's screech continues driving through my head, he's also wildly gyrating his own head. It's going up, down, and around in circles. He's standing up, then sitting, then standing again on my shoulder on one foot. I think he's doing the "Funky Chicken!" Or, maybe it's the "Funky Parakeet." He finishes his big solo in style:

"Spar---ky Bird! Pret---ty Bird! *Sparrr-ky Birrrd!"*

While the word *"Birrrd..."* trails off, Sparky flies up again, makes a few circles around the room, and lands back on Susie's shoulder. Wow, this guy knows how to finish a solo on a high note!

"Oh, Mr. B, Sparky's saying he likes you!"

"Cool, Susie. Thanks, Sparky! I like you, too. But...how am I going to explain to my Larry bird about all of these parakeet feathers being on my shoulder?"

*

Rocky has to be the meanest Chihuahua in the history of Chihuahuas. He doesn't like *anybody;* not the family that he lives with, not his neighbors, and certainly not me. Maybe that's because Rocky is not the most handsome dog around. The top of his head is bald, and his eyes bulge out a little too far, somewhat like a fish. He's small in size, too...even for a Chihuahua. I bet he's not quite a foot long, although I've never gotten close enough to him to measure!

Rocky and his human family live in a third floor walkup, in an apartment building with six units. I don't mind going up and down all of those stairs once a week to teach my student, Rebecca. She and her parents are very nice, and Rebecca is a dedicated trumpet pupil. The thing I dread about Rebecca's lessons can be summed up in one scary word: *Rocky!*

Now, I must say that normally I like dogs a lot. Altogether, I bet my students collectively have at least fifteen dogs, a dozen cats, and several birds. Not to mention Grimy, the late Salafoofer (may he rest in peace after being swallowed and then barfed up by a cat). I enjoy being around all of those animals, and they like me, too. Most of them seem really happy to see me, except for a few of the more aloof cats. Not Rocky, though.

You've heard about a dog's bark being worse than his bite? From what Rebecca and her parents tell me, that's not the case with Rocky. He gives equal billing to the barking and the biting. Each member of the family has been bitten by Rocky many times, and they say he bites at least one of them almost every day!

Fortunately for the mailman, the mail just goes into the slots at the ground floor entrance to the building. He's seen and heard Rocky a few times as they pass each other going in and out of the foyer, and he's heard of Rocky's reputation. But, at least he doesn't have to go up and say hello to Rocky every day. I would guess that the Postal Service might even require Rocky to live on the third floor. I've met that mailman a few times, and we've gossiped about Rocky. He just rolls his eyes, and laughs when I say how I just came from Rocky's apartment. It's easy for him to laugh...he doesn't have to go up there! Rocky's family has also told me that he's bitten every neighbor he's ever met, as well as everyone who's ever set foot in that apartment...except me. I'm now #1 on his "be sure to bite" list, and I can tell by the way he glares at me that he knows it.

Rocky's bark is something to hear, too. I think it's about the highest sound that a person can hear. Once Rocky begins to bark, I don't think he takes a breath for about a minute. The barks are very fast, and very close together; something like the sound that Hitchcock used in the shower scene of "Psycho." And, Rocky's bark is *extremely* loud. Let's see...try to imagine a "Hitchcock-ian" air horn going off right next to one ear, while a pig squeals at the top of its lungs into the other ear. That's Rocky. No one can get him to stop either...I've heard the family try. *Rocky* is the only one who decides when *Rocky* is finished barking.

The apartment building where Rocky lives faces a busy street, so I always have to park around the back in an alley. He seems to know by the sound of the car door closing if you're going up to his place to bother him. Here I am now, pulling into the alley. As my car door shuts, it sets off Rocky on his routine. He starts his barking/shrieking/porky/"Psycho" noises. I can hear him even though he's up on the third floor, and the apartment windows are closed. It sure seems like he knows that it's me. I can feel the hair on the back of my neck standing up already. Geez, *this* is why I became a trumpet teacher? Calm down now, genius. You're here to help Rebecca, remember?

As I enter the building, I have to ring their doorbell so the family can buzz me in. After that, I get to traipse up the three flights of steps to their door. From the time I shut my car door to when I actually knock on their front door takes about five minutes. It's a good thing, too, for it can take a long time for the family to catch Rocky and then put him behind one of those expanding wooden baby gates for safe-keeping. Not only is this dog very short, but he can barely jump, so a visitor is somewhat secure. Rocky usually stops yelling after I come in and finally sit down. After that, he'll just squint his eyes and stare at me (picture Clint Eastwood as a bald, short, mean Chihuahua...sorry, Mr. Eastwood, I'm a big fan of yours, actually!).

I walk into the building's entryway, and ring their bell. Rocky's been sounding off since I got out of the car. I pass one of the neighbors in the foyer. She smiles and nods her head:

"Good luck up there."

"Thanks. Rocky sounds hungry for an ankle today. Hope it's not mine!"

She holds out her bandaged hand:

"He got me the other day when I tried to pet him. Never again. They should evict that dog!"

"Thanks for the advice."

Rebecca buzzes me into the inner door of their entryway, and I start up the stairs. Even from the bottom step, I can hear scurrying and shouts of *"Rocky!"* and *"Owww!"* coming from above. They're trying to catch him, but he's biting them back. This dog is so small and fast (and angry) that catching him is a pretty difficult job to accomplish. I can also hear Rocky screaming. His voice gets louder and higher if you get close to him, so I can tell when they're about to grab him. Nope, they're not close yet. I continue up the stairs, and finally knock on their door. All I hear is more scurrying, more shouting, and more squealing. Sometimes it takes them five minutes to catch him, and I guess today is one of those times. I'm waiting, and waiting, and...hold on...there goes Rocky's voice, up higher, faster, and louder. I think they're about to---

"OUUUCH!!"

"WEE-YEE-YEE-YEE-YEEEEE!!!"

Then, silence. Rebecca opens the door: "Hi Mr. B. We got him...it's OK to come in!"

I look around cautiously, and I can see Rebecca's dad shaking his bitten fingers while trying to hold a squirming Rocky.

"Uh, OK, thanks." I reply.

Rebecca's dad deposits Rocky behind the baby gate as I sit down. I always try to keep an eye on him until I can see that he's safely back behind there. As I get out my trumpet, I can hear the next phase of Rocky's routine begin. He walks back to the other side of the room, and then charges at the baby gate like a mad ten-inch-long bull.

"BOOM!!"

"Pitter-patter-pitter-patter *BOOM!!"*

With one final angry glare in my direction, Rocky circles a few times, and finally lies down.

"Good boy, Clint...I mean, Rocky."

Without picking up his head, his eyes look up defiantly at me:

"Go ahead, punk, make my day."

I try to come prepared for Rocky, in case he does get loose and bites me. Even in hot weather, I always wear my thick, rubber, tall black boots to Rebecca's lessons. Ann calls them my "shit-kickers." I also wear two pair of long, wool socks. This can look ridiculous on a day like today, when it's 90 degrees outside and I'm only wearing shorts and a t-shirt. Rebecca's family, however, has never asked me about my strange attire. I think they know the canine motivation behind my sartorial splendor. Since Rocky can barely jump, I'm safe as long as I don't bend down very far. But, if I happen to drop my trumpet mouthpiece for instance, and Rocky's gotten out, well...forget it. I'd rather just get a new mouthpiece.

Rebecca's trumpet playing sounds great again today. She's having another excellent lesson. Rocky is sleeping behind the baby gate, and I can even hear him snoring a little, when, suddenly, the door buzzer rings from downstairs...Rocky wakes up like a shot, squealing wildly. He's probably mad at himself for not hearing the car door closing in the alley. I hear Rebecca's mom ask who it is through the intercom, and then she tells the person to come up. Rebecca says that her uncle is visiting. He lives overseas, and hasn't been back in years. Uh-oh, I wonder if he's ever met Rocky? I hope they warned him!

Rocky is still behind the gate, but Rebecca's dad picks him up to try and get him to calm down and stop shrieking. He's squirming like crazy to get away from her dad. Rebecca's uncle arrives at the door, and she lets him in.

"Uncle Joe, I'm so happy to see you! This is my trumpet teacher. His name is Mr. B."

"Hello, Uncle Joe. It's nice to mee----"

Oh, no...with one more decisive squirm and squeal, Rocky has escaped from Rebecca's dad. He's on the loose!

"Rocky! Rocky!" calls Rebecca's dad.

"WEE-YEE-YEE-YEEEEE!!" replies Rocky (I think that's the F-word in Chihuahua-speak).

"Rocky, come here." implores Rebecca: "Help us catch him, Mr. B. Help, Uncle Joe!"

"WEE-YEE-YEEEEE!!"

Rocky starts to zip by me, and in the heat of the moment I stupidly hold out my hand to try and grab him. He's so small, and light. How hard can it be?

"Here, Rocky. I got you n----*YYOWWW!!"*

"WEE-YEE-YEEEEE!!"

Rocky has bitten my hand, right in the fleshy part between my thumb and first finger. He sneers at me as he lets go of my hand and runs away. He seems to be smiling while he sneers. Either that, or that's a piece of my flesh sticking out of his mouth. My hand begins to throb, and when I look down at it I can see blood oozing out onto the floor. Rocky got me good!

"Don't worry, Rebecca, I'll get him!" Uncle Joe bellows out in a Darth Vader-like voice.

He sounds way too optimistic for me. Rocky continues to whiz wildly around the room. Joe makes the mistake of leaning over to try and capture Rocky, and the biting Chihuahua jumps as high as he can (which is about 3 inches) and grabs a hold of Uncle Joe's unmentionables. Joe starts serpentining around the apartment, and Rocky is *still* attached to Joe's private parts. Rocky is hanging there, about three feet off of the floor, parallel to the ground. Uncle Joe is a rather large man, and his pants are pulled up to just below his chest. He tries to swing his hefty torso back and forth as fast as he can in order to throw Rocky off.

Rocky's eyes begin bulging even more as he dangles to and fro, and what little hair he has on his head is standing up...he's totally enjoying this moment. The two of them continue their dirty dancing scene for what seems like several minutes:

Joe's swinging (he looks like Jackie Gleason).

Rocky is dangling.

Joe keeps swinging ("and Awaaay We Go!").

Rocky is still dangling.

Joe's dangling (at least some of his gentlemanly body parts are).

Rocky is swinging.

They're both screaming so loudly, and in such a high pitch, that no one can tell which voice is which, and there's no way Rocky is letting go.

Rebecca's dad had dialed 911 after he saw Rocky bite my hand. I've now taken a seat, with my hand still bleeding. I didn't know I'd be treated to such a floorshow at this lesson! The paramedics have just arrived after climbing up the three flights of stairs. They are there to check on me, and they didn't even know about Uncle Joe's anatomical mambo with Rocky. One paramedic runs over to me, while the other two stand there, transfixed by Rocky and Uncle Joe's gyrations. They can't believe it, either. Rebecca's dad grabs Rocky's behind from behind. Finally, after stifling their laughter, the paramedics give Rocky some kind of shot to knock him out (I would have used a rubber hammer myself). Joe keeps screaming, and they manage to get him into a chair. Even though Rocky is asleep, his teeth are still attached to Joe's "Jones." Rocky's teeth must be locked in that position. The paramedics now give Uncle Joe a shot, too, and he gradually calms down and falls asleep. They don't make rubber hammers big enough to do that.

Next, we all begin the long journey down the stairs and out to the ambulance. I'm feeling better, but the paramedics want me to go to the hospital for a possible rabies shot. Can't wait! Uncle Joe and Rocky continue to be intimately involved. The three paramedics somehow clunk them down the three flights on the gurney, but they're both out cold, anyway.

Rocky is going on a fun ambulance ride today, but he doesn't even know it! The paramedics and I are staring at Uncle Joe and Rocky, but they're trying not to chuckle in front of me. After a short journey, we pull up to the E.R. door. Dog gone it...I wish I had my camera! The paramedics must have radioed ahead, for it seems like every doctor and nurse in the entire hospital is there to greet us. They whisk me into one E.R. station, and I can tell that they've put our two connected friends into the adjacent one. While I'm being bandaged up, and given a shot, I can hear the rest of the doctors and nurses laughing on the other side of the wall. They're finally able to extricate Rocky's incisors from Uncle Joe's manhood. I would have loved to have seen them to do that...then again, uh, maybe not.

Good thing the doctors were quick, too...Rocky is waking up, and he sounds really scared:

"WEE-YEE!! WEE-YEE!! WEE-YEE!!"

The nurses give him another shot, and he's out again. Uncle Joe is still asleep, and I can hear him snoring through the partition.

Rebecca's dad had followed us to the hospital in his car, and now he wants to drive all of us back to the apartment. One small problem remains, however: who is going to hold Rocky? Joe continues to snore as they load him into the car, so I guess it's going to be Rocky on my lap.

I pleaded with the nurse to give Rocky one more shot, just in case he wakes up in my lap, but she said that they've already given him enough to kill a horse. Uh–oh, Rebecca's dad seems to be driving *VERY SLOWLY.* I don't think he wants Rocky to wake up, but I wish he'd go faster! As we finally pull into the alley by my car, Rocky gradually begins to stir. Little by little he squirms and squeaks on my lap. I'm trying to open the car door to get out, but I'm holding Rocky in one hand, and my other hand has a gigantic bandage on it. C'mon, man, I gotta get outta----

"WEE-YEE-YEEEEE!!"

Too late. Rocky's awake and angry. Rebecca's dad keeps parking. Rocky slithers out of my grasp, and makes a huge Chihuahua leap from my lap right towards my face. I close my eyes, hold my breath, and brace myself.

Wait, wait...nothing happens! I slowly open my eyes, afraid that this serial Chihuahua might be waiting to scratch them out. But...Rocky is nowhere to be seen. Did someone grab him? Could it have been Boo Radley? No, I hear a high-pitched, squeaky voice shouting:

"I got you now, you little sonofabit---"

"Uncle Joe...it was you!" I exclaim. "I can't thank you enough! Are you OK? Is your voice all right?"

Joe answers in his new shrill, soprano tone:

"Well, not really. I'm going upstairs to rest. But, it was fun meeting you. Have a nice day, Mr. B."

"You too, Joe."

I struggle trying to drive home with my clubbed hand, but I still think that I'm much better off than poor Uncle Joe. At least my hand will heal. I'm not sure about Joe's manly accessories, or about his voice, either. And, to think, a ten-inch dog did all of this damage. Oh, the humanity!

Ann sees me walk in, and she can't help but notice how my hand is all wrapped up.

"What happened to *you*?"

"I'll give you one guess."

"Rocky got you?"

"Yep."

"Are you all right?"

"I think I'll be fine. The E.R. doctor said there's no permanent damage."

"The E.R. doctor? Permanent damage? *What?*"

"I can tell you the details later. But first, you won't believe what happened to Rebecca's Uncle Joe. He got the worst of Rocky by far. Oh, and by the way, if Rebecca's family calls here to check on me, Uncle Joe is changing his name to Josephine."

*

Dave's house is an extremely fun place for me to give lessons. Dave is one of eight trumpet students that I teach from the same high school, and they all are great kids with very nice families. They are all also excellent trumpet players, and are very interested in learning about the history and theory of music. They've all ranked high in state music competitions, and they've even attended summer music camps just because they are so much into music and playing the trumpet.

Each week, I'm able to play and teach some very sophisticated trumpet literature with these students, and I know that they will all practice this material during the week. Obviously, to have this many fine students from one school is quite unusual. I've been teaching all of them at their homes since they were in the fifth grade, so Ann and I have gotten to know their parents rather well over the years, too. These parents are terrific people, and they have been exceptionally kind and generous towards us.

I have another reason that I enjoy teaching at Dave's house. Dave and his parents have pet birds, and the birds are a riot! There are four parrots that live in the kitchen. Dave's parents keep the kitchen door closed during the lessons, so I don't get to see the birds that much. But, I sure get to hear them all the time, and they are always having lots of fun! They are all constantly talking to each other, and responding to any human who talks to them. Often, I'll hear one of them mimic something that I've just said. When I'm in the living room teaching Dave, I sometimes forget that these guys are actually birds, and not four more people sitting around and conversing in the kitchen.

As Dave opens the front door, I can hear the four of them yakking away in their sing-songy, fluctuating voices. Their names are Flappy, Rosemary, Peaches, and Garfunkel. Their voices are distinct enough so that even I can tell them apart, although I only get to hear them once a week. They tend to all talk at the same time, and they don't seem to listen to each other, but I know lots of people who are the same way. They are also very opinionated:

"Baaar...Birrr---ds are best!" announces Rosemary.

"Governor's-a-dope! Baaar...Governor's-a-dope!" Peaches stated. She hates politicians.

"Cats drool!" That must be Flappy; he's very territorial.

"Baaar...Truuu---mpets rule!" Garfunkel chimes in. He's the music lover of the bunch.

"Misss---ter B! Baaar...Misss---ter B!"

That's Flappy again. He seems to like me, and he always nods his head up and down as he calls out my name. I guess he recognizes my voice more than the other birds do, and he looks right at me when I talk to him. He's a friendly guy!

Dave says the parrots know that it's me when I come in, and that I should say hi to them before his mom shuts the kitchen door.

"Hi, guys. How ya' doin'?"

They sit up tall and ruffle their feathers for me. I think they do recognize my voice, and they all begin moving their heads and jabbering together:

"Baaar...How ya-doin'? How ya-doin'?"

"Rub-my-head!"

"Baaar...Birrr---ds are best!"

"Koo-koo-ka-choo! Koo-koo-ka---"

"Baaar...Feelin' Groovy! Feelin' Groovy!"

"Plastics-my-son!"

Their necks are really gyrating around now:

"Baaar...She stole my parsley. Stole my parsley! Stole my---"

"Naaaht---me! Naaaht---me!"

"Rosemary parsley! Rosemary pars---"

"Baaar..."Misss-ses Robinson!" That's got to be Garfunkel.

"Boys and girls, calm down now." Instructs Dave's mom. "Mr. B is here to teach Dave. You know that."

"Baaar...Misss---ter B! Misss---ter B!" There goes Flappy-Bird once more.

"Hi, Flappy," I reply, "how's my buddy?"

Dave's mom closes the kitchen door, and Dave and I begin his lesson. As usual, teaching the trumpet to Dave is lots of fun. After about fifteen minutes have gone by, Dave asks me about Larry, his neighbor. Larry is in fifth grade, and he's ten years old. Larry and his parents just moved into this neighborhood a few months ago, right before school started. They have all heard Dave practicing his trumpet several times, and on Dave's recommendation, Larry's parents decided to call me to teach Larry, too.

Unfortunately, I'm not sure if that reference was a good thing or not! Unlike Dave, and the other high school students I teach from this suburb, Larry is *very* lazy. He doesn't seem to care about playing the trumpet in the least. He tells me that he doesn't like anything about school, actually. He's only interested in playing video games. He would talk about video games for the entire lesson if I let him. And, sorry to say, Larry is not very good looking, either. He's short, chubby, and for lack of a better term, ugly.

Oh, and one more important thing. On top of being lethargic and unattractive, Larry is an obnoxious smart aleck, and is often disrespectful towards me. He constantly interrupts what I'm saying, changes the subject, makes fun of playing the trumpet, and whines for practically the entire lesson. I always picture Jerry Lewis at age ten when I'm with Larry, except that Larry doesn't have the intelligence part of Jerry Lewis, just the whining part. It's a real pain for me because I teach Dave first, and experience a great lesson. Then, I have to go and teach Larry, who proceeds to spoil my day (and my love of teaching) completely. Here's a typical exchange between Larry and me:

"OK, Larry, let's play #13, the one I wanted you to practice."

"Ah, I hate #13. I didn't play it, and I don't like the **number** thirteen, either. Why didn't you want me to play fourteen? I would have played that one. It's your fault."

"Well, Larry, I didn't give you #14 because you still can't play #13, even after a month. How does that make you feel?"

"Ah, who cares? Did you see that new video game that's coming out? It's called *'Dead Army Ninja Crotch-Kick 4.'* I've got versions 1, 2, and 3, and this one's supposed to have extra secret codes so you can crotch-kick longer and deeper."

"No, Larry, I don't know that game. How about if we play Jingle Bells from your other book?"

"Trumpets are stupid."

"How would you know, Larry? You don't practice enough to find out."

OK, that's enough of Larry. Now, back to Dave, who is asking me how Larry is doing with his trumpet lessons:

"Well, Dave, please don't repeat this, but Larry's lazy, and he hasn't learned a thing so far. Plus, he's a smart-ass, and he won't listen to me. I don't like him, at least yet. But, thanks anyway for recommending me."

I say the last sentence while I'm smiling. Dave knows me well enough to know I'm only half-kidding.

"Oh, sorry, Mr. B. We hear him talking back to his parents all the time, too. And, I heard that he gets in trouble at school a lot. He says nasty things to me and my parents, until I threaten to punch him out. We've never even let him in the house. Don't worry, the whole neighborhood knows all about Larry."

Just then, the doorbell rings, and Dave's mom opens the door:

"Hey, laaady!"

Oh my God, it *is* Jerry Lewis! No, it's really just Larry.

"My dad sent me over. He says to give him a hammer. He needs one for something."

"Now Larry, what's a nice way to ask?" responds Dave's mom.

"Who cares. Got the hammer, *laaady?"*

"Just a minute, Larry. Say hello to Mr. B."

"Yeah, I know him."

"Nice to see you, too, Larry. Does your dad need a hammer to pound some nails into his he----"

"Laaar---ry's lazy! Laaar---ry's lazy!"

"Hey, who said that?" demands Larry.

We all just shrug.

"Heee'---sa smart-ass! Heee'---sa smart-ass!"

"What's going on?"

Now Larry's really starting to freak out. All he sees is Dave, me, and Dave's mom. We're all just standing there with our mouths closed.

"Baaar...I don't like him! I don't like him!"

"Trouble at school!"

"Baaar...Naaa---sty! Naaa---sty!"

"Weee---know about Larry! Weee---know about Larry!"

"Punch him out! Baaar...punch him out!"

For the first time that I can remember, Larry is speechless, and he looks awfully scared.

"Uh...this is spooky...*I'm outta here!"*

Larry turns and runs out the door as fast as he can.

"Keeep the haaammer, you kooooks." Larry exclaims as he's disappearing into his own yard.

"I think that's the last we'll see of our friend Larry for a while." says Dave's mom.

"Hey Dave," I ask, "I take it Larry doesn't know that you have pet birds?"

"Nope. Not a clue. I wish I had videotaped that."

Dave runs over and opens the kitchen door. The birds start squawking and calling out:

"Dave's here! Baaar...Dave's here!"

"Dave's cool!"

"Cooo---lest dude! Cooo---lest dude!"

"That was great, guys." Dave answers. "You ran off that little piece of----"

"Language, Dave."

"Yes, mom."

"Laaan---guage Dave! "Laaan---guage Dave!"

"Right, guys."

After this bizarre episode, Dave's lesson time is about up, and his mom comes over to hand me the check. I feel bad about taking money for this lesson, since I really only taught him for a little more than half of the thirty minutes. Plus, I got to witness Larry's comeuppance, and that was worth more than the price of the lesson to me! But, Dave's mom insists on paying me:

"Mr. B, you've given Dave extra time almost every week for all of these years. Go ahead and take the check. Also, I have a question for you. We know how much you enjoy seeing and talking to our birds each time you come over. Since we have four of them, we were thinking of downsizing a little, and we were wondering if you and Ann would like to have one of them?"

"Oh my, I don't quite know what to say. That would be great...I'm sure Ann would agree. We'd be happy to pay you for one of them. Can you let us know what would be a fair price?"

"Oh no! We just want you and Ann to take one. We've been talking this over for a while now, actually, and we think it would be fun for both of you, as well as for the bird. We wouldn't charge you...it would be our pleasure. Whoever you decide to have, we'll make up his cage and tell you how to feed him. You can take him home next week if you'd like."

"Wow...that's amazing! Thank you so much. I wonder which one we should tak---"

"Misss--ter B! Baaar...Misss--ter B! Tru---mpets Rock! Tru---mpets Rock! Laaar---ry's lazy! Laaar---ry's lazy!"

That voice sounds like...Flappy-Bird! He sure is responsive when I'm around, plus he helped to chase Larry away. What more could I ask for?

"Flaa---ppy Bird! Flaa---ppy Bird! Misss--ter B! Misss--ter B! Flaa---ppy Bird! Pretty Bird!"

"Well," I tell Dave and his mom, "that settles it. I think someone has already made up my mind for me. We'll take Flappy-Bird. I can't wait to tell Ann. Thanks again!"

"Flaa---ppy Bird! Pretty Bird!"

Trumpet lessons at home

CHAPTER SIX

Well, here we are. Finally, after all those years of living in the apartment, Ann and I have moved into our own home. At last, we'll be able to try and start a family. We'll also have much more space to live in, plus we now have our own yard to enjoy. And, we don't have to constantly stare out of our apartment window at Mr. and Mrs. Bluto, and at all their little Bluto's. That was always unbelievably frustrating to see them, their house, and their yard right below our apartment window. *WE DID IT!*

Of course, this also now means that if we want to, we can teach some or all of our lessons at *our place,* instead of driving from house to house to meet the students. While I've always liked teaching the kids at their own houses, it is very tough on the car, and is also wearing on me physically. Right now, I spend an awful lot of time driving between the lessons, and if I can teach at home instead, I can schedule the students back-to-back, without any of this wasted time. I can probably teach one or two more students each day if I give the lessons at my house.

Being at home, I could grab something to eat or drink whenever I wanted to. That sounds like a refreshing idea! I may even be able to schedule a half hour break around the dinner hour to actually eat at a normal time, instead of eating at 10 o'clock at night like I often do. What a concept!

I could also use the bathroom---my own bathroom---if I have to. Wait a minute...*eewww*...I just had a scary thought: what if one of my students wants to use my bathroom? I'll have to think about that one. Maybe I could rent a porta-potty and leave it outside? Nah...Ann wouldn't go for that!

I could even sneak a peek at the TV to see what game is on, especially if my student hadn't practiced that week and sounds like a wounded bear. I can just hear it now:

"BRAP-BRAP-BRAAAPPP." Followed by:

"SOX WIN!" Or...

"CUBS LOSE!"

I've been going from house to house for several years now, and I do get worn out, especially in the winter! The process of putting on my gloves, boots, scarf, etc., scraping off a frozen windshield, and jumping into a cold car six or seven times a day is getting tougher each year. By the time my car heats up, I'm often already at the next student's house. Why not have *them* fight the elements and come to *my* house, at least some of the time?

Because of these reasons, I've decided that when any new students call me for lessons from now on, I'll teach them at my own abode. I'll continue to go to the houses I've already been teaching at, but over time those students will graduate, and eventually I can have all the lessons at my place.

However, I still have mixed feelings about doing this. There are many things that I'll miss about travelling to student's homes if I do end up teaching all of them at my house. When I'm in the kid's own environment, I can get a sense of what they're really like, of what's important in their lives, and how they relate to their parents (both good *and* bad).

I can see what toys my students like, and how well they take care of their stuff. That's not to mention all of the dogs I can pet, and all the food I can eat when I look hungrily at the parents around dinnertime (yes, I know that's pathetic, but it's rewarding). I can also charge more money for going to their house. Plus, going to different places is a nice variety, especially when compared to sitting in a tiny practice room every day at a high school, where I usually have to give lessons in a glorified closet with no windows.

There was one evening of lessons that really influenced my thinking about teaching at home. It had been snowing for most of the day, and I left home about 2:45 to begin my teaching rounds at 4:00. I drove our Jeep that day, figuring that type of vehicle would help me to get through the snow. Normally, it would take me about forty-five minutes to drive to my first student's house, but this day I allowed for some extra time because of the snow. I certainly didn't want to cancel any lessons, and none of the students or parents had called me to say that I shouldn't try to come because of the weather. Could it be that the kids were outside playing in the snow, and just forgot about me? And, their parents were all stuck in their cars in a snow bank anyway?

I got on the highway to start the ten mile drive up to the suburb where all of this days' students live...the road looked fairly clear, and I couldn't see much traffic. After about a mile, I figured out why there weren't very many cars. The snow began coming down harder, with more wind, and the visibility became less and less as I drove north. I made it about halfway to the first student's house, and I could barely see the car in front of me. But, I figured it was silly to just turn around and go home. By the time I did that I could be at the student's house anyway! I'm not even sure if I could turn around, or where I could get off of the highway, since I couldn't see any exits. And, of course, there were no cell phones in 1985, so I had no way to communicate with anyone.

I forged ahead slowly up the highway. The snow had come down too fast for the plows to keep up, so I was trying to create my own lane, since I couldn't see the white lines. I can see cars in the ditch scattered along the side of the road...I wonder if they're trumpet teachers, too? It's taken me over an hour just to go about eight miles, and now it's 4:00. I'm already late for the first lesson, and I've got seven students scheduled today. *Finally*, I come to the exit for this suburb. I've taken this road dozens of times, but this is the first time I haven't actually been able to see it!

As I started to drive up and around the exit loop, I had to accelerate to make it up the hill. I began to slip and slide and I hit the retaining wall a couple of times. Ah, no harm, no foul. Thank goodness I'm in the Jeep! I kept on plodding around the exit ramp, and finally made it onto the street. I should be there in about five minutes.

I noticed that this normally busy street was almost deserted, and the snow was drifting across the road, with the wind even rocking the Jeep a little bit. I slid up to a red light at a big intersection, and I was barely able to stop. No other cars were anywhere in sight. This is normally a long light, and I thought about just going through it---who would know or care in this weather? I waited for at least a minute, and now it's 4:15, so I've already missed half of my first lesson. *Just great.*

Off to the right, I could barely begin to see a short, 2-door car starting to swerve through the intersection. It looked like some kind of a sub-compact. He still had the green light, so I'm glad I didn't try to go through my red light. I saw the driver trying to speed up to make the light, but when he accelerated he just started spinning faster and faster. *WATCH OUT!* He came right towards me, but there was nothing I could do to get out of his way. I would have just spun my wheels trying to move that quickly. Through the blowing snow, he was getting closer every second. Oh, no...I could see the terrorized look in his eyes, and his mouth was opening wider and wider. He was staring at me, shaking his head and shouting something, all while trying to turn his out-of-control tiny car. *WHOA!!* What can I do---?

"BOOM!!!"

I heard his car hit me, but with the size difference in our autos, I didn't feel a thing! I think the top of his car might have hit my rubber Jeep fender, but I'm still not sure. His car just bounced right off of mine, and went spinning on down the street. As he drifted away, he turned his head in my direction. His mouth and eyes were still *WIDE* open, but now he showed more of a quizzical expression. I waved at him and gave him a big "thumbs up." His astonished face and car became smaller, gradually disappearing down the street as he spun into the blizzard of snow.

Because of this "bumper-cars" experience, I missed my short green light, and so I'm still sitting at this intersection. Now it's 4:20...*FORGET IT....I'm going through this red light!*

Even though I was way behind schedule, I continued on and eventually taught my first three lessons of the day. All of the parents were nice enough to let me call ahead to my next lesson and tell them that, while I was late, I was still coming over. It was a pain putting on my boots, gloves, and scarf every thirty minutes, and I had to brush off the car after each lesson, too. Now it was dark, and the temperature was dropping.

My fourth lesson of the day featured Butch, the beagle. He was very friendly, but he also drooled constantly wherever he waddled. I liked him a lot, and he always seemed to be smiling at me as he dribbled on my hand or leg. I had left my wet boots by the front door, and I didn't realize how much Butch would love to investigate all that snow on those boots. As I walked to the door after the lesson, there was Butch, salivating profusely on, around, and inside my boots. After sloshing through the snow in between students, my socks had finally dried by the end of the lesson, and now I had to put these slobbery boots on over them. Oh, man...I had no choice! I slipped them on *very slowly,* and felt my feet squish down into them. I can imagine that Butch was busy attacking my boots for the entire lesson, since they were awfully wet inside. I squeaked and squished out the door:

"Thanks Butch! See you next week, buddy!"

By the end of my fifth lesson of the day, I was almost forty minutes behind schedule. All of the parents were very understanding, and I did get to eat several cookies and two hot dogs while teaching their kids. They tried to tell me to just go home, but I explained that since I was already in their neighborhood, I might as well come over. I obviously wanted the money, too, but I didn't tell them that.

Going out to my car after the fifth lesson, I noticed that the wind was even stronger, and it was getting to be bitterly cold. C'mon, now...just two more students to go, then I could take my time going home. I put my key into the door lock, but it had frozen. Remember, there's no such thing as a remote car entry in 1985! I thought I had left the other door open, so I was lucky enough to get into the car that way. I just had to climb over the tall gearshift in the middle of the two seats, while trying not to smash my trumpet. Finally, I lumbered my way into the driver's seat, and started the car. I turned on the defroster full-blast, and went to open my door so I could go out and scrape off the windshield.

No such luck. I got the driver's door unlocked, but the door was completely frozen, and even banging on it with my shoulder wouldn't open it from the inside. So, I climbed back over the gearshift, gingerly maneuvered around my trumpet, and went back out the passenger side to start scraping. By the time I finished this procedure, and began backing out of their driveway, I had wasted about ten minutes, and my feet were still oozing inside my boots from Butch's adventure.

My sixth and seventh students lived only a couple of blocks away from the fifth one. I was really lucky when I set up my schedule in that I was able to teach all of them in a row. When the weather was nice, I sometimes parked the car in between their three houses, and walked to all of them. *Not today!* The snow was mounting up higher, and the plows had created huge walls of snow along the sides of these narrow suburban streets. All I had to do was drive one block, turn right, and drive another half block to get there. The first block went fine, but while turning right I skidded, spun, and slid into a giant snow bank. No damage to me or the Jeep, fortunately. I put the Jeep into 4-wheel drive and tried to back out, but even though it was a Jeep, it had still gotten stuck in this drift. *AARRGGHH!!* I was only about three houses away from my next student's home. My sixth student saw what had happened, and he came out with his dad to try and help push me out.

We all struggled with the car for a while, without any success, and then we just decided to rest. By now, my sixth lesson should have been long over, and I was even way late for my seventh, and last, student of the evening. It was 9:15, and I'm usually done with all seven students by 9 o'clock. Obviously, I was extremely tired and cold. My mustache had icicles dripping off of it. My car was stuck. My feet were soaking wet from Butch, and I hadn't even gotten any food from Butch's house (he had eaten all the leftover people food). My student's dad and I decided to cancel the lesson, and then I called Ann to tell her I was stuck and that as soon as I got the car out, I'd come home. I had no idea how long that might take.

They let me call student number seven to cancel his lesson, and when he heard about my wedged car, he got very excited.

"Mr. B, this is going to be really cool! I'll be right there!"

Since he lived so close to where I was, he dragged his dad out and they both offered to help me. This was going to be loads of fun for my students! I'm not sure how excited their fathers were about the idea, but they were generous about helping, too.

When I went back outside towards the car, I started to notice more and more kids and adults coming out of their homes with shovels. I found out later that my students had called all of their friends from the block. Here it was, still snowing like crazy, with the wind howling up and down the street. The temperature must have been about 5 degrees. It was late in the evening, especially for the kids on a school night (I never found out if their school had a snow day the next day). With all of the people walking towards me, carrying shovels through the snowy night, I must say that they looked like a mob who might be coming to tar and feather me. This multitude also seemed somewhat like a bunch of zombies staggering around in a horror movie. Pretty soon there were around twenty people surrounding my Jeep: they were all there to help push me out! The kids were screaming with delight, and telling me how much fun they were having. I wish I could have said the same to them.

Naturally, I was extremely grateful to all of them. It was so nice of this entire neighborhood to help me. Because of the snowstorm, I'm sure they had all had a terrible day, too. And...to think, most of these people didn't even know me. This whole scene was rather amazing.

I climbed back into the Jeep from the passenger side, and once again gently stepped over the gearshift and around my trumpet. After just a few minutes of shoveling and pushing by the crowd, my Jeep became free of the snow bank! Everyone began waving their shovels in the air, and the entire throng let out a big cheer. My students shouted:

"Thanks, Mr. B!"

Thanks for what, I'm not exactly sure. I didn't quite know what to say, but I kept mouthing the words "thank you" and waving from inside the car. You see, I still couldn't get my window down. These windows in the Jeep had manual cranks, and they always froze in severely cold weather. I hope that the people were able to at least see my relief and gratitude, even though they couldn't hear me.

As I was saying goodbye to all of my helpers, I saw one man's face that seemed familiar. He wasn't the father of one of my students, but I sure recognized him from somewhere. I kept looking at him, and thinking of different places I might have known him from. Finally, when my car began moving, and I was turning it around to leave, it hit me....*this was the guy in the sub-*

compact who caromed off my Jeep just a few hours ago! He must live in this area, and he came to help push me out. I'm sure he had had enough of my Jeep for one day, and wanted it out of his sight. Let's see...not only did we get into an accident today, but then I also got my car stuck right by his house. He probably thinks that I'm the "Ugly American" who came to act boorishly in his suburb.

I was stunned for a moment, and just stared as I drove past him. I think he recognized me, too...he smiled, waved, and gave me a big "thumbs up!"

*

Last week, I got my first call for a new student since I decided to teach at my house. Ricky is a twelve-year-old seventh grader who's been playing trumpet for over three years. Ricky's mom said that it would be fine for her to drive him over to see me. They just live one suburb over, and she'll wait in the car during his lessons. He's coming today at 4:10. I've had to rearrange my schedule to fit him in, since the rest of my lessons today are still at the student's houses. I'll first go to Julie's house for her regular 3:30 appointment, then quickly drive home to teach Ricky, then hustle to go out again to my other five student's houses of the evening. It's going to seem really strange to drive to my own house to give a trumpet lesson!

Julie is one of the finest students that I've ever taught. Our schedules have always worked out where I've been able to give her a trumpet lesson right after school, every week, for about five years. She always practices a lot during the week, and is quite serious about music and about playing the trumpet. Julie's lesson is one of the easiest for me to teach, since she absorbs musical material like a sponge, and is very enthusiastic. I imagine she may go into trumpet playing and music teaching as a career someday.

Today's lesson has been another super one for Julie. The time flew by, and now I have to rush home to meet Ricky and his mom for Ricky's first session. It's now 4:00, and I have ten minutes to spare, but I only live about five minutes away. I just have to get over these train tracks, and...*DAMN!!!*...the train gates are coming down. I can see a train coming, and naturally, it's a freight train. Oh well, I should still make it home in time...hopefully. Ann knows that Ricky and his mom are coming over, and she said she'd let them in and get him set up for the lesson. I hate being late for things!

Fortunately, this train doesn't have too many cars in it. There goes the caboose...good. It only takes me a few more minutes to make it home. As I pull up, I see a strange car in our driveway...it must be Ricky's mom's car. No one is in the car...they must be inside already. The clock in my car says 4:08...good...I sure didn't want to be late for his very first lesson!

I rush into my house, and Ricky's mom is waiting for me inside.

"Hi, I'm Mr. B. I see my wife let you in, and—"

"You're late! We thought you'd never get here! I have things to do, you know!"

"Uh, it's nice to meet you, too. Actually, it's just 4:10 now. I'll get started with Ricky's lesson right away. You can wait in the car if you'd like, as you told me you'd do."

She's already made me so discombobulated that I can't even think of her last name at the moment...let's see...Ricky's mom...maybe it's "Mrs. Lucy!" I sure don't want her barking at me anymore, at least not for a while. I don't see Ann, either. I bet after meeting Mrs. Lucy, Ann went upstairs to hide, and I can't blame her.

Mrs. Lucy harrumphs at me, still using an angry tone:

"All right. I'll be in the car!"

She brushes past me and shuts the door in my face. That's my own front door! I haven't met Ricky yet, but I sure hope this apple fell *extremely* far from her tree. Maybe the apple even rolled down the hill to get farther away from her.

As I turn and go into our living room, I can see Ricky. *Wait...what's this? He's got his feet up on my coffee table! Take a deep breath, now...try not to explode.*

"Uh, hi Ricky. How 'bout if you put your feet down on the floor?"

Ricky just grunts back at me, without opening his mouth:

"mmMM."

He doesn't look in my direction. He grudgingly takes his feet down.

"OK, Ricky, let's go downstairs and get started!"

He grunts again:

"mmMMM," and still doesn't look at me.

My first lesson at my own house, and after all of these years of imagining how cool this moment would be...thanks to Ricky, this is turning out to be *just terrific!*

After trudging down the stairs to my basement, and sitting down by the music stand, I try to converse with Ricky. Our witty repartee gets faster and faster:

"OK, Ricky...get out your trumpet. I'll get my horn out, too, and we can play some songs together."

Ricky stares at the floor, and the only response is yet another:

"mmMM."

"Do you have the trumpet books your mom bought? I'll take a look at them."

"MMMmmm."

"Can I see your school music?"

"mMM!"

"Take out your mouthpiece and trumpet."

"MMMmmm!!"

"Do you like Band?"

"MM-mm."

Good...that's the closest he's come to giving a real answer so far. He still hasn't opened his mouth, moved a muscle, or even looked at me. We continue our quick banter:

"Get out your trumpet, Ricky…let's play!"

"mmmMMMM!!"

"What songs do you like?"

"MM-mm."

"Can I see your trumpet?"

"mmMMMMM!!"

I do believe I'm teaching *"Very* Young Frankenstein!" Let's keep going; I'm having too much fun to stop now.

"How old are you, Ricky?"

"mm."

"Do you have friends in Band?"

"MMMMmm."

"Do you know your pants are on fire?"

"MMMM."

"Your mom is really a 'biotch,' don't you think?"

"mmm-MMM!"

Actually, I didn't ask that last question, but I sure wanted to. I did ask if his pants were on fire, and even that didn't get a rise out of him. Twelve whole minutes have passed, and I've had enough of Ricky already. I'm not going to put up with this nonsense, especially in *my own house!* He's probably a tremendous trumpeter, but how would I know? Actually, I just don't care anymore.

"OK, Ricky, I think that'll do it for today. Your lips must be very tired by now. Let's go out and see your mom…I can't wait to tell her how much we accomplished today."

Ricky slowly turns his head towards me, and gives me a sinister squinty evil-eyed glare. I guess he enjoyed the lesson, too! Step-by-step, we gradually head up the stairs and outside to greet Mrs. Lucy. I am quite upset, but I'm also a little scared of this family…and now they know where I live! When I talk to Mrs. Lucy, I better try to be diplomatic when I tell her that I don't want to teach her son again.

"Hi, Mrs....uh (I still can't remember the right name). Well, uh, we didn't get much done today."

"What do you mean?"

"Actually, Ricky refused to take out his trumpet or his music, and he wouldn't answer any of my questions, either."

"WHAT! How can you say that?"

This woman doesn't just speak, she shouts everything.

"Well, like I said, Ricky wouldn't get his trumpet out, and he wouldn't talk to me. Maybe he doesn't feel well?"

"Doesn't feel well? Ricky, are you sick?"

"mmmMMM!"

"Well of course, teacher!" (she can't remember my name, either) *"He's sick...just look at him!"*

Ricky's giving me that menacing glare again. I know he's not sick...I should never have mentioned that to give him an excuse. C'mon, I can't lose my nerve. I have to keep trying to fire him as my student:

"Well, Mrs...uh, I'm not sure if trumpet lessons are really a good idea for him. I don't think he's that interested, and I think you should talk to him at home before he---"

"Do you want to talk about it, Ricky? Maybe you just don't like this teacher?"

"MMMM!"

"OK, teacher, we'll talk and let you know!"

Wait a minute...I can't let Mrs. Lucy be the one to decide...I want to be the one to tell her what an obnoxious kid she has. I better try and put it in a nice way, however:

"You know, I just don't think Ricky's quite ready for private lessons. Maybe he'll mature more later on, but I won't be able to teach him anymore. It wouldn't be worth your money or my ti---"

"REALLY! Ricky, are you immature now? Do you want to go home? Then you'll be mature by next week?"

"MM-mmm."

"No, wait." I try to explain. "I don't think he'll be mature by next week---I mean, I just don't think---I mean, he *was* very disrespectful towards me."

"WHAT!!! Now you're saying that my little Ricky is sick, immature, and disrespectful!"

"Uh...well yeah, actually, now that you mention it."

Good...maybe she *finally* gets it. Mrs. Lucy begins to drive away, and as her car moves forward she starts talking faster and faster:

"OK, teacher, thanks for the update. I'll call you about next week... ...bye! What do you say, Ricky?"

"mmm-MMMM!"

Mrs. Lucy and Ricky speed down the street.

WHAT! That's it? I don't want to teach him next---wait a minute...she didn't even pay me!

"Mrs. Lucy....Loooosey! Riiickkky! BABALOO!"

Oh, forget it.

As I head back inside, I can't help but think...is this what teaching lessons at my own house is going to be like all of the time? Are most of the students who come over going to be Ricky-types? Do I really want more "Rickys" and "Mrs. Lucys" coming into my home?

MMMMM-mmmmm!!!

*

Several months have passed since the Ricky episode, and I now have six new students coming over for lessons every week. They're all nice kids, and *most* of their parents are easy to deal with. Thank goodness, there's been no phone call from Ricky or Mrs. Lucy, either. Who needs that nonsense? I think this teaching-at-my-house-thing may work out yet.

I teach my lessons in our unfinished basement, and it's a very functional workspace with plenty of room. It's not the most glamorous teaching studio, however. Our house has these old wooden steps leading downstairs to a concrete floor. Concrete is perfect for trumpet players, since we have to blow the spit out of our trumpets every few minutes. Are you surprised about the spit? What would you expect to be inside of a trumpet after we blow as hard as we can for a long time into these metal tubes? Especially with some of my boy pupils, who probably haven't brushed their teeth since their last baby tooth fell out.

I've been in the middle of lessons when students stop playing because they can't make a sound. When I look inside their mouthpiece or front trumpet pipe, it's *completely* blocked! I can't see through it at all, but I sure can tell what they had for lunch. There are all sorts of candy bars and bologna trying to be forced through these pipes and it all ends up getting stuck. And, maybe a little piece of brawnschwager, too. Who wants a fancy carpet for that spit to end up on?

Also in my basement are several beams that are holding up the house (so far, anyway). Up above in the rafters, Ann and I have stored lots of our own music, as well as a plethora of toys for our young sons. In my teaching area, I have one bare light bulb above the lawn chairs that we use for the lessons. Hey, it's a 100 watt bulb, at least. And...I've put cushions on these lawn chairs, since it gets fairly cold down there when the heat isn't on.

The laundry area is on the other side of the basement, so occasionally we can hear the washer and dryer running during lessons. Sometimes Ann will be folding clothes on our old metal laundry table, which is covered in white contact paper. Usually, though, she tries to stay out of the basement during the trumpet lessons...she can already hear plenty of blaring trumpet noises when she's up on the first floor.

While these conditions may seem rather Spartan, they're not uncommon for a teaching studio. In fact, some of the greatest music teachers in the world have similar set-ups for their students, with bare bulbs, concrete floors, etc. This seems to be especially true of brass instrument teachers like the trumpet and the tuba. For some reason, many brass players don't seem to be too concerned about outward appearances...they just want to play their instruments! I figure if it works for these elite artists, then it should be fine for my junior high and high school students, too. Most of them don't seem to mind it at all, and one boy even told me:

"Mr. B, you've got the *best* basement. I love coming over to your house!" So...NO COMPLAINING!

It's into this setting that Mrs. Van Bevington brings her son, Ernst Van Bevington III, for his lessons. I like Ernst III. He's only ten, but he's a good trumpeter for his age. Ernst III also loves my basement.

"The cracks in your cement floor look like moon craters, Mr. B. Oooh...this is so neat!" he tells me.

Mrs. Van Bevington, on the other hand, is not that enamored with my basement. The first time she called to set up Ernst's lessons (try saying Ernst's three times in a row), she actually said to me:

"And you know, Mr. B, I'm an important lawyer. You'll provide a table and chair for me to do my work during the lessons?"

"Sure," I said, "come on over."

I told Ann that we might be in for another Mrs. Lucy with this one, and Ann went right upstairs to hide. When Ernst and Mrs. Van Bevington got inside my house, Ernst bounded down those wooden steps, and almost hit his head on a beam as he jumped up and down:

"Oh, look mom. Isn't this the coolest place?"

Mrs. Van B. showed Ernst a look of disdain. She was dressed to the teeth. Her clothes probably cost more than a thousand dollars, and I think her shoes were worth more than my car. Throw in the fancy hair, nails, and jewelry and you get a good idea of what's important to Mrs. Van Bevington. Seeing her in my basement reminded me of the way Ginger always looked when she was stuck on Gilligan's Island...more than a bit out of place.

"Mom! Come on down!"

Ernst was excited. Mrs. Van B. was hesitant. She took off her high heels. I don't think she even wanted to touch the creaky banister, but she slowly made a serpentine motion down the stairs.

"Eeww, eeww, eeww, eeww,..."

She murmured at each step, until she had made it down all ten stairs. She started to let out a big sigh, but then her stocking feet hit the cold concrete:

"Oh… my…*God!"* she said scornfully as she quickly hopped from one foot to the other.

"Ooh-ooh, Mom...there's toys…and trumpets...and stuff up there...and cement...and--"

"That's nice, Ernst. Now, Mr. B, is that table and chair ready for me? I have to prepare some papers for a significant trial."

This was way before laptop computers, so she would be writing everything out herself.

"Walk this way, Mrs. Van Bevington."

I felt like the butler in a Three Stooges episode. I watched her eyebrows go up as she approached our laundry table. *Oops!* I had forgotten to take all of the dirty laundry off the table, so I just slid it over to the corner. I did put a brand new White Sox seat cushion on a lawn chair that I had placed by the laundry table, and I switched the light bulb that's up above it from a 60 to a 100 watt bulb. I know the dryer was still running right next to her, but what more could she want?

Ernst and I began the lesson, and I could tell that he had a happy disposition, plus lots of energy. He has a high, squeaky voice, and he talks very fast.

"Hey Mr. B, do you know I'm Ernst the Third? But some of the other guys at school call me Ernst the Turd. I don't mind. Hey mom, did you know they call me Ernst the Turd? Remember how Johnny said I was *Ernie Tur---"*

"Yes, Ernst! Now go ahead with your lesson."

Looking over, I could see that Mrs. Van B. was uncomfortable sitting at the laundry table. Her cold feet were dangling in the air.

"Oh, are your feet cold, Mrs. Van Bevington? Here...put your feet on this."

I took an old carpet square that we had kept, and placed it under the laundry table. Uh-oh, I think there was some dried cat barf on part of the carpet. Oh well, I don't think she saw it.

Ernst and I had a really fun lesson, and he scooted quickly up the stairs.

"Mom, I can't *wait* to come down to Mr. B's basement again!"

Mrs. Van B. wasn't quite so enthusiastic. She disgustedly stomped up the steps.

"Mr. B, I didn't get *any* work done! I couldn't concentrate at all. There were so many distractions. Now I'll have to miss dinner at the club in order to finish my work!"

Gee, I couldn't imagine why she didn't finish. Maybe it was the noise of the trumpets? Or the dryer? Or the cold floor? Or the dirty laundry? Or the cat's barf? What does she expect? This is someone's home, not the Hilton.

I was really hoping she'd say that she would stay out in the car during Ernst's lessons from now on. Ernst III is a neat kid, but Mrs. Van B. is a piece of work. All she said, though, was:

"Mr. B, when we come over next week, I'd like some coffee and sweet rolls. *Try* to have that ready when we get here."

At your service, Mrs. Van Bevington.

*

Ann and I each give lessons to one of the O'Hara twins. Timmy plays the flute, and Mikey toots the trumpet. I still have trouble telling them apart when they're not holding their instruments. Even though they're just beginners on their instruments, their mom wants them to have private lessons. That way they can learn at a faster pace than they'd be able to in their larger school group. We teach them at the same time, in order to save their mom an extra trip. Ann teaches Timmy in the dining room, while I give Mikey his lessons in the basement.

Timmy and Mikey are very cute little guys, with red hair and freckles that announce their presence as soon as they enter our house. They're nine years old, are a little over four feet tall, and they're in fourth grade. They also have friendly, outgoing personalities, and are *extremely* competitive with each other. I think they must constantly argue in the car on the way over. By the time they get to our house, whatever happens to be the issue of the day spills over into our living room. They look at us and smile when they arrive, but they usually can't say hello right away. They're too busy bickering. I can't wait to hear what they'll be discussing today. Here they come:

"Timmy, your Cubs *stink!* Ryne Sandberg retired, and the other players are no good."

"Oh, yeah? Well, Mikey, the White Sox can't hit, except for Frank Thomas. *They won't make the play-offs, either!"*

"Yeaahh? Well, the Sox are still better than the *Packers,* Timmy!"

Wait...they've switched the argument from baseball to football without missing a beat.

"Bears are *terrible,* Mikey."

"Yeaahh? Well...you're *ugly!"*

"You're *uglierrr!"*

Guys...be careful treading into "ugly" territory... remember, you're identical twins, right?

The cool thing, though, is that they can go right from yelling at each other to having bright smiles again. They always start talking to Ann and me as if nothing had happened:

"Hi, Mrs. B!"

"Hi, Mr. B! We practiced a lot this week."

"Yeah, we like those songs you gave us to play. Come on, let's start the lessons!"

"Yeah, let's get going!"

Mikey races down the stairs to get his trumpet and music set up.

"Hurry, Mr. B...I want to play my first note today before Timmy does!"

We can hear some flute notes coming from upstairs...too late, Timmy has started already.

"RATS!" exclaims Mikey.

"Oh well, let's make some buzzes, Mr. B!"

"OK, Mikey."

I begin almost every lesson by having the student make some sounds on a short, metal pipe called the mouthpiece. When you hold the mouthpiece up to your lips, keep your lips close together, and blow fast air, the lips will vibrate the air and then sounds come out of the mouthpiece. These "buzzing" sounds are especially fun for the younger trumpeters to make. It's a good way to exercise the lips, before trying to play tones with the entire trumpet. I'll usually demonstrate some mouthpiece buzzes, then I'll try and have the students copy the different kinds of sounds I'm making: slow, fast, high, low, whatever. This requires tightening and loosening your mouth muscles, and using lots of air. It's a fairly standard warm-up for trumpeters, and for all brass players, too. Mikey really gets into his "buzzes."

After we finish warming up, Mikey and I start reviewing "Hot Cross Buns," which I had assigned to him to practice last week. This song is from their school band method book, so every instrument in the band has it in their method book, too.

"This is fun, Mr. B...*let's play!"*

We begin blaring the first few notes:

"Baaa...Baaa...Baaa."

Uh-oh, we can hear Timmy and Ann playing the same song upstairs on their flutes:

"Tooo...Tooo...Tooo."

"Oh no!" Mikey shouts at me.

"I can play it better than Timmy!"

He plays louder:

"BAAA...BAAA...BAAA!"

But, between every note, we can still hear Timmy and Ann. Mikey is getting annoyed, and then Ann comes up with a good idea. She hollers into the heating duct in the floor that connects with the basement:

"Hey, trumpet guys down there! Let's play the song together, OK? One, two, ready, go!

"BAAA-TOOO...BAAA-TOOO...BAAA-TOOO..."

The flute and trumpet sounds mix together nicely. Mikey sounds great, and he's happier now, too.

"That was cool, Mr. B. Tell Mrs. B that was a good idea!"

After playing our "Buns" off, Mikey and I go back to doing some trumpet-only exercises, and I can hear Ann and Timmy playing flute studies upstairs. The twins are both wiggly little guys, and they have typical attention spans for age nine, which means their concentration doesn't last very long---*LOOK---A SQUIRREL!!* You get the idea. All of a sudden, Mikey and I hear:

"BOOM!" coming from up above.

"What was that, Mikey?"

"Oh, I bet Timmy fell off his chair. He'll be OK...he does that all the time at home. His butt is bouncy, Mr. B."

Mikey doesn't seem concerned, and I don't hear Ann say anything, eith---*"BOOM!"*

Timmy must have fallen off again. I know these folding chairs we use are a bit slippery, but---

"BOOM!"

I look over, and Mikey's now fallen off his chair!

"You OK, Mikey?"

"Oh, yeah...I just wanted to see what it felt like to fall off the chair, too. I liked it...I bet my butt's bouncier than Timmy's!"

There's only a few minutes left in the lesson now; just enough time for one more song.

"What do you want to play, Mikey?"

But before Mikey can answer, we begin to hear the flutes playing "Jingle Bells."

"Ooo, Mr. B, let's play 'Jingle Bells,' too. I can play it faster than Timmy!"

"That's OK, Mikey. It's not a race. Santa gets to everyone's house eventually, you know. Let's start. One, two, ready---

"Mikey, *you stink.* Did ya hear me? I can play it better than you!"

It's Timmy, shouting through the vent.

"You're *ugly,* Timmy!"

"And you're *STILL* uglierrr, Mikey!"

Enough of this sibling rivalry, and enough venting through my vent!

"Mikey, let's go upstairs. We can all play it together."

As Mikey and I climb up the steps, and then turn to go into the dining room, we can see that it's starting to snow outside. Mrs. O'Hara has been parked in our driveway, so Ann invites her in to hear the boys play. Ann conducts our little Band of elves as the snow falls:

"One, two, ready, go..."

"BAA-TOO...BAA-TOO...BAA-TOO..."

Even though the boys have only been playing for a couple of months, their enthusiasm carries them through the entire song. Of course, Ann and I were playing along, too, so I think that helped to make it sound just a little better.

"Mrs. B, that was the *BEST!*

"Yeah...can we do that every week, Mr. B?"

"Sure, guys. At least until January."

Mrs. O'Hara liked it, too:

"That was so thrilling to hear them play...what do you say, boys?"

They respond in unison:

"Thaaannnkkks."

"Come on, boys. We'll see you next week, Mr. and Mrs. B."

As the twins follow their mom through the snow and out to the car, Ann and I can hear them starting up their arguing again. Their excited voices trail off as they get farther from our front door:

"Notre Dame *stinks,* Mikey!"

"Yeah? Well, you don't know what you're talking about. Michigan is the worst this year."

"Yeah? Well, your freckles make the shape of Idaho!"

"Yours do, too!"

"Oh yeah? Well,..."

*

As I look more closely, I can see Dino's car coming around the corner towards my house. Boy, do I look forward to seeing that car every week! I can also hear it as it thunders closer. It's a 1970's model Chevrolet Monte Carlo. It's also a convertible, and it's black. I don't know much about cars, but Dino's been telling me some facts about his Monte Carlo. It's got a 454 horsepower V8 engine, which is *huge!* It's such a gas-guzzler that I guess they stopped making it in the mid 1970's after the energy crisis. It's also got the Turbo Hydra-Matic transmission. I have no idea what the heck that is, but it sure sounds cool!

The all-white inside is something else, too. There are swiveling Strato bucket seats, plus a floor shifter. A floor shifter? *Wow!* But, Dino explained to me that the floor doesn't really shift. And, the instrument panel is black, to match the exterior. Dino's got the top down today, and it looks really sharp zipping down my vanilla suburban street. What a great chick-magnet car this must be!

Dino's an eighteen year old high school senior. He's a great kid...always smiling and in a good mood. Although he goes to one of the most affluent old-money high schools in the country, he never brags about his house, or going on trips, or about belonging to a country club like so many of the other students from that school. He doesn't even seem concerned with what the other kids think and do, which is very refreshing for me.

Dino wants to improve his trumpet playing, and he does practice fairly often between his lessons. I've been teaching him for a few months now. However, he also has other interests besides the trumpet, with his car being the most important. He told me that he bought the car with his own money from working at a car repair garage after school. His car is about fifteen years old, and Dino said he didn't pay that much for it since it was falling apart at the time. What he means by 'that much' I'm not sure. He's done a lot of work making the engine more powerful, and he has also put in many hours repairing the body and painting the exterior.

Every week, I eagerly anticipate seeing something new or different about the car, such as bumpers or tires. Unlike several of his high school classmates, who only hire people to work *for* them with their parent's money, Dino says that he's done all the repairs himself. He tells me that he can get parts for practically nothing from the garage where he works, and that they don't mind him using their equipment, too. I really admire his handyman abilities, since my own mechanical skills are about equal to The Three Stooges when they were plumbers.

Besides his car, Dino just looks like a very "cool kid," too. In fact, with his clothes and his hair, he resembles the John Travolta character from "Grease" quite a bit. He doesn't say much, but he smiles and nods his head a lot. And, as I mentioned, he doesn't care what his wealthy classmates do or think, although from what the other kids tell me Dino is extremely popular in school. He really has his act together for a teenager, and he's in a positive frame of mind almost all of the time. I must admit that I'm somewhat envious of Dino, especially his hair...you see, I lost most of mine many years ago!

He's pulling up to the curb now. As he shuts off that roaring engine, I can see that new white wall tires are on it this week.

"Way cool tires, Dino."

"Thanks, Mr. B."

As Dino walks up to my front door, I start to see some of my neighbors walking this way. It looks like several fathers, walking with their little boys. There are maybe about fifteen people, and they're heading towards Dino's car. Many of them wave to me and say hello:

"Hey, Sam....mind if we check out this car?"

I turn and ask Dino, and he just shrugs and says:

"OK."

"Go ahead," I say, "but don't touch."

Dino smiles, but doesn't speak. I imagine he's used to the attention he gets about his car.

We turn to go into the house, but...wait....now I can see some more neighbors heading over. There's about a dozen ladies in this bunch, with some younger girls, too. They don't appear that interested in the car, and I know they're not there to talk to me.

"Hello Sam...is this one of your students?"

Dino and I turn around.

"Yes...this is Dino."

Almost in unison, the women say:

"Hiii, Dino."

Again, Dino shrugs and smiles. He waves, but still doesn't say anything. I can guess that he's used to this type of attention, too! Now my front yard has almost thirty people in it. Half of them are staring at Dino's car, and the other half are staring at Dino. I've never even *seen* some of these people before. This scene reminds me of that old joke:

"I feel like the world is a tuxedo, and I'm a pair of brown shoes!"

"While you're all here, would you like to mow my lawn?" I ask, only half-kidding. One of the kids replies:

"No, but can we wash this car?"

I turn to Dino. He just shrugs again, but then he shakes his head no while looking back at me.

"Sorry, guys, the top's down." I tell them. "Can't this time."

"Ohhh, too bad." the boys shout. "Hey mister, we can wash it next time!"

Once more, Dino shrugs. He's got all of these people mesmerized, and he hasn't even said a word to them! We turn again to go inside, as one of the ladies calls out:

"Hey Sam, how long is the lesson?"

"About a half hour." I answer.

"Is it *every* week at this time?" another woman asks.

"Yeah."

The ladies again reply in unison:

"OHH-KKK."

I catch Dino out of the corner of my eye. He's smiling and shrugging again, but he still doesn't say anything. Finally, we turn and go in to start his lesson. As I glance back, I can see Dino's groupies... they're continuing to hang out on my front lawn. The least they could do is pull some of my weeds!

Ann has walked uptown to do some errands today, so Dino and I are staying in the dining room for the lesson. Usually, Ann stays home if she knows Dino is coming over for a lesson. She somehow makes it a point to always answer the door for him, and also to say good-bye to him on his way out. And, I've noticed that when we're having the lesson in the basement, Ann seems to be on the other side doing laundry all of the time, too. I can see her sneaking a few peeks at Dino. I'll have to ask her about these "coincidences" someday! Since Dino and I are staying on the first floor today, I can listen for the doorbell when my next student, James, arrives. James goes to school with Dino, and he's the one who gave Dino my name to call me for lessons.

After about ten minutes of Dino's lesson have passed, the doorbell goes off. It can't be James just yet. I open the door, and it's one of the younger neighbor boys. He looks like he's about seven. I don't even know his name, and he's never spoken to me.

"Hey mister, can you get that other mister who's in your house with you?"

Assuming that he wants to talk to Dino, I wave for him to come over to the door. The boy asks Dino:

"Hey mister, what's that big pipe in the back of your car? It's *shiny!"*

Dino shrugs, and explains to him in a soft tone:

"That's an extra exhaust pipe, because the car has a big engine."

"OK!"

The boy runs back out to a group of kids standing by the car. I can hear him trying to explain to them what Dino said:

"He said it's an egg-sauce pipe, 'cuz it's got big energy."

The group responds:

"OHHHH!"

What? Whatever, I guess. I close the door, and Dino and I resume the lesson. A few minutes later, the doorbell rings again. Maybe James is way early? Nope...when I open the door this time, it's a little girl from around the corner. She shyly announces to me:

"Excuse me, sir. My mom wants me to give these cookies to the man who's sitting over there. Is that OK?"

"Yes, come on in."

But, as I open the screen door to let her in, about seven or eight more girls brush past me. They must have been hiding on the side of my house. They're all carrying brownies or cookies, and they're giggling loudly as they scurry over to see Dino.

"Hi, sir. Our moms made these for you. Here you go."

Dino smiles, and says:

"Thanks, girls. And thank your moms, too."

"Tee-hee-hee-hee. You're welcome, sir! We'll tell our moms...they'll be *so* happy. *Tee-hee-hee.* Can you hold the door, sir?"

They all squeal together, and then they almost knock me over as they hurry back outside.

Again, Dino and I try to continue the lesson. We play our trumpets for about five more minutes, and then I hear yet another person at the door. I've suddenly become the most popular guy on the block, but somehow I don't think I'm the reason why. Could it be James at the door this time, do you think? Nah...I doubt it.

"Hey Dino, do you want to get the door this time?" I ask.

When he opens it, I can see that our guest is the same little guy who was here before.

"Hey mister, what are those glass things on the front of your car?"

After another shrug, Dino replies:

"I have special blue headlights. I can turn them on and off with a different switch."

"OK."

He runs back out to tell the rest of the gang:

"He said he's got blue head lice, *just like Billy at school!* He said they have a special itch when he turns them on!"

"Yeah, Billy's blue head lice itches like that, too!" one boy exclaims.

"OHHHH!"

Dino and I finally finish his lesson, but we sure didn't get much done. I was going to start him on a new trumpet solo, but I had to give up that idea when all of his fans kept coming to the door. I'm surprised there weren't paparazzi taking pictures through the windows, too. Now I have to help Dino carry all of those homemade desserts out to his car.

As we head out my front door, and make our way to his car, I can see groups of people lined up on both sides of the sidewalk. There are several seven or eight year old boys on one side who are all pointing towards the car. Behind them are some of their dads. On the other side are about ten young girls, with a few of their moms mixed in. This bunch is staring at Dino, not the car. As Dino and I gradually move closer to his car, it's starting to remind me of a gauntlet. All of a sudden, one of the girls calls out to me:

"Hey sir, can you make sure that *he* gets those cookies?" pointing to Dino.

"Yeah."

"Pleeease, sir?"

"Sure thing." I reply.

Geez, why don't you just throw rose petals at his feet, too? The boys and their fathers step towards us as we reach the car. I've noticed that many of the more balding dads have now put on baseball caps. They must have gone home to retrieve the hats...could it be they want to pretend that they are still part of Dino's generation? Maybe I should also look to see if they have cigarettes inside their rolled up shirt sleeves? As they speak, the dads try to make their voices resonate about as low as they can go, I guess to sound more manly:

"Here, son, let me hold the door for you."

"Sure like your car, young man."

"Oh, hi Sam."

Gee, someone is actually talking to *me!*

Finally, Dino gets in and starts his car. I hand him the bags of treats. He shrugs at me one more time, but it's not in a conceited way. He's just trying to tell me that he has this happen to him all the time, and that there's nothing he can do about it. As he drives away, he smiles at the people, and gives a big wave. They shout and wave back enthusiastically:

"SO LONG, SON!" roar the men, trying to imitate James Earl Jones.

"GOOD-BYE, SIR!" the little girls giggle with a nervous laugh.

"SEE YA, MISTER!" scream the younger boys.

"Nice Seeing You, Young Man!" the ladies say, in a rather flirty way. I notice that several of them now turn and shoot dirty looks towards their husbands.

I begin to stagger back inside, when some of my suddenly friendly neighbors pepper me with questions:

"Hey Sam, he's coming back next week, right?"

"Yeah...is he?"

"Same time, Sam?"

"Does he come over every week?"

"Yeah, Sam...is it every week?"

"Yes, yes, yes, yes." I keep replying like a broken record. "Nice to talk to you, too."

Here comes Ann walking around the corner. She sees this strange throng on our property:

"What's happening? Oh...was Dino just here? *Did I miss him?*" I nod.

"Oh well, I'll be sure to be here next week."

She smiles and shakes her head:

"So...I see that you have a bunch of new friends."

Finally, I reach my door and go in. The crowd is still lingering on my front lawn, talking and pointing in the direction where Dino's car was. After a few more minutes, I notice James driving up to the house. He wades his way through Dino's remaining groupies, and makes it to the front door.

"Hi, Mr. B. There are a lot of people standing in your yard. Was Dino just here for his lesson?"

"Yes he was, James. How did you know?"

James doesn't answer. He just smiles at me, and shrugs.

Gifts, sons and Christmas morning

CHAPTER SEVEN

"Here you go, Mr. B."

Uh-oh. William hands me a package, and I have a sneaking suspicion about what might be in it.

"Oh, uh, gee, uh, thanks, William. Should I put it in the fridge when I get home?"

"Yeah, my mom said you should. She made her special *'Chocolate Guacamole Mint Brownies'* again this year for the holidays, Mr. B. She wants you to let her know if you like them better than the ones from last year."

Well, considering that my stomach was lurching from these nauseating delicacies until around February last year, I'm not sure how to respond to that. But, I'll take the bait:

"Uh, OK, William. How are they different from last year's batch?"

"Oh, she said that she also put extra pepper in them this time, to spice 'em up a little. We all love 'em...even my little brother! We actually ate them all, so my mom had to make some more just for you and Mrs. B."

After throwing up in my mouth a little, I hurl out a reply:

"Wow...tell your mom thanks, William. Mrs. B. and I can't wait to try these again!"

William's revolting brownies are just the first of about fifty holiday gifts that Ann and I will receive from our students again this season. As we travel from house to house to teach lessons, and develop a good relationship with all of these families like we have over the years, we tend to get some really cool and interesting presents.

Often, we'll be given the baked goods that are part of a family tradition, like William's family brownies. Last December, William didn't bother to tell me about the guacamole portion of the ingredients, so I could only see the chocolate and mint parts on the outside. Being the pig that I am, I ate a few of them in the car on the way home before the guacamole seeped through into my system. After holding my head out of the car window like a dog for several miles, I finally arrived home:

"Hi Sam." Ann said. "How was your da---"

"Can't talk now, hun! I'll be out later!"

"What happened, Sam?"

"Noth...ing...yetttt!" I reply as my voice makes its own Doppler effect while I run through the room. I then hurriedly slid my anatomy onto a first name basis with the Kohler company for the next half hour.

Don't be disillusioned, though, because almost all of the food presents that we receive are terrific. I confess that I've consumed lots and lots of them while driving home. Occasionally, though, we get some that we just can't swallow. And, we seem to get these treats as repeat gifts *year after year!* I recall one fruitcake that is always so hard; I think it was originally the cornerstone in one of the Pyramids. For five straight Decembers, I've come home with a brick-like package, and Ann always says:

"I see you got that fruitcake again. Good...we could use another doorstop."

Sometimes, there seems to be a weird correlation between how bad my student is, and how good the gift is that the family gives to me. Maybe the parents feel guilty that they have tormented me with their kid's laziness and horrible trumpet sounds for a whole year, and now they just want to make up for it? I'm not sure, but I always get great presents from at least two or three of my lousiest students every year.

I'm on my way now to Jon's house. I've been teaching Jon for over two years. Actually, I should say that I've *tried* to teach Jon for over two years. He's never been interested in the trumpet, and he never practices. None of his friends are in the band at school, and Jon fancies himself as a jock, even though he's only about four feet eleven inches and in the seventh grade. I've come close to firing him as a student several times, since it's such a waste of my time and their money. This past September, I told his mom that I was going to "put him on probation." In other words, if he didn't show any progress in the next couple of months, then I wouldn't teach him anymore. His mom agreed; she realized how futile it was to keep going with the lessons when Jon is so lazy.

Jon's lessons for the rest of September and October were still excruciating to my ears. He hadn't practiced, and showed no improvement. Worse yet, he just didn't seem to care, either. The probation idea hadn't helped to motivate Jon, and I was thinking of firing him soon. By the beginning of November, I had had my fill of Jon's attitude, not to mention his lame-o version of trumpet playing. Jon's mom asked me if I thought he was getting any better:

"Well, to tell you the truth, not really. I've given him several fun things to play, including some popular songs and a jazz duet. Almost all of my students enjoy these. But, unless Jon starts to practice regularly, he'll never make any progress. I just don't think these lessons are a----"

I was about to tell her that this would be his last lesson, but then I remembered something. Last December, Jon's mom gave me and Ann a huge container of fudge, and it was incredibly delicious! They gave us so much of it that it lasted until March, even though it seemed like we were eating it constantly. Hmmm...maybe I should keep teaching him until after the holidays? Can I sacrifice six more weeks of aural angst, just on the hope of getting some more of that fudge this Christmas? Well...*SURE!!* I tell Jon's mom:

"You know what? Let's keep going with the lessons until the end of the year. Then I'll let you know about continuing."

For the rest of November, and on into December, Jon kept having awful lessons. There's just no way for him to hide the dozens of wrong notes that he is playing. I always played along with him, but the clashing of our different notes (my notes are the right ones, I reminded myself) kept giving me the chills. I even wore my earmuffs through one of Jon's lessons. Well, I *was* chilled!

In addition to his plethora of "clams" (that's trumpet-speak for cracked or incorrect notes), Jon gets a sound out of his trumpet that reminds me of a wounded donkey. Plus, he never bothers to empty his spit valve until I remind him to do it every five minutes or so. From constantly blowing into the trumpet, saliva (trumpeters say "spit") collects inside the slides. And, so do particles from whatever the trumpeter has recently eaten. We regularly have to empty out all of that junk by opening a lever on our trumpet, and then blowing air through it (the polite term is "water key," but we all say "spit valve"). Since Jon never does this, he always sounds like he's playing his trumpet underwater. It's hard to describe, but Jon's every note sounds something like this, with the letters accelerating as the spit flows faster through his trumpet:

"T-A-D-A-L-AD-L-D-L-DLDLDLDLDLDLDLDLDLDLDL!"

"Blow out that spit, Jon! No...not on my foot, you stu---!"

Sometimes, we refer to the type of trumpet tone that Jon conveys as being able to "take the paint off of the walls." Believe me, Jon's walls are definitely down to the bare plaster by now.

During these last few lessons, I've spent this dreadful time blissfully thinking of that fudge. Sometimes, while mired deep in chocolate musings, growling noises would interrupt me:

"r-r-r-R-R-R-LDLDL. r-r-r-R-R-R-LDLDL."

Oh, that's just my stom---no, wait, that's Jon's trumpet soun---
no, that *is* my stomach ---no, no, *it is* Jon playing. Ugh...I should
have fired him months ago---but, I just couldn't. *I really want that
fudge!*

All right, I've made my pact with the devils food...uh, devil.
Finally, I'm here now for Jon's last lesson before the Christmas
break. Hopefully my taste buds will be rewarded for all of these
months of audio torture. I ring the bell...*ha*, that will be the nicest
sound I ever hear coming from this house!

"Oh, hi, Mr. B. You here *again?*"

"That's right, Jon. Almost every Monday for the last two years.
Let's get on with it."

I've decided that if today is going to be my final Jon
experience, then I'm definitely going to play my own trumpet as
loud as I can. Hopefully, I'll be able to drown out Jon's musical
belches. Once again, I get through his lesson dreaming of fudge,
and listening to myself play, instead of hearing Jon's clams. We're
now down to just five minutes remaining, with maybe time for one
final piece. I look through Jon's book of popular songs for trumpet.
I'd sure like to find one last song that *I* want to play. Let's
see...how about... *"Something Stupid."* Yeah, the old Sinatra tune
that he sang with his daughter, Nancy. That would be *perfect* for
this situation!

"Hey Jon, you wanna play *'Something Stupid?'* "

"What, Mr. B?"

"Yeah, Jon, I know. We do that every week."

I point to the beginning of the page:

"OK, Jon, here we go. One-Two-Ready-Breathe:"

*"Blorr-bp-bp-BleeorrLDLDL.   ToeeoeeoooLDLDL.   Blap-
Bloop-BlopLDLDL. Weeerrr-splaaatLDLDL..."*

"Jon...we made it! That really was *'Something Stupid.'* Let me
just brush these paint chips off of my shoes, then we can go
upstairs and find your mom."

As we get to the front door, Jon's mom is there to meet us:

"Hi, Mr. B. Jon, give Mr. B his check, and also give him the present that we made for him and his wife."

Jon grudgingly hands me a large package.

"Oh my, is this what I think it is, Jon?"

He answers in his usual grumpy tone:

"Yeah, it's the fudge *again.* Merry Christmas, I guess."

"Wow...thanks so much! I have one more student tonight, but I'm sure I'll eat some on the way home."

I turn towards Jon's mom:

"It looks like you gave us a lot of fudge again this year, and do we ever appreciate it! Oh, and by the way, I won't be teaching Jon anymore. This was his last lesson. *Bye!"*

I scurry out the door holding my little chocolate slabs of delight, and drive off quickly. *PHEW!* That worked out even better than I had hoped. I'm not sure what I'm more pleased about, having the fudge, or getting rid of Jon as a student. Let me just try some of this fudge before I make up my mind.

*

During this last week before Christmas, I receive oodles of edibles from the twenty-five other houses where I teach. This happens every year, and Ann and I are very grateful. We may not get paid very much for doing this job, and we don't get sick leave or medical benefits, but we sure are full around the holidays!

Let's see, this year there have been dozens of cookies, several popcorn tins, and three packages of that really good sausage that you can order through the mail. Plus, I get lots and lots of chocolate, in all shapes and forms: chocolate Christmas trees, chocolate cakes, assorted chocolates, chocolate mints, and even two chocolate sheep for a manger set. And, chocolate covered *everything* (raisins, marshmallows, coconut, etc.), chocolate cocoa, chocolate shaped trumpets, and, of course, those chocolate guacamole mint brownies from William's mom. Hmmm...maybe I'll send them anonymously to Jon as a going away present.

In addition to all of these tasty treats, Ann and I have received *tons* of other elaborate gifts from our students and their families. Some of these include a crystal salad set, a terracotta chip and dip bowl, a crystal salt and pepper set, and a polished granite clock. We've also been given several very nice picture frames, pen and pencil sets, and a really neat "Personal Butler," which is a snazzy silver key holder to put my keys in when I come home.

Plus, I can't even begin to count the number of wonderful notes of appreciation that we've gotten from the families, with many of these having been written by the students themselves. We've kept them all down through the years, and we are always exceedingly thankful and proud that they took the time to write them. Many other fine pieces have come our way, too, including money clips, belt buckles, and reading lamps. I also remember a nice young man who was a flute student of Ann. His family did not have a lot of money, but when he finished his four years of lessons, they gave Ann a splendid sterling silver heart necklace.

*

Last week, I received one of my more unusual gifts. The package was rather sharp on one side, and it had already torn through the wrapping paper by the time I got home. I went ahead and opened it:

"Hey hun, look at this nice silver pen that I got."

"Oh, that is really nice, Sam. It's one of the top brands. And, it's from a very high-priced department store. I bet this cost a lot of money. You'll have to start using it with your students."

"Right, right. I sure will."

I notice that there is a small button at the top of the pen. I wonder if that opens it up to put in a refil---

BOI-YOI-YOING!

"WHOOAA!"

"Watch out, Sam!"

Wow! A small (but very sharp) switchblade just popped open, grazing my nose like a nervous mohel.

"Huh. Would you look at that! I've never seen anything like this before. Uh, Sam, you better be careful with this. Uh, on second thought, how about if I take this back to the store and exchange it for something that you could really use? Since this seems to be so expensive, I might be able to get several things for you. Would that be OK?"

"Sure, hun. Go ahead...I already have plenty of pens, and what would I use that knife for at the lessons anyway?"

Hmmm...maybe just to keep Rocky the Chihuahua away from me? I can just imagine the knife opening up inside my back pocket, and slicing off a little rump roast. Or, worse yet, having the knife in my front pock---oops, better not go there. I'd sure like to hang on to all of my appendages for a little longer.

"OK, Sam, I'll go to the store next week, and let you know what I can get for it."

*

Of course, Ann and I have received a few "white elephant" gifts along the way, too. We have no idea what some of these things really are, and no one that we ask can tell, either. We've tried hanging them on the walls, placing them on top of a desk, or searching for some kind of function in the kitchen for them. Uh-oh...as I drive to Ethan's house tonight, I recall that for the past two years his family has given me presents, but we've never figured out what they were! Ann thought one of them might have a use in the kitchen---the kitchen of the *Spanish Inquisition!"* The embarrassing part for me is when I came back for Ethan's first lesson after Christmas. Ethan is an excitable little boy, and he couldn't wait to ask me what I thought of his gift. The conversation went something like this:

"Mr. B! Mr. B!"

"Hi, Ethan."

"Did you like the present?"

"Uh, yeah, it was very nice of you to give us that---that present."

"Cool! Did your dog like it?"

"Well, Ethan, we don't have a dog. We have a pet bir---"

"Oh, that's OK. It's good for lots of stuff besides dogs! I bet your car liked it! It's great for cars, too!"

"My car? Uh, yeah, sure, Ethan. My car liked it a lo---"

"Cool! How about your backyard! Did it like the present?"

"My backyard? And my car? And my dog? Oh, yeah, the backyard thought it was a neat present, Ethan."

"Cool! And, and, it works the best on your feet! Do you need help with your feet, Mr. B?"

"Uh, well, I guess so, Ethan. Sometimes my foot does get stuck in my mouth."

"Really? That's cool, Mr. B. The present will sure help with that!"

"OK, Ethan, maybe it will start helping right now? Uh...thanks for the present."

"You bet, Mr. B. I can't wait to give you something new next year!"

Let's see: what do you get when you cross a dog, a car, a backyard, and a foot? Let me know if you figure it out.

I'm pulling into Ethan's driveway now. I wonder what type of white elephant is in store for me this year. I knock on the front door:

"Mr. B! Mr. B!"

"Hi, Ethan."

"Mr. B, I've got your present here. MOMMM! Come on down, Mr. B's here! Open it now, Mr. B! It's even cooler than last year's present! Oh yeah, did you ever get your foot out of your mouth?"

Ethan's mom interrupts:

"Now, Ethan, Mr. B can open it at home, on Christmas morning, if he wants."

"Aawww. But Mom, can't he open it now? I don't want to wait two weeks until Mr. B comes back after Christmas, and you said I

can't call him on the phone on Christmas morning at 6:30 like I did last year."

I remember that phone call *very well.*

"Can you open it now, Mr. B? Can you?"

"Excuse me, Mr. B." Ethan's mom says. "You can do what you want, Mr. B. I have to go upstairs to make a phone call."

"OK, Ethan, I'll open it now. Here goes."

I reluctantly unwrap the package, and I end up holding this--- this object. It looks like that thing that Jackie Gleason tried to sell on *"The Honeymooners,"* a combination of a corkscrew, wart remover, and skate key. What the heck *is* this thing?

"Mr. B, do you like it? Do you know what it's for?"

I try to stall Ethan, as I start thinking as fast as I can: "Well, uh, Ethan, is it, maybe, uh, a thing that a dog would like?"

"Nope, that's not it."

"How about something for my car?"

"Uh-uh, Mr. B."

"My backyard?"

Ethan giggles:

"No, that's not it!"

"Well, maybe---maybe it will help my feet somehow?"

"That's it, Mr. B! It's a foot polisher! Isn't that the coolest? It works on your right foot, and it's supposed to work on your left foot, too."

Well, that would explain the wart remover and skate key sections of this thing that I'm holding. I still can't figure out the corkscrew part, though.

"Do you know how to use it, Ethan?"

"No, but my mom said she'd show me tomorrow. Does your foot need polishing, Mr. B? Maybe after you get it out of your mouth?"

"Yeah, uh, sometimes my right foot does need a little polishing, Ethan. Not sure about my left. Thanks a lot, I could use one of those. I'll show it to Mrs. B. right when I get home!"

*

Now, it's Wednesday of the week before Christmas, and Ann is pulling into our driveway. She's just gone to that ritzy department store to try and exchange my fancy silver writing/surgical utensil (i.e., the pen/knife combo). Ann said that it looks expensive, so I'm hoping she was able to get a few shirts, or a couple pair of pants, or maybe even some dress shoes for it.

"Hey Hun, was it worth a lot of money like you thought?"

"It sure was. About $75."(And that *is* a lot for 1988)

"Cool! What'd you end up getting for it? Some shirts?"

"No, no shirts."

"Maybe some shoes?"

"No Sam, no shoes."

"How about some pants, then?"

"Well, you won't believe this. Just one shirt was $125. And, all the pants and shoes were well over $150. *Everything* in that store is way overpriced."

"Well, OK then, what *did* you get?"

"A pair of socks!"

*

I'm really looking forward to the four lessons that I have this evening. I've taught all four of these boys for at least three years. These guys are also good friends, and their families are friendly with each other, too. I started out teaching just one of the boys, and he kept referring me to his friends. Now, I have four students who all live in this same neighborhood. The boys like the fact that they all take trumpet lessons from me, and each one always asks me how the others are doing. They are somewhat competitive, but they keep it fun and positive. They all want to improve, and no one wants to fall behind any of the others in their trumpet playing acumen. These lessons are truly easy for me to teach, and I enjoy them immensely!

I've also been fortunate to receive some outstanding holiday presents from all of these families over the past few years. Some have included really well made scarves, gloves, and hats. We'll see if I'm lucky in the gift department again this year! I arrive at Keith's house first. The thirty minutes go by fast, and as usual, Keith has a fine lesson. On my way out, I pause to put on the leather gloves that his family gave me last year.

"These gloves are great, Keith. Thanks again."

"Sure, Mr. B. Merry Christmas!"

"Merry Christmas to you and your family too, Keith. Well, uh, I guess I'll see you in two weeks for your next lesson."

"OK. Bye, Mr. B."

"Bye, Keith."

Hmmm...that *is* strange. No gift, and no card either. I always get *something* from them. Oh well, maybe next year!

Next, I head to Ryan's house. It only takes me about a minute to drive from one of these houses to the next.

"Hi Ryan." I say, as I take off the spiffy wool hat that he had presented me the year before.

"Hi Mr. B. Did Keith finish learning his solo?"

"Yes, he did. Now it's your turn, and I bet you'll finish it, too."

"I sure will, Mr. B. *Let's go!*"

Ryan does very well during his lesson, and as I'm leaving, I put that hat back on.

"All right, Ryan. I'll be back in two weeks."

"OK, Mr. B. Merry Christmas! Bye."

"Bye, Ryan, and Merry Christmas."

Huh...this is getting weird. No cards or presents from either one of them. Was it something I said? All right, on to Brett's house.

"Hi ya, Brett."

"Hi, Mr. B. How did Ryan do?"

"Oh, both Ryan and Keith finished learning the solo. You ready, too?"

"You bet, Mr. B!"

After hearing Brett play, I can tell that he had really practiced hard this week, too. I'm standing in his front hallway, slipping on the fancy knit sweater that Brett's family had given me previously.

"Nice job, Brett. The next lesson will be in two weeks, right?"

"Right. And, oh, Mr. B..."

My ears perk up. Oh boy...maybe he's going to give me a present!

"Yeah, Brett?"

"Can you tell me if Thomas finishes the solo, too? That would be *so cool* if all four of us did it in the same week! Bye."

"Oh, OK." I reply rather dejectedly, as I pull the sweater over my head. "I'll let you know. Bye, Brett."

WOW...this is really odd. I'm not sure what to think. Am I truly that greedy and shallow of a person? Don't answer that. At least I still have lots of that gooey fudge from old "Spit Valve" Jon to feed my sorrows. And, I no longer have to try and teach Jon, either! Well, here I am at Thomas' house:

"Hello, Mr. B. Tell me who finished the solo tonight! I'm ready to try, too. And I want to start the next solo, too. Can I, Mr. B?"

"You bet, Thomas. All the other guys finished the solo, and they said that they hope you do, too! I can't wait to hear you play it. Let me just take off this nice scarf that you gave me last Christmas."

Just like my three previous students tonight, Thomas sounds great on his trumpet, and he completes this solo as well. At the end of his lesson, I even have time to start him on a new piece, which puts him a little ahead of his friends. That makes Thomas *very* happy:

"That's *great,* Mr. B! I'll call the other guys and tell 'em I learned *more* than they did. But, I bet they'll catch up quick. We can all practice together over Winter Break."

"Sounds good, Thomas. Well, I'll be back in a couple of weeks. Is your mom home?"

"No, she had to go out. But, she left me your check. Here it is."

"Thanks, Thomas." I adjust the scarf back around my neck. "OK, bye."

"Bye, Mr. B."

Now I'm downright depressed. These are four of my best students, and four of the nicest families, and I didn't get one little present from any of them. All right, you materialistic trumpet tutor, get back in the car. I think I'll go home and start in on that fudge. I should watch out, though. The fudge tin looks a lot like the container of those nuclear "guac brownies." I sure don't want to mix *those* up. Oh, maybe I'll just stop off for a Mountain Dew at that gas station around the corner on the way ho---

"Mr. B! Mr. B! Wait...wait!"

"Oh. Hi, Thomas. Are you OK?"

"Yeah. I forgot! I forgot!"

"No, Thomas, you gave me the check. Here it i---"

"No, no! I forgot something else. Come back in."

"Oh. OK, Thomas."

"Here, Mr. B! Here's your present! And, and, it's from all of us!"

Thomas hands me an envelope. Yea! At least I finally got one gift tonight!

"Oh, that's really nice, Thomas. Tell your family thanks very mu---"

"Oh no, Mr. B. It's from all four of us!"

OK. Thomas, his sister, and their parents. That makes sense.

"Right, Thomas. Thanks a lot, that's very thoughtf---"

"No, no, Mr. B! I mean it's from all four of your students tonight: me, Ryan, Keith, and Brett. And from all of our parents, too. Since I'm the last one, they gave it to me to give to you. They decided not to say anything to you as a surprise. Are you surprised?"

"Why, yes, Thomas. I'm *very* surprised. Tell all the guys thanks from Mrs. B and me, will y---"

"Mr. B! Mr. B!"

My name is suddenly being shouted from behind me. I turn around, but it's dark out, so I can't quite se---

"It's us, Mr. B."

"Keith."

"And Brett."

"And Ryan, too."

"Wow...hi guys. You just walked over here now?

"Yeah." calls out Brett. *"We want you to open the present."*

"Can you see it from on the porch?" asks Ryan.

"Yeah, sure." I reply. "OK, here goes."

I rip open the envelope. It looks like a gift card, to...to only *the* most expensive restaurant in this suburb! And, it's for an awful lot of money. This would definitely be more than enough money for two complete dinners for both me and Ann!

"Oh my goodness, guys! I don't quite know what to say. This is so nice of all of you...thank you so much!"

"You're welcome, Mr. B." says Thomas. *"My parents said that we all corrobolated together to get this."*

"No, that's not it, Thomas." replies Brett. *"My mom says we all cobborolated together."*

"No, no!" shouts Ryan. *"We all carbureted together!"*

"No, my dad said we all collorobated." declares Keith.

"OK, guys. I think I get it. Each of your families paid for part of this gift card. You collaborated on it."

"Right! That's it, Mr. B." yells Thomas.

"Have fun at that restaurant with Mrs. B!" hollers Keith.

"Yeah!" the boys all scream in unison.

"Thanks again, guys. And be sure to thank your parents, too. I'll see you in a couple of weeks. Keep practicing, OK? Merry Christmas, guys!"

"Don't worry. We're gonna practice together. Merry Christmas, Mr. B!"

*

"Oh Sam, he's sooo cute!"

"Ooh...he's absolutely adorable!"

"He looks *so* much better in his tux than you ever do, Sam."

"Why, thank you, I think."

Our first son, Sean, was born in November, and one of the baby gifts he received is an infant size tuxedo. He does look very cute wearing it, and since I usually put on my own tuxedo for gigs two or three times a week, Ann took our picture together. Naturally, I've been showing it off to everyone that I see. I wonder if Sean will be interested in music someday?

My students and their parents have been very encouraging during the months that Ann was expecting Sean. Every week, they would ask me:

"How's Mrs. B?"

"Is she feeling OK?"

"Call us when the baby is born, so we can get the right kind of present if it's a boy or a girl."

And, here is my favorite comment that I heard often from several of the moms. They would say something like this right in front of my student. I *think* they were kidding, but I wasn't always sure:

"Tell Mrs. B. not to worry. I bet your child won't give you any trouble. Not like my lazy one does!"

That would usually elicit this response from my student:

"I know, Mom. *I know.*"

Since Ann and Sean came home from the hospital, these students and their parents have all been very generous, too. Some brought over meals, some offered to shovel if it snowed, and others said that they could babysit for Sean when he gets a little older.

And, I can barely count all of the gifts we received for Sean! Ann and I teach over sixty students, so, of course, that means over sixty baby presents have come in since he was born. Again, we're very grateful to all of these families!

One fashionable gift genre for our November born son has been a plethora of "Baby's First Christmas" items. He's received rattles, blocks, and sweatshirts with that printed on them. And also many Christmas tree ornaments of all shapes and designs that say "Baby's First Christmas." And more ornaments. And...well, you get the idea. We've hung them up all over the tree, and they have helped to give the holiday a special meaning this year.

Sean's gotten several teddy bear type items, too, such as socks, booties, and a very cool hand painted teddy bear switch plate that can be placed around a light switch. Ann and I enjoy looking at that switch plate every day, and we know Sean will too as he grows up.

Another quite unique gift that Sean received is a small box, in the shape of a tooth. It's painted to look like a giant tooth, and it's supposed to hold Sean's baby teeth when they fall out. We can put the tooth into the box, tell Sean we're leaving it under his pillow for the tooth fairy, and then put some money back in it for Sean. What a neat gift idea! By the way, is a dime per tooth still enough, like when I was a kid? Probably not.

The area that we live in is full of Chicago Bears fans, and the team is really popular, especially since they just won the Super Bowl a few years ago. Being born in the middle of the football season, Sean has been given tons of Bears winter clothing items to wear, including baby size snowsuits, hats, pajamas, and sweat suits. Plus, Bears t-shirts, a Bears bathmat, and a Bears quilt. And, naturally, a Bears football!

Unfortunately, the Bears lost the other day, so their season has gone down the proverbial you-know-what. Oh well, maybe they'll get back to the Super Bowl soo---

"Crreeeecck!"

Huh...someone is opening up our screen door. Oh good...it's a large container that's covered in wrapping paper; looks like yet another present for Sean! I call upstairs to Ann:

"Hey Hun, we got a big package here."

"OK, Sam, go ahead and open it. I'll be right down."

I rip open the paper. Here's the card:

"To Sean, and Mr. and Mrs. B. We didn't want to ring the bell and disturb the baby. Congratulations, from Billy and Mrs. Bottogly!"

Ann calls down:

"Sam...who's it from?"

"Mrs. Bottogly dropped it off."

"Oh yeah, I know her, Sam. That was nice of her. What is it?"

I finish tearing off the wrapping paper. Oh, what perfect timing for this gift:

"Hey Hun, you'll love this...it's a Bears diaper pail."

*

Kevin, our second son, was born in early July, about two and a half years after Sean. Just like his big brother, Kevin is a happy little guy almost all of the time. Sean is enjoying having a baby brother to roll around with, at least for the time being. We'll see what happens as they grow up. Ann says that just like Sean, Kevin kicked inside her stomach every time she was performing on her flute, and he also kicked every time any kind of music was playing. Maybe he'll like music, too, when he gets older?

Ann and I continue to teach dozens of students each week, and we've known many of these kids and their families for years; even way before Sean was born. As always, these people have been extremely kind towards our sons and us. It's a great feeling for us to receive baby gifts from our same students for the second time, and the families seem very happy for us, too.

Being born in July, my students have been giving Kevin several presents with a patriotic theme, with different designs of the flag on infant sized shirts, caps, and pants. Plus, Kevin has received a tiny flag that he likes to hold. He's been waving it around a lot this summer.

Since Kevin's gotten all summer season clothing, Ann and I are hoping that he can still fit into all of the winter Bears stuff that Sean received from our students when he was a baby. I don't know, however, since Kevin will probably be too big to get into them. The other problem is that the Bears haven't been very good lately, so I'm not sure I'd want Kevin to be seen too often wearing Bears clothes.

Instead of all those Bears items, Kevin has received tons and tons of baseball clothes, specifically Cubs material. The Cubs are unbelievably popular around here, which is fine, *except that I'm a big White Sox fan!* My grandfather was, too, and he helped me begin my interest in the Sox when I was a kid, even though most of my friends were Cub fans. I think my students and their families know that I'm a White Sox fan, but almost all of them are Cub fans anyway, regardless of what I think. I'm probably outnumbered around here by Cub fans by about 10-1. I'm used to that, but inside my house now are baby sized Cubs shirts, hats, socks, jackets, and pants. Plus, there are Cubs pennants, posters, pictures, and even a clock that shouts *"CUBS WIN! CUBS WIN!"* every time the alarm goes off. *AARRGGHH!!* Worse yet, Kevin has gotten absolutely nothing that says White Sox on it. Just like I did with Sean, I'm going to have to quickly brainwash Kevin into being a Sox fan, or he'll get swept up into the Cub mania around here.

I do have a predicament here, though. All of these students that gave Kevin the Cubs clothes are going to want to see him wearing them. After a lot of thought, I did come up with an idea that might avoid having Kevin wear any Cubs clothes in public. We'll see if it works.

OK, Kevin, here we go. Let me just put your left leg inside these pants.

"Goo-goo-goo."

Good...now you're right. OK, and now your arms. That's it.

"Gaa-gaa-gee-gee."

All right. Looks great! Now, Kevin, I have the camera to take your picture. Just lay right there. I'll tickle you a little bit so you'll smile...there you go---

"FLASH!"

"GOO-GOO-GAA-GEE!"

Perfect, Kevin! You look terrific in this baby tuxedo, just like your brother did.

"Gaa-gaa."

Now, all I have to do is show this picture around to all of my students for the next few weeks. I can just tell them that we haven't yet gotten any pictures developed of you wearing any of the Cubs stuff. Yeah...that should stall everyone for a while, don't you think, Kevin?

"Gee-Gee-Gee!"

It's already September, and football season is starting up. Maybe I'll just dress you more in those Bears clothes that your brother had, OK? You won't mind, will ya?

"Goo-gaa-goo-gaa."

Hopefully, the Bears will make all of my students and their families forget about these Cubs items until next spring, and by then you'll be much too big to wear them! All of the families that is except for the super Cubs fan Mrs. Sckaanck. I bet she'll ask me every week about that Cubs cap she gave to you. Oh well, this plan is worth a try. What do ya, think, Kevin?

"Gooooooo! Gooooooo!"

"DING-DONG!"

"Hey Hun, can you get that? Kevin and I are busy."

"OK, Sam."

"Who is it, Ann?"

"Oh, whoever it was just left a package in the door. I'll open it."

C'mon, Kevin, let's go downstairs and see. Maybe you got *another* present!

"Gaa-Goo-Gaa!"

Ann finds the card inside the gift-wrapping:

"To new baby Kevin, and Mr. and Mrs. B. We want you to start rooting for the *correct* team right away! From the Tottertates!"

"Goo-Gee-Goo!"

"Sam, who are the Tottertates?"

"Oh, Thom Tottertate is one of my newer students."

"Sam, did you pronounce that "Thom", using the "Th" sound? Isn't the "h" supposed to be silent?"

"No, not for him, hun. His family does say the "h," so it does sound like "Th-om.""

"OK, Sam, whatever. Let me finish opening it, all right Kevin?"

"Gaaaaaa. Gaaaaaa!"

"Sam, it's a...a...Cubs rubber bed pad, in case Kevin wets the bed. Do you like it, Kevin?

"WAAAAH! WAAAAH!"

"Oh, Kevin, you don't like it? That's too bad. What do *you* think, Sam?"

"WAAAAH! WAAAAH!"

*

Now that our boys are getting a little older (they are ages four and two), Ann and I are actually able to go out once in a while, when we have a little energy and money left over. We just want to go see an occasional movie, or grab a bite to eat. We're still performing on our instruments at several gigs each weekend, so we don't get to step out very often. Usually, we're able to get Ann's mom or sister to babysit for the boys, but sometimes they're not available.

Fortunately, Ann and I have found that one of the most valuable perks of our being teachers is that we have now amassed a large stable of built-in babysitters for Sean and Kevin. Altogether, we've probably hired about a dozen of our students to watch our kids. Of course, some of them are girls who are really into babysitting. They do a terrific job, and Kevin and Sean have a great time with them. Also, since the vast majority of my trumpet students are boys, we have found that quite a few of these 12-18 year old young men really enjoy coming over to babysit for our little guys. My students have loads of energy to play with Kevin and Sean, and our sons absolutely love it when one of their pretend "big brothers" arrives to join in on the fun!

Ann and I perform in several outdoor band concerts every summer, in various parks throughout the city. We often try to bring the boys along, with one of our students as their babysitter. While we're playing in the concert in one part of the park, the boys can play on the playground equipment, and our student can still hear the concert. What's very interesting for all of us are the rides home. We talk about the cool swings and slides that Kevin and Sean got to romp around on, and we can also discuss the songs from the band performance with our student. They really enjoy hearing their teachers playing in a professional concert. Two students in particular come to mind. Not only are they both tremendous babysitters for the boys, but attending these concerts has also helped them to develop a highly sophisticated interest in music, as well as in playing their own instrument. Ann and I are extremely proud of them!

I've already mentioned about the great relationships that Ann and I have been able to achieve with the parents of our students. Because we are so familiar with these parents, we are confident that we can trust the parents to be immediately helpful if there is any kind of an emergency for our student/sitters. We're very lucky in this regard. Compared to most parents of young children, we can have far fewer worries about our kids when we do go out.

Since we'll be seeing our student's parents the following week at their lesson anyway, we can almost always get an honest report about how things went when Ann and I were out. Our students can't lie to us if there were any problems. Well, they can try to lie, but they can't get away with it because we'll be talking to their parents right away!

I'll be arriving at Raymond's house in a few minutes for his lesson. We used him last Sunday night to babysit for the first time. I wasn't sure if Raymond was all that interested in the job, but we had gone down our list, and we were having trouble finding someone who was available. His name was next in the order, so we thought we'd give him a try. Raymond's parents are very nice, and I've known them for a few years.

As I drive, I'm still a little confused about something that happened when Raymond was babysitting. When Ann and I got home on Sunday night, we stepped in a large sticky spot on the floor right by the front door. Obviously, something had spilled, but with the dark wood floor, we couldn't tell what it was. It's strange that it would be sticky, because our boys don't drink soda, at least not yet. The Mountain Dew is all for me! When we got home that night, I had asked Raymond:

"Hey Raymond, did someone spill a drink right here?"

"Oh, uh, no, Mr. B. I didn't see anything."

"Dad, Dad!" shouts our Sean. "That's not twue. Waymond bwought a can of Coke with him, and he spilled it wight there!"

"Oh, weally---I mean *really?* Thanks, Sean. Is that what happened, Raymond?"

"Oh, no, Mr. B. I don't know what happened."

"OK, Raymond. Get your coat...I'll take you home."

When I get to his house today, I think I'll ask Raymond's mother if she heard anything about the "Coke-gate" spilling incident. She greets me at the door with Raymond:

"Hello, Mr. B. Raymond had a good time babysitting for your sons the other night. Thanks for calling him."

"Oh, sure. You're welcome, Raymond."

"Now, Mr. B, Raymond has something he'd like to say to you. Go ahead, Raymond."

"Uh, Mr. B. Uh, my mom wants me to tell you that I did bring a Coke over to your house, and, uh, I did spill it on the floor. Uh, I'm sorr-rry."

"Very good, Raymond." his mom adds. "He told me about it after he got home, Mr. B. But, I do hope you will continue to call him to babysit."

207

"Oh, thanks for telling me, Raymond. We'll keep you on our babysitting list."

However, I think we'll be moving Raymond down *several* places on the list.

*

Tonight should be really interesting and unusual. Ann and I are going to an art exhibition, and it's being held on the grounds of a beautiful park and gardens near where we live. The interesting part for us is that the artist who is having the showing is the father of one of my students. Mr. Matthews has another occupation during the day, and he is also an outstanding artist, painting mostly floral still life and landscapes.

On top of that, we've hired the Matthews' son, Brian, to babysit for Sean and Kevin tonight. Brian is a freshman in high school, and I've been going to his house to give him trumpet lessons for about four years. He's a really friendly, easygoing kid, and my boys are always super excited when Brian is their sitter. Through these four years of lessons, I've also gotten to know Mr. and Mrs. Matthews pretty well. They have always been interested in Ann and my performing careers, and they were a big help in offering to watch Sean when Kevin was born. I know our little guys will be happy to see Brian tonight. They're waiting for him by the front window. Here comes his mom now, dropping off Brian in our driveway:

"Hi, Mr. B." Mrs. Matthews says, as Brian gets out of the car.

"We'll see you over at the gardens."

"We'll be there soon!" I reply.

"Brian! Brian!" Sean shouts.

"Bwian! Bwian!" Kevin adds.

"Hi guys. Hi Mr. B."

"How ya doin', Brian? The boys are sure glad to see you."

Sean leads Brian into the playroom:

"Brian, come in here. We want to show you the farm and train station we're building."

"OK, Sean. Be right there."

"All right, Brian. Have fun." I say. "Mrs. B. and I are excited to see your dad's exhibition. We'll be leaving now. See you guys later!"

"*Bye Mom! Bye Dad!*" they screech in unison.

The park and gardens are only a short distance from our house. Ann and I arrive, and we head into the viewing area. Already, there are a few dozen people walking around. The paintings are phenomenal! Many of them are quite large, and would take up a big portion of a wall in someone's home. Flowers larger-than-life of all hues and types just make us feel like we're in a fragrant garden. All of the art is for sale, and the pieces have already been framed very nicely, too. I overhear other people saying that they think the prices being asked for Mr. Matthews' paintings are exceptionally fair, especially for ones that are this well done and this size. I can imagine that the frames alone would be worth a lot of money.

Ann and I catch a glimpse of a few of the price tags, and we can tell right away that the paintings cost way more than what we could afford. They are terrific works of art, and I sure wish we could buy one for the house. Oh well, maybe someday! That's OK, though. We're here not only to view the art, but also to support Mr. and Mrs. Matthews, who have always been so kind to Ann, our sons, and me. It is a private exhibition, but Mrs. Matthews invited us personally to come and see it.

After viewing the entire display, we find Mr. and Mrs. Matthews:

"These are unbelievable paintings, Mr. Matthews!" exclaims Ann. "Thanks so much for inviting us."

"Yes, they're just great." I add. I know slightly more than nothing about art, but even I really like the colors that Mr. Matthews uses in his paintings. I continue my ignorant bluster:

"The colors are so bright, and they stand out very well against, uh, the background of the lighting and the walls, and...uh, the frames that are the ones next to the flowers---"

Uh oh, be careful. I'm on a slippery slope here. I realize that I'm sounding like an artsy idiot, and I can't seem to stop myself:

"---and the water fountains, too, with all the colors, and...uh, especially that one next to the bathroom---"

I'm beginning to sweat like crazy:

"---with the light shining on it, and, uh, did you like those little rolled up hot dogs they were serving, and...uh, I think I may have dropped my keys over there. *Excuse me!"*

That was brilliant, you genius! Why can't you just say a little bit, and then shut up?

Ann grabs my arm before I can escape (or find a hole in the floor to disappear through):

"Uh, what my husband means is that even *he* can distinguish all the colors, and he's partially colorblind."

Oh, boy. Thanks, Ann! Good thing she interrupted me before I said something that sounded truly stupid.

"Uh, right, Mr. Matthews. That's what I meant."

"Well, thanks very much." Mr. Matthews replies. "And, thanks for coming tonight, too. I appreciate it a great deal."

Mrs. Matthews concurs:

"Oh yes, we really do appreciate it."

Mr. Matthews then asks:

"Is there one painting that stands out to you?"

I *should* let Ann answer (since I'm the dummy of the group), but instead I blurt out:

"Yeah, we really like the one with the red and white flowers sitting on the glass table. Even I can see the sharpness of the color combinations. That's an amazing painting."

"Why, that's very nice of you. Thanks."

After a few more minutes of conversation, Ann and I decide to leave and drive home. I have to take Brian back to his house. As

I'm sitting in the car, waiting in our driveway, Brian starts to come out:

"Bye, guys." he says. "See you next time."

"Bye, Brian! Come back and play soon!"

That's Sean voice, but I can't see him because the screen on the front door is still taller than Sean is.

Kevin pipes up next, and since he's even shorter, there's no way I can see him. I just hear his squeaky two-year-old voice:

"Yeah...come and pway, Bwian!"

*

A week has now passed since Mr. Matthews' art exhibition, and I have about an hour left before I start my teaching rounds today after school. I sure hope that Mr. Matthews was able to sell some of his work. Those are fabulous paintings; I just wish we could afford to buy one. It did look like there were several high rollers in the crowd that evening, so maybe he had some luck. The phone rings...*oh great, it's probably one of my students cancelling his lesson at the last minute.*

"Hi, Mr. B, it's Mrs. Matthews."

"Oh, hi, how are you?"

"Just fine, thanks. Are you and your wife going to be home in about twenty minutes?"

"Uh, yes. We'll be home for a little while. Do you need something?"

"Oh, no. I just wanted to make sure you'd be home."

Huh. I wonder what that was all about. Brian's lesson isn't until tomorrow.

"Sam, who was that on the phone? One of my students?"

"Uh, no Ann, it was Mrs. Matthews. She just asked if we'd be home in twenty minutes. Do you know what she meant by that?"

"No, I have no idea."

Oh well. I get to watch *Jeopardy* today, and after that's over I still will have a few more minutes to make it to my first student's house on time. Since Ann and I moved into this suburb, I now live a lot closer to many of my students. That does make it quite a bit easier on me, and also on the car. OK---good, here's the Final Jeopardy answer now:

"DING!"

"The bloodiest battle in American history was fought near this creek in Maryland. 30 seconds, players. Good luck!"

"DAH-DEE-DAH-DOH-DAH-DEE-DAAAH. DAH-DEE-DAH-DEE..."

Oh, that's an easy one: "What is Antietam?" I wonder if any of these three drone contestants will get it righ---?"

"DING-DONG!!"

What? Did the *Jeopardy* theme song suddenly add some more bel---?

"DING-DONG!!"

Oh, wait. That's *my* doorbell, you dope. I look out the window. Huh, it's Mr. and Mrs. Matthews. And, he's carrying a large package.

"Hey Ann...it's the Matthews' at the door!"

"Hi! Come on in. How are you?"

"Oh, we're fine, Mr. B." Mrs. Matthews says. "Is Mrs. B. home, too?"

"Hi, I'm here." Ann responds. "It's nice to see you again. What can we do for you?"

"Well...my husband and I were talking. After the showing the other night, we know you mentioned that you liked that painting of the flowers on the table, and..."

Mr. Matthews unwraps the package, to reveal *that very painting, in its attractive frame.* The richness of the floral painting's colors makes our living room about a hundred times more beautiful. Mrs. Matthews declares:

"Well, here. We want you to have it...here it is!"

Ann and I are practically speechless.

"Oh my goodness!" Ann cries. "We don't know what to say! That *is* the painting that we both admired so much. You really shouldn't do this."

"That's right, you really shouldn't." I add. "This is part of your business, and, and we know that you're selling these, and we wouldn't be able to pay you what you're asking, particularly with it already having been fram---"

"Oh, no no. That's quite all right." Mrs. Matthews states. "We don't want any money for it. We just want you to have it because you're such nice people, and we know that you'd appreciate it. We were so glad you came to the exhibition."

Then she asks:

"We hoped you might have a place for it?"

Ann points towards an empty wall in our living room, and says:

"Well, right over there would be *perfect!* Wow...we just can't thank you enough."

"Oh, it's our pleasure." replies Mrs. Matthews. "We're happy that you will be the ones to have this painting."

Sean and Kevin hear us talking, and they bound into the room:

"Hey guys, look at this cool painting that Brian's parents are giving to us! Brian's dad is the artist. What do you think?"

"oooOOOooo!" they utter in unison.

They're impressed, but Sean also has another question:

"Hey Dad, did Brian come, too?"

"Oh, no, Sean. Not today. But he'll be here again sometime to babysit for you guys."

"Aawww."

The boys are sad. Sean glances at Mr. and Mrs. Matthews:

"Can you bring Brian next time?"

Kevin chimes in:

"Yeah, *pwease bwing Bwian, and mo fwowers, too! I wike 'em!"*

*

"zzzZZZ!"

"Daaad!"

"zzzZZZZ!!"

"Daaaad!!"

"ZZZ---oh, oh, sorry, Sean. Right, right. Uh, I know you want to act as Santa today, so go ahead and keep opening the presents."

It's 7:15 on Christmas morning here at the Bennett house. Our sons Sean and Kevin are now ages five and three, and needless to say they are both *extremely* excited about Christmas. Sean woke up Kevin at 6:30 this morning, and they ran down the stairs (well, Kevin crawled down) to see if Santa had stopped at our house. Indeed, the bearded jelly-bellied man in the big red suit had been here, and he has left several presents for the boys. Santa also munched on the cookies that Kevin and Sean had left out for him, too (actually, I'm the one who devoured those cookies).

For the past few weeks, Ann and I have been placing under our Christmas tree all of the presents that we've received from our students. That is, except for those Chocolate Guacamole brownies from William's mom. Those went right out in the trash, along with the obligatory fruitbrick...er, fruitcake that another student gave to me (the garbage bag was awfully heavy that day). My boys have been checking out the bottom of the tree every day to see what new gifts have arrived, and it's getting pretty crowded under there. So far, though, they've been disappointed with what they've seen:

"Daaad, this one says: 'For Mr. B' again."

"Aawww...it's: 'For Mrs. B,' Mom. Are we gonna get some presents, too?"

Ann replies:

"Now, you know guys, Santa comes down the chimney the night before Christmas. That's why none of your gifts are under the tree yet. All the elves are still making your presents in Santa's workshop at the North Pole. Don't worry, when you wake up on Christmas morning, your gifts will be there."

"OK, Mom. We know." they sadly respond.

Finally, late on Christmas Eve, well after the boys had gone to sleep, Ann and I placed all of Sean and Kevin's gifts under the tree. The tough part of celebrating Christmas for me and for Ann is that Christmas Eve and Christmas morning are *very* busy work times for us as performing musicians. For years and years, before the boys were born, we played our instruments at several church services on December 24th and 25th. Usually, on the afternoon of the 24th, we would perform at masses beginning at 3pm and 5pm, and then stop at our friend the "Colonel's" house (yes, I do mean Colonel Sanders) to grab a bite to eat. Believe me, there are very few restaurants near us that are open in the evening on Christmas Eve!

After resting at home for a short while, and maybe watching a little of *"It's A Wonderful Life,"* or *"A Christmas Story,"* Ann and I would then leave again to perform at yet another church service. This one would actually start at midnight. The Midnight Mass usually lasts longer than most church services, so we would often get home a little after 2am. Because of all the adrenaline that's flowing from performing, on top of the excitement of this special mass, a musician can often feel wired after a presentation like that. It's very tough for me to fall asleep right away. On Christmas Eve, I like to turn on the TV channel that just has the one camera constantly zoomed in on that Yule Log. Ah, what classic entertainment that is! If I'm lucky, I may doze off at about 3am.

Then, *BOOM,* on the morning of the 25th, we'd get up at about 5:30 a.m. and go play at the 7am, 9am, and 11am masses. Ann and I would finally get home and collapse around 1pm on Christmas Day. This routine was exhausting even before we had kids! Sometimes all of these services have been at the same church, but there have been lots of times when we've had to drive quickly to get to different places. Ann and I don't always have the opportunity to work together, either. There have been many years where we each performed in separate churches for at least some of these masses.

As you can imagine, Christmas can be quite a lucrative holiday for musicians! Ann and I have always been reluctant to turn down the chance to play at any services. There are dozens of other trumpeters and flutists who are also trying to earn a living performing on their instruments, and they would be more than happy to take our place. And, once you turn down a gig, the employer may be hesitant to call you again.

If you even say no to just *one* of the six Christmas Eve and Christmas day masses, the church music director may want to hire someone else to play at *all* of them. They usually prefer to have the same musician playing at them all, so that they don't have to worry about several different people coming in and trying to figure out the music. Plus, it's a lot easier for a church music director to just make one phone call to book a musician for all of the masses, instead of many calls to hire someone to play at only one or two masses each.

When Kevin and Sean were infants, and didn't know much about Christmas or Santa, we were able to have them stay overnight at Ann's Mom's house. The boys didn't care; they were simply happy to be with their grandmother. Now, however, Sean and Kevin are old enough to start really enjoying the whole Christmas spectacle. For weeks, they've been looking forward to coming downstairs on Christmas morning and opening presents with us. Of course, Ann and I want to be with them, too!

So, this year we decided to turn down playing at the 7am mass this morning, but we're still performing at all five of the other services. Ann's Mom is staying with us overnight, so she watched the boys while we went to the two Christmas Eve services yesterday afternoon. We got home from picking up the Colonel's traditional Christmas fare (to us that means *Original Recipe*) at about 7 last night, but after we all ate, the boys were still much too excited to go to bed. Around 8:00, I announce:

"OK, guys, time for bed."

"Oh, Dad, can't we stay up for a while?" asks Sean. *"We want to see Santa!"*

"Yea, pwesents fwom Santa!" Kevin shouts.

"No, sorry guys. You're going to get up early, remember, so you need to go to sleep now. The sooner you go to sleep, the sooner you'll wake up. *(Wait...that makes no sense at all! But, it usually tricks the boys.)* Head on up now and start getting ready. I'll be right up."

"Oh, OK Dad. Goodnight, Mom."

"Boys, did you leave out the cookies and milk for Santa?" Ann asks.

"Yep. Do you think he'll see them?" Sean wonders.

"Oh, don't worry. He'll see them. I'm *sure* they'll be gone in the morning." *(Hey...how does Ann know that!)* "Goodnight, boys. Tomorrow is Christmas!"

"YEAH!!"

Ann and I are lucky; Kevin and Sean are very good boys, and they never give us any problems with these parent/child power struggles. They reluctantly go upstairs to get ready for bed. I'll tuck them in, while Ann starts wrapping the boys' presents and putting them under the tree.

We're already tired from playing at the first two masses of the day, and Ann and I should really rest up for the big Midnight Mass performance. Not only can these gigs be physically demanding, but they are mentally draining, too. We have to concentrate hard during the entire performance, and we can't speak to the other musicians very much without it being too obvious to the audience, especially in a quiet church setting. Consequently, most communication is done through non-verbal signals. The musicians are constantly trying to read each other's minds about who plays which part, and when, and you're always anticipating what part everyone will play on the next song. Ann and I have to leave for the church in about two hours, since we have a rehearsal before this mass. But, we need to get as many of the boys' presents ready as we can right now, so that we don't have to do it when we get home later. And, I do mean *much later!*

My job tonight is to put together a model train set, which is one of the boys' biggest gifts. I'll try and place the tracks around the tree, because we want to have the train up and running when the boys come down in the morning. The picture of it on the box looks really cool, and at our local "mom and pop" toy store we saw it all set up and working. There are four train cars, two-dozen pieces of track, and lots of little people and animals to ride in them. The owner of this store is really great; he seems to like playing with the toys even more than the kids! Ann and I went to the toy store without the boys, of course. This will be a big surprise for them.

I think I've already mentioned that my handyman skills are comparable to *The Three Stooges*, but I'm even worse at wrapping things. So, it's going to be me versus this train set. Fortunately, this model is a rather large scale, so even I can hopefully achieve success in putting it together.

I start to position the pieces of track, and they seem to fit into each other rather easily. Good! Now I just have to make them into a circle that's large enough to go around the Christmas tree. Let's see, there are twenty-four pieces of track all together, and they're supposed to form a nice, big circle. Here's track number twenty-one going in, now twenty-two, and twenty-three, and finally---wait a minute!

"Sam, how's that track coming along?" Ann asks.

"Uh, just fine. Should be done soon."

I *should* be, except that my circle looks more like a pretzel. This can't be right! Let me check the numbers on those track pieces again. OK, numbers one through ten are correct. But, oh, now I see. I mixed up eleven and nineteen. All right, I'll just switch those two. OK, now I'm back up to track twenty-three again, and---*WHAT?*

"Sam, I'm almost done wrapping the boys' other presents. Need some help with the track? Remember, you have to put the train cars together, too. Then we can see if it runs. I can't wait to look at the boys' faces when they see it in the morning!"

"Uh, yeah, right. I'll let you know if I get stuck."

Hmmm. I switched tracks eleven and nineteen, but now three of the other tracks are heading off on their own, making it look like a big number "6." *That ain't right!* Eewww...now I can feel remnants of the Colonel's feast starting to churn around in my stomach. OK, try it again. One through ten, all correct. Eleven through---uh-oh, seventeen is backwards. *That's got to be it!* Just turn that around, and---now I have the shape of a giant number "9." Come on, now. Keep trying. Take off the stem of the "9," twist that piece the other way, and---now it's an oversized "3."

Aargh! OK, once again...maybe start with track number eleven this time. I'm *sure* the first ten are correct.

There...there...right...good...*wrong! The tracks are now in the shape of the infinity sign!* No, no...The Colonel is quickly being demoted down through the ranks of my digestive system. I better get up to the bathr---

"Sam, are you done yet? We have to leave in a little while. Let me take a peek---*oh, my,* the tracks look like a...*a croissant!* Here, Sam, how about if I finish the tracks?

"Uh, OK, Ann. I'll be right back. I have to go to the bathroom."

By the time I finally come back down, Ann has finished putting the tracks together. She is really good at mechanical things like this. She actually got them to be in the shape of a circle!

"Here, Sam. Can you connect the train car pieces, and set them on the tracks? And then, can you start putting the people and animals all around? You might have to connect some of them, too, if they come in several parts. I'll finish getting ready so we can get to that rehearsal."

"All right, hun...I'm on it."

It looks like we have about twenty minutes before we have to leave for the church. Here goes...wow, the tops of these train cars are snapping nicely onto their wheels, and they sure look cool sitting on the tracks. That was easy, even for me! Five minutes are left now before we have to leave. OK, how about setting up the little people and animals. Oh, brother...I see lots of tiny heads and separate body parts. I guess I'm going to have to finish this when we get home. Ugh...so much for resting before the Midnight Mass. I'm beat already, and we've got three more performances in the next twelve hours! Well, at least we got most of the boys' presents ready (or Ann did, anyway).

*

As usual, Ann and I made it home about 2am after playing at the Midnight Mass. *Oh man, am I tired!* I'm not sure how Ann feels, but I'm wondering if I can get through this schedule again next year. We may have to give up playing at some of these masses so that we can devote more energy and time to the boys, and to their Christmas celebration. *I can't even imagine how lousy I'm going to feel by the time I get home tomorrow!*

Let's see, Sean and Kevin are getting up at 6:30, and Ann has already gone to sleep. Well, I better hurry up and put these teeny railroad inhabitants together. Some of them go inside the train cars, too; I have to be careful to place them in the right spots. All right, that guy's head and body snapped together easily. And, that pig did too, and both of those cows, and...and...

zzzZZZ. zzzZZZ. zzzZZZ!

Uh...uh...*sheesh!* I must have fallen asleep. What time is it? *3:30! Oh, that's just great!* I still have about thirty of these miniature creatures to go. Hmmm...I'm going to need some help in order to finish putting these pieces together. Let's see what I can come up with...

...*Ahhh...that's much better!* There's nothing like sitting in my living room at 4am on Christmas morning, snapping together miniscule heads and torsos, sipping on a cold Mountain Dew, and watching the Yule Log burning the night away on TV.

Buurrpp! Oh, excuse me. I guess the Colonel came up for another visit, too.

Now, that's what the holidays are all about!

*

"Dad, this present says: 'To Mr. B, from Arnold Higginbottom.' Who is that?"

"Oh, he's another one of my students. Nice kid. OK, what's the present, Sean?"

"Ugh. It's *another* gift card to a coffee store."

Well, we're back again at the Bennett house, at 7:15 on Christmas morning. Ann's Mom is staying over, too. She's sleeping now, but she'll babysit again when Ann and I leave for work later. I finally got to sleep at about 4:30 last night, and then Ann and I got up at 6:15 in order to beat the boys downstairs. I wanted to get the movie camera set up early. That way I could get a good shot of the looks on their faces as they came down and saw how everything was set up. The boys absolutely love the train set, and it's continuing to run around the tree while we open our presents. Sean is pretending to be Santa, and he's passing out the gifts to everyone. I'm in charge of making a list of who gave us each present. That way, when Ann and I send out our thank you notes, we can match the correct gift with the correct student.

There are still lots and lots of packages under the tree from our students, but Ann and I have to get dressed soon and get our instruments and music ready. Remember, we have to go back to the church again in less than an hour. We still have to perform at the 9am and 11am masses, even though we gave up playing at the 7am service this year in order to stay home with Kevin and Sean. We're both exhausted, and I really think we'll have to reconsider doing all of this again next year. Right now, however, we want to try and keep wading our way through all of these gifts, because I know that Ann and I will feel even worse later on today. I finish writing the name on the "thank you note" list:

"Higg...in...bott...om."

"OK, Sean, what's the next one?"

"To Mr. B, Merry Christmas from Louis Svincterd. Is he another student, Dad?"

"Yep. You know him, guys. That's Louis, one of your babysitters. Good guy."

"Oh yeah, Louis. He's nice!" Kevin shouts.

"Uh, that's an interesting last name, Sam." Ann says.

"Yeah, his mom told me that it's a family name, and they didn't want to change it. But, she said when the family originally came over from Europe, the people at Ellis Island added the "d" on the end for some reason. All right, Sean, what's the present?"

"Oh, Dad, it's a gift card to a bookstore."

"OK, Sean. Let me add him to the list...Svinc...terd."

Ann and I always receive *tons* of gift cards to bookstores and coffee places each year, and are we ever grateful to our students and their families! However, I know that opening all of these is a really boring part of Christmas for Kevin and Sean. Naturally, they are much more interested in opening their own presents, which we finished doing first.

"All right, guys. Are you getting bored?" I ask.

"Yeah, Dad." Sean states forlornly.

"Yeah, this is bowing, Dad!" adds Kevin, as he plays with the trains. He continues:

"Dad, how come this pig's head is on top of a man?"

"Yeah, Dad. And, how come the train conductor's hat is on the cow's head?" Sean utters.

"Oh-uh-well, I guess Santa was a little tired last night, and he must have mixed them up. I'll speak to him about it next year. Uh, OK, boys. Let's just open a couple more, then Mom and I have to get ready for work. What's the next one, Sean?"

"This one is from Leon Snarfgblatt. Is that how you say it, Dad?"

"Well, the 'g' is silent. What is it?"

"It's a gift card, but this one says it's to a l-i-q-u-o-r store."

"Oh yeah, way to go, Leon! His parents must know how tough it is for me to be his trumpet teacher. Snarf...g...blatt. Next, Sean?"

"It looks like another gift card. Wait, these are tickets to something."

"To what, Sean?"

"I can't tell. Here, Dad."

"Oh my, look Ann. Ha...they're Lottery Tickets! I wonder if this student is going to quit soon, and his parents just want to help me out. Who's it from?"

"To Mr. B, from Eddie Glorp."

"Oh yeah, good old Eddie. He won't be involved in the trumpet world for much longer. *He's super lazy!* Thanks, Eddie! Gl...o...rp. How about just one more, Sean?"

"Oh, OK, Dad." Sean reluctantly grabs for a cube shaped box.

"I bet it's another mug, Sam." Ann says.

Over the years, Ann and I have been given about twenty-five Christmas variety coffee mugs from our students. Some are red, or green, or both, or they have Christmas trees on them, or pictures of Santa, etc. Knowing that we're a musical family, our students have also given us a couple of mugs that have Christmas Carol verses and notes written on them. Ann gets them all out every December, and they are lots of fun to look at and to use.

"OK, Sean, open it up."

"Look, Mom, it's a mug that says *'We Wish You a Merry Christmas'* on it. That's *cool!"*

"Great, Sean. Who's it from?"

"It says: 'Merry Christmas, Mr. B, from the Bierfahrt family.' "
Kevin and Sean start to giggle.

"I wike that name, Dad!" Kevin declares.

"Yeah, that's a good one. Here, let me see that mug."

As I lift up the mug, music begins to play. Wait...it's the tune to *"We Wish You a Merry Christmas."*

"Hey, Hun. Listen to this."

Ann grabs the mug off the table, and it starts to play the song again.

Ann is momentarily startled:

"Ha! I guess every time you lift up the mug, the music plays! It must have some kind of chip in the bottom of the cup. That's really neat. And, every time we hear it, we'll also think of the Bierfahrt family. Right, guys?"

"That's right." I reply. "I better write their name down on our thank you list. Bier...fah...rt. Got it! OK, boys, Mom and I have to drag ourselves back to work. We'll be home around 1 o'clock, so mind your grandmother."

*

Finally, *finally,* Ann and I are pulling back into our driveway. It's 1:15pm, and we've just finished performing at five masses in less than 24 hours. And, to think that we always used to perform at six of these masses up until this year, when we thought we'd try doing both "the working" and "the being a family" parts of Christmas. We're both so tired, and also mentally drained, that we can hardly drag ourselves back into the house. I can tell from looking at Ann that she is thinking what I'm thinking, too: we're going to have to give up *all* of our performing on Christmas Eve and Christmas morning, for the sake of our family.

Of course, we *want* to be home with the boys for the entire time on these two holidays. That's obvious. We want to have all of these memories of them coming downstairs to see if Santa had stopped at our house, and we don't want to have to rush off to work again. And, we want to be around Sean and Kevin without being preoccupied about getting our music and instruments ready, or worrying about resting enough, or trying to put train parts together at 3:30 in the morning.

Ann and I are still somewhat torn about what to do, however. Being professional musicians means we are self-employed, and unlike many other vocations we don't make any money unless we are actually working. Playing at all of these services is a nice chunk of our income, especially since school is out and we only teach a few lessons during the last two weeks of December. The money we earn from performing goes a long way towards buying Christmas presents, too.

Also, Ann and I have spent years developing great relationships with many of these church music directors, and if we turn them down for all of the Christmas gigs, we may not get called back in the future. We may not even get called again to play at other church services either, such as Easter, Confirmation, or any weddings at the church. Unfortunately, I can envision our income dwindling for the next several years if we give up performing on Christmas. That's why Ann and I are so undecided about this whole situation; while we'll be able to be home with the boys, we won't have much money to do anything, or to buy many presents!

Oh well, I think our minds are made up. Ann is going upstairs to take a nap, and I'll drag myself over to a chair by the Christmas tree to crash for a while. I'm guessing that when the boys are teenagers, they won't care about this whole Christmas morning scene anymore. Maybe Ann and I can try and get back into the gigging circuit at that point. Que sera sera!

As I settle into the chair, I notice that under the tree there are *still* two more student gifts remaining to be opened.

"Hey Kevin and Sean. Can you guys help me open these last two presents?"

The boys are still busy playing with their new train set, as well as with all the teeny people and animals that go with it.

"OK, Dad. Uh, Dad, you look bad. Are you OK?" asks Sean.

"Yeah Dad, you look sick!" shouts Kevin. Are you OK, Dad?"

"Yeah, guys, I'm just a little tired. I'll be OK."

Sean has another question:

"Hey Dad, why is this horse's head on top of a bed in the train conductor's house?"

Kevin pipes up, too:

"Dad, how come this man doesn't have a head on?"

"Oh, uh, remember how I told you guys that Santa was super tired last night? He must have gotten them a little mixed up."

"Oh, that's OK, Dad." Kevin replies. "I like this guy with no head...he's fun! I'm gonna call him Hawwy!"

"That's a good idea, Kevin. Now, can you hand me that package from behind the tree?"

"Here, Dad." says Sean. "It's shaped like another trumpet!"

Another trumpet, oh my! During my teaching career, I must have been given about thirty or forty different kinds of decorative "trumpet" gifts from my students. Many of them are very fancy, and are made out of brass or crystal, with engraved messages from the family. A lot of them are ornaments to be placed on the Christmas tree, or to be hung on a wall during the holiday season. One is a giant sized wreath in the shape of a trumpet that we hang outside on the front door. I've also received trumpet designed pens, doorknockers, money clips, belt buckles, shoehorns, and bottle openers. They are all wonderful gifts, and are very thoughtful ideas, and I appreciate having them all! I can't even imagine what kind of "trumpet" this next gift might be!

"Go ahead and open it, Sean."

"Look, Dad, it's a...trumpet lamp!"

Oh...that's cool! I've had people tell me that I should make my own trumpet into a lamp, but I always hoped they were kidding. Let's see, this one is about two feet tall, and is in the shape of a trumpet. t would make a great desk lamp.

"Who is this one from, Sean?"

"It says: 'Merry Christmas, Mr. B. From Jerry Berryperry.' "

"All right, let me write that name down for the list. Jer-ry-Ber-ry-per-ry. Got it! Now, there's only one gift to go. Open it up, Sean!"

"OK, Dad. It's a big package. I think it's a...wreaf."

Sean's still missing a few teeth, you understand.

"You mean a wreath?"

"Yeah, a wreaf, Dad, full of music stuff. It's pretty!"

Sean hands it to me...*WOW! This is amazing!* It's an ornamental red, green, and white Christmas wreath. It's about twenty inches in diameter, and it's got three layers of ruffles, red and gold lace, and gold beads. There are even music notes sewn into it, along with a red velvet bow. And, attached to the wreath is a little brass trumpet. I wonder where they found something like this?

"Sean, let's go show this to Mom."

We head upstairs to wake up Ann. I know that she wants to sleep, but she'll be happy to see this wreath (I hope).

"Mom, look."

"Uh, uh, what is it, Sean?"

"Mom, look at this *cool wreaf!*"

"Cool what?"

"The wreaf, Mom!"

"Oh...oh my! That's *wonderful*. Where did we get it?"

"From Dad's student Barry and the Finnegan family."

"Oh, that makes sense. Doesn't Mrs. Finnegan run that sewing business, Sam?"

Ann studies the wreath more closely:

"Just look at all the detail in this. Sam, I bet Mrs. Finnegan sewed this herself by hand. That's an *unbelievable* present. Thanks for showing it to me, guys, but can I please go back to sleep now?"

"Sure, Mom! We'll be quiet!"

Sean and I go back downstairs. I'm thinking that I can finally collapse into this chair for a while, but Sean has another idea:

"Dad, can I play that *'Fantasia'* video again? I want to conduct some more!"

"Oh, I guess so, Sean. But, please keep the sound down very quiet because your Mom is sleeping, OK? And, Sean, I may snooze in this chair for a little while, too. It's just because Mom and I have had to work really hard these past two days. But, you can go ahead and start it."

Sean got the movie *"Fantasia"* for his birthday in November, and one of the scenes in the film has the Philadelphia Orchestra performing a Bach piece, under the direction of the famous conductor, Leopold Stokowski. The movie shows a camera that's looking from behind Stokowski while the Bach piece is being played, just like the view an audience would have of the conductor at a concert. Sean has become fascinated with this scene, and he just loves to conduct along with the great "Leopold."

To get ready for his conducting, Sean grabs a toy stick from one of his building sets, and then climbs up on our old typewriter box. The announcer opens with something like this, with Sean mimicking his voice:

"And now, the Philadelphia Orchestra, under the direction of Leopold Stokowski, will perform the Toccata and Fugue in D minor, by Bach."

Sean contorts his face into a very serious expression, to match the tone of the song. Leopold and Sean both raise their hands in preparation, and then the piece begins with a fortissimo flourish:

"Da-Da-Laaaa! Da-da-la-da-laaaa...Dat!"

The Great Maestro and the "Future Great Maestro" (Leopold and Sean) wave their arms passionately in unison while the orchestra belts out the piece. Sean grimaces, wrinkles up his nose, and flails his eyebrows up and down wildly throughout the entire song. It's a fabulous thing to watch, and I've already taken a movie of him doing it. I can't wait to show it to him when he's an adult!

"That's great, Sean." I exclaim, as I try to stay awake to watch him. "You'll make a terrific conductor someday!"

Ann must have heard the music, too, because she comes back downstairs to gaze at Sean's conducting.

"Go, Sean, go!" Ann shouts.

After several minutes, the piece ends with a very long chord. Sean clenches his teeth, and makes a giant arm wave in partnership with Leopold as they both cut off the orchestra. Sean steps off of his podium...er, typewriter box, then he turns, puts his hand on his stomach, and takes a big bow.

"Yeah, Sean!" yells Ann. "Sam, remember how before Sean was born, he would always kick inside my stomach whenever he heard music? I think he must have been conducting!"

Sean wants to know, too:

"Hey Dad, what do you think?"

"*zzzZZZ...zzzZZZ!!*"

End of the house-to-house era

CHAPTER EIGHT

"Well, Sam, it looks like we can't go to the show."

"What? Oh no, do you mean that he really does hav---"

"That's right, Sam. He does have the chicken pox. So, I guess at least some of us won't be able to go."

"Oh, man...that's too bad. Maybe we can figure out something."

Shoot...this *is* going to be a problem. We have tickets to see a very popular musical, *"Joseph and the Amazing Technicolor Dreamcoat,"* starring Donny Osmond. It's supposed to be really cool, and we read where Donny Osmond even flies around the theater on wires during the bows at the end of the show. It sounds to me like what they do at the conclusion of *"Peter Pan."* Ann and I were going to take both of our boys to see it, but now we've found out that Kevin, our three year old, has the chicken pox. Our son Sean, who is five, has had them already, so at least he can still go.

Poor little guy...even though he's only three, Kevin is really into music and singing and he's been noticing the ads for this musical on TV. Boy, is he going to be bummed! We've all been looking forward to seeing *"Joseph"* for a while, but not only can't Kevin go, either Ann or I will obviously have to stay home with him, too. How can we possibly get a babysitter to stay with Kevin when he's sick like that? *AARRGGHH!!*

Oh yeah, I just thought of something else, too. Ann and I are also going to have to change our teaching schedules around because Kevin has the chicken pox. We've been teaching more and more of the lessons at our house over the past few years, and for the most part it's been a good experience. Of course, we can schedule more students at home than we could if we drove to each individual student's house. That's really helped to save the wear and tear on our cars, and on us, too, especially in the winter! I'm sure that's cut down on our car repair expenses, as well as on gas purchases. Obviously, we can also make more money that way, since we can schedule the students back to back at home. However, we can't charge as much for a lesson at our own place as we do when we go to the student's home, since they are the ones taking the time to come to us. So, I guess we probably don't make that much more money in the long run.

Since we're not going from house to house for lessons as much, we've noticed that there have also been some other drawbacks. The biggest downside is that we haven't built the same kinds of relationships and friendships with the families that we used to when we would go visit them every week. It's fun for us to see the kids interacting with their parents and siblings, and to get a sense of what the family dynamic is like when they're all on their own turf. Sometimes they all have a good rapport, and other times they don't, but at least Ann and I can see what kind of environment our students are coming from.

There have been many, many parents of our students that we've become friends with over the years, simply by having conversations with them each week. We don't have nearly as much of that type of connection with the parents when they come to our house. Now, they just drop off their kids, and pick them up at the end of the lesson, and maybe we'll get a wave or a quick honk of the horn from them. We do miss getting to know all of them.

And, of course, we miss playing with all of our animal friends, too! All of those countless dogs, cats, birds, salafoofers, and "what-the-heck-are-those-things" that were so much fun to play with each week. Believe me, I often recall the pet of the house with much more fondness than I do the student. I wonder if those "guys" miss seeing us as much as we miss being around them.

All right...now, with our little Kevin sick, I better get started on my phone calls to cancel the lessons this week. I can't imagine that very many parents would want their kids to be exposed to a three year old who has the chicken pox, even if their child has already had them.

My first student is Ken, who is a high school senior. I've been teaching Ken for almost seven years now, and when he was younger, I would go to his house for the lessons. Since Ann and I moved into our own place, and I began having more students at home, Ken is now old enough to drive himself over to my house. For all of these years, Ken has been a terrific student...well-prepared, very talented, and interested in improving. And, his family is unbelievably supportive and generous towards Ann, our sons, and me. We even use Ken often to baby-sit for Kevin and Sean. They always enjoy having him come over, since he plays so well with them. My guys think of Ken almost as a (really) big brother.

Because Ken comes to my house now for his trumpet lessons, I miss not being able to see his family as much as I used to. Hmmm...I have an idea. Maybe I can teach Ken at *his* house again while my son is sick? That just might work. Hey...how about if I try and teach almost all of my students at their houses for these next couple of weeks? I'll call Ken first, and see what he says:

"Hi Ken, it's Mr. B. Guess what? My son Kevin has the chicken pox! So, I won't be having any lessons at my house for a while. Can I teach you at your place, at least until he feels better? The lesson would be on the usual day."

"Oh hi, Mr. B. I'm not sure, but I'll ask my mom when she gets home. I can call you back later, if that's OK?"

"Sure, Ken. Talk to you later. Bye."

"Bye, Mr. B."

I gradually work my way down my list of students, calling all of them to see if I can teach them at their own house for the next week or two. I've had to cancel a few of the lessons because we just couldn't work out a time, so I'll lose some money. But, I have been able to rearrange many of them at their place. By the time I reached everyone on the phone, or waited for them to call me back, the whole scheduling process has taken a couple of days. Plus, either Ann or I will have to stay home and babysit while the other one of us goes out, so we have to be careful when we make our teaching plans.

Actually, I think going to these houses again should be a lot of fun for me! I'll be going to several of the homes that I used to travel to regularly, and I'll get to see many of my old animal buddies again.

Let's see, first I'll be visiting Dave and the parrots. Ann and I still have Flappy-Bird at home, so I'll be sure and say hi from him to the other parrots. Then, I'll be going to Danny's house. I know that he still has Sport, that wild terrier.

Sometimes I can see Sport bouncing around in the car when Danny's mom drops him off at my house. That dog still has loads of energy! And, I can't even imagine what new kinds of lizards and slimy creatures that Danny may have by now; there's probably a Grimy IV oozing around in Danny's room.

After that, I'll get to see my singing beagle pal, Samantha, at Josh's house. It should be a really enjoyable day; at least until I realize how tired I am because I'm going from house to house to teach once again.

I'm still waiting to hear back from a few students, and one of them is Ken. I hope he calls soon, since I only have one time slot left when I'll be in his neighborhood. Over the years, I've always tried to teach the kids back to back that live close together, but because of all of the different activities of each family, that was a rare thing for me to accomplish. So, I generally ended up driving back and forth, going from one side of a suburb to the other, or from one suburb to the next and back again. This is one of the toughest things about scheduling lessons at the student's homes, and I sure don't miss that part of it *at all.* Oops...there's the phone. Maybe it's Ken:

"Hi, Mr. B."

Yep, I recognize Ken's voice (remember, there is no Caller ID yet):

"Oh, hi Ken. What's up?"

"Well, my mom said you don't have to come over."

"Oh, does she want to cancel the lesson this week? That's fin-"

"Oh no. She just meant that I can still have my lesson at *your* house."

"But, did you tell her that my son has the chicken pox? She probably wouldn't want you to be expo---"

"No, no, Mr. B. Actually, my mom said that I only had a mild case of the chicken pox when I was little, and the doctor wasn't sure if I still might get them again. My mom *wants* me to come over and try to get exposed to them. She said it's better if I have them now and get it over with, since next year I'll be away at college. So, I can come for my lesson tomorrow at the regular time, if that's OK?"

"Really! Well uh, sure. I guess that's fine."

"OK. And, my mom said that I could babysit for Kevin anytime during his chicken pox, if you want. She wants me to hold him and play with him a lot."

*"Oh man...*that's great, Ken! I'll talk to Mrs. B. about the babysitting."

"OK. Uh, can I talk to Kevin, Mr. B?""

"Sure, Ken. Hang on."

"Hey, Kevin. Your friend and babysitter Ken is on the phone. He wants to talk to you."

"Oh, OK Dad."

I listen in on the conversation, as Kevin glumly picks up the phone:

"Hewwo?"

"Hi Kevin. This is Ken. I heard you are sick. That's too bad."

"Yeah. I have lots of chicken pots all over."

"Oh, I'm sorry, Kevin. How would you like it if I came over sometime to play with you?"

"Weally? That would be *cool!*"

"All right, Kevin. I'll see you tomorrow. Put your dad back on the phone, OK?"

"OK. Bye Ken."

Kevin starts shouting at me:

"Dad! Dad! Ken's coming over to pway with me tomowwow! Yea!"

"That's great, Kevin! Let me finish talking to Ken."

"Thanks, Ken. We'll see you tomo---"

"Tomowwow, Dad!"

Ken's hung up the phone already. Huh...isn't that something! I know that Kevin has been really upset about all of this, and I sure can't blame him. Not only does he have to miss going to this cool musical (while some of us do get to go), but the doctor said that his case of the chicken pox has been unusually severe, and it has made him even more sick than a typical child normally gets. Kevin will sure be happier when Ken comes over to play with him!

"Hey Ann! You won't believe this! Ken just called. He said he only had a very weak case of the chicken pox as a kid, and that his mom wants him to come over tomowwow so he can be exposed to them now. They're not sure if what Ken had was enough to make him immune, and they don't want him to get them when he's away

at college. His mom even wants him to baby-sit, too! What do you think of that?!"

"*Wow!* I'm not sure what to say, Sam. I think I should still stay home with Kevin while you guys go to the show. But, I know Kevin would love it if Ken paid him a visit! And, did you just say 'tomowwow?' "

It should be quite an interesting day tomorrow. First, I'll teach Ken his trumpet lesson, then I'll take our boy Sean to see *"Joseph"* while Ann, Ken, and Kevin, our poor little chicken-man, hang out here. Today, I'm making my teaching rounds at all of the student's houses, and I'll get to reacquaint myself with my old pet cronies. I haven't been back to some of these houses for years. I'm ringing Dave's doorbell now. He starts to open the door:

"Hi, Dave. It's nice to be back here agai---"

"*Misss-ter B! Misss-ter B!*"

"*Baah...trumpets rock!*"

"*Baah...howz Fla-ppy Bird? Fla-ppy Bird?*"

"Hey, Mr. B." Dave says. "The birds are glad that you came over. They had some things that they wanted to tell you."

"Hi guys!" I reply to my aviary buddies. "It's great to see you! Flappy is fine, and he says hi, too."

In unison, the birds answer:

"*Baah!!*"

*

After Dave's lesson, I drive next to Danny's house. As I knock on his door, I can hear Sport:

"*Yipe-yipe-yipe-yipe-yipe!!!*"

"Hey Sport, how ya doin', boy?" I ask through the closed door.

"*Yipe-yipe-yipe-yipe-yipe!!!*"

I think Sport recognizes my voice. Danny opens the door:

"*Ooh-ooh, it's so cool you came over, Mr. B. Look at my new guy!*"

"Hi, Danny. Who ya got now?"

"Ooh...it's a cousin of the foofer family, but he's really more of a feefer than a foofer, Mr. B. Can't you tell? His name is Rhymy, 'cause it rhymes with Grimy. I thought of it all by myself. Isn't that a good name?"

"Yeah, Danny, that's a real cool nam---*look out Danny, Rhymy's getting loose!"*

"Oh, there, I got him! Thanks, Mr. B, that was close! Remember how I couldn't find Grimy after that time he got away? That made me sad."

"Yeah, Danny, I remember. But, now you have Rhymy."

Shhh. I never did tell Danny what happened to poor Grimy.

*

And then, I continue on to Josh's house. His crooning beagle Samantha greets me at the door, with her bottom half and tail wiggling vigorously:

"ohrrr-OHRRR-OHRRRRRRR!!!"

"Hi Mr. B." Josh says. "I think Samantha wants to know if we can play a jazz duet today. She's missed her singing practice since I started coming over to your house for my lessons."

"Sure, Samantha. We can play one right now, OK?"

"ohrrr-OHRRR-OHRRRRRRR!!!"

*

What a fun day that was for me yesterday! But, since I was travelling from house to house, I am a lot more tired after teaching that I normally would get when I stay at home to give the lessons. And, I wasted enough time in the car that I could have taught two more students, if all of the lessons had been at my own house. Oh well, it sure was nice to see my animal cohorts once more!

Here comes Ken now for his lesson. With his face full of chicken "pots," Kevin sees him driving up:

"Dad, that's Ken! Yea!! Hi Ken!"

"Oh my, Kevin, look at all of those chicken pox!" Ken exclaims. "How do you feel?"

"OK, I guess. Can we make set-ups now, Ken?"

Uh-oh, I better interrupt:

"Well, not just yet, Kevin. Ken's going to have his trumpet lesson first, remember?"

"Oh yeah, Dad. *Huwwy up, OK!"*

"OK."

Ken and I "huwwy up" through his lesson, and then Sean and I go to the theater to check out *"Joseph."* As we leave, I can see that Kevin and Ken are already busy making set-ups. Maybe Ann can finally get a little rest after taking care of our chicken pox tyke for the past week.

*

A few months have now passed, and Ken is over at my house finishing up his final trumpet lesson. He's leaving for college in two days. I tell him:

"Ken, good luck, man. You've been a tremendous student, and you're family is terrific, too. And, you've become a great friend to my sons. We can't thank you enough! Oh, and, by the way, whatever happened with you and the chicken pox?"

"Oh, I never got them, Mr. B. The doctor said that the minor case I had years ago must have been enough to make me immune. But, I sure had lots of fun that day playing with Kevin, and I'm still glad that I came over!"

My sons hear Ken's voice, and they come running into the room. Sean shouts out:

"Are you done with the lesson yet, Dad? We wanted to say good-bye to Ken!"

"Yes, we're done. Tell Ken what I told you, OK?"

Sean is forlorn:

"Oh, yeah. We're sad you're leaving, but good luck in college!"

Then Kevin adds, in a rather gloomy tone:

"Yeah, Ken, good wuck in cowwege. Can you pway with us when you come home?"

"You bet, guys. I sure will."

*

Two other students that I have been teaching at my home are the Ford brothers, Scott and Luke. Scott is a high school junior, and Luke's an eighth grader. Both boys are very respectful, and have kind personalities. They look me in the eye when I'm talking, which is not always a very common trait amongst students. At their lessons, they'll try and implement my suggestions about how to improve their trumpet playing, and then they'll go home and work on these ideas, too. They don't want to disappoint me the following week.

Since the brothers live about thirty minutes from my house, their dad drives both of them over at the same time to save himself extra trips back and forth. Scott will wait upstairs while Luke has his lesson, and then they'll switch. They usually bring some homework to do, or a book to read while they're waiting. I've also noticed lately that they've been getting more interested in doing other recreational activities when they're waiting upstairs.

Now that our sons Sean and Kevin are ages five and three, they have *lots and lots* of toys spread out all over the floor of our house. They do have a toy chest to put them in, but the toys are often still scattered around the first floor when Scott and Luke arrive at 6:30 in the evening. Most of our son's toys are Legos, building blocks, and Playmobil sets. The boys love to build cities, train stations, towers, zoos, and all sorts of combinations of these places. They call these combinations their "set-ups." Here's a typical conversation that occurs several times a day:

"What are you gonna do now, guys?" I ask.

Sean puffs out his chest:

"I'm gonna make some more set-ups!"

Followed by Kevin, who emphatically adds:

"And I'm gonna help!"

As part of these toy collections, Sean and Kevin also have dozens of "citizens" to inhabit these different lands, and these people run the gamut of history from the medieval era through futuristic space-age adventurers. The boys get a kick out of mixing up these townspeople in strange ways. I might see an astronaut riding on a horse, or a knight sitting inside of a train. They can combine their clothes, too. I especially like it when there's a space helmet being worn by a 13th century monk. And, there are also plenty of farm and zoo animals that are part of these toy sets.

Kevin and Sean usually play quietly with each other when I'm teaching in the basement. Ann and I often take turns playing with the boys when the other one of us is teaching. I can hear my guys using different voices, softly pretending to be some of the many characters in their "set-ups."

As I'm teaching Luke today, I start to hear some unusual sounds coming from upstairs. Our living room is directly above my teaching space in the basement. We have hardwood floors on the first floor, and they're only covered by area rugs. Because of this, my students and I can hear every voice, footstep, crashing toy, and wooden floor squeak that's coming from upstairs.

Like most other days, I can hear Sean and Kevin's voices from above, but this time I also hear another boy speaking...a boy with a much lower tone:

"I'm going to steal your cows and pigs. *You can't stop me!*"

This is followed by Sean's higher pitch:

"Oh no you won't. My knights are riding in from the train station to stop you! Clip-clop, clip-clop, clip-clop."

Then, I hear some shooting sounds:

"Pzsh-Pzsh-Pzsh-Pzsh!"

Next, I can identify the lower voice again:

"No, you missed. Your knights are out of bullets. My astronauts are taking your pigs on the boat down the river. Splash. *Row-row-row, astronauts! There they go!*"

And now, Kevin chimes in. His three-year-old voice is rather squeaky:

"Aaahhhh! Here come my cowboys flying in the space ship. They'll get my pigs back!"

I'm in the basement, trying to explain some type of musical concept to Luke. When I hear this crazy conversation, however, I just stop talking, and Luke and I smile at each other. The low voice belongs to Scott, of course, who is playing with my sons. Scott is sixteen, and he'll be in college in a year-and-a-half, but I can tell that he's down on the floor having a great time playing with the set-ups. When Luke's lesson is over, he passes Scott coming down the basement steps. I'm sitting in my lawn chair around the corner, and Scott can't see me.

"Luke, you take over, OK?" Scott whispers.

Luke replies softly:

"Sure. Who ya got?"

"I've got the astronauts and some monks, and they've got the cowboys and knights. Watch out, 'cause they like to hide some elephants behind the train station. Then they bring them out to smash my dinosaurs."

"OK, Scott, got it."

What? I am *totally* mixed up by this point. Knights are riding in trains and shooting guns. Astronauts are on a boat. Cowboys fly in spaceships. Elephants are fighting dinosaurs. What type of *"Twilight Zone"* universe am I in?

When Scott sits down for his lesson, I ask:

"What were you guys doing up there?"

"Oh, just some homework, Mr. B. Luke has homework, too."

I guess Scott doesn't want me to know about the big adventures that are going on upstairs. That's OK. Now, as we begin Scott's lesson, I can hear Luke playing with Kevin and Sean, too.

"Keep your T-rex *away from my elephant!"* shouts Sean.

Since Luke is thirteen, his voice is in the process of changing, and he cracks every other word. He sounds like a cross between a yodeler and Foster Brooks:

"My tricera-uh-atops will sma-uh-ash your kni-uh-ights. *Boom-boom. Boo-uu-oom. AA--uu--aahhhh."*

This is followed quickly by my Kevin's high voice:

"No...here's my polar bear hiding in the barn. He'll win. *Ggrrrowwwwlllll!"* That's the squeakiest bear growl I've ever heard.

"I'll ge-uh-et those co-uh-ows. Here comes the *mo-uh-onk."* replies Luke.

This goes on throughout most of Scott's lesson. When we head upstairs afterwards, Luke tells him:

"Dad's not here yet.....*let's play!"*

Scott gets down on the floor, picks up a donkey, and pretends that it's kicking some middle-ages serfs. The four of them banter back and forth for a while. First I can hear Scott's low voice:

"Out of my way, you lowly serfs!"

Next, Sean chirps up in his five-year-old tone:

"Not so fast, donkey!"

This is followed by Luke's puberty-throated crackling remarks:

"T-re-uh-ex rules!"

And then three-year-old Kevin screeches:

"Pigs on a train! Pigs on a train!"

The four of them continue to play for a few minutes, until their dad arrives and rings the doorbell.

"Hi guys. Are you ready?" asks Mr. Ford.

"Aawww, can we stay a little longer, Dad?" *Pleeease?"* they ask in unison.

"No boys, we have to get going. And I'm sure Mr. B. would like to relax now, too."

Both of my sons chime in together:

"Can't they stay, Dad?"

"Sorry guys, but they'll come back next week."

Mr. Ford then inquires:

"Did you get your homework done, boys?"

"Yes, Dad."

Don't worry, I'm not going to spill the beans.

"OK, Mr. B. We'll all see you next week. Say good-bye."

All four of the boys reply sadly:

"Byyyye."

As they pull out of my driveway, I start to think...isn't this the coolest situation? Just imagine, here you have two teenage boys playing with my little guys. Not only are Luke and Scott being nice to Kevin and Sean, but these "big kids" are also enjoying themselves like crazy! I actually think they might be having more fun playing with my sons than they do during their trumpet lessons. They're excellent trumpet students, too, so I won't take that personally! On top of that, my boys are having a terrific time. It's like Sean and Kevin have two new big brothers coming over every week. How great is that? We're definitely going to call the Ford brothers for babysitting!

*

My sons have built their toy "set-ups" all over the house, including some in the basement, and most of our students are used to seeing them. Like the Ford brothers, I think many of my other boy students would like to play with Kevin and Sean's toys, too. The older kids all seem fascinated by the amount of possible combinations that you can make with these toys. Sean and Kevin change them around all the time, and my guys can remember which students have seen which "set-ups." When the students come in, they start asking my sons questions on how the "set-ups" work:

"Hey, Kevin. Where'd that pig go from last week?"

"Oh, he's sitting on that elephant over there. See him?"

Or, I might hear:

"Sean, who's riding in the train today?"

"The dinosaurs are inside. See their heads sticking out?"

"Yeah, but didn't the dinosaurs get run over by the knights and horses last week?"

"Yeah, but they're better now."

"Oh, OK."

Kevin and Sean just love to stand there and show off their creations in front of these big kids!

In addition to these cities, farms, stations, etc., my sons also play with oodles of toy cars, trucks, and Hot Wheels. At first, they just had a few of them. The boys put them all into a line, like in a parade. But, their collection kept growing as they received some birthday presents and hand-me-downs from older neighbor boys. Now, after a couple of months, there are almost one hundred of these vehicles lined up. My sons move them around often, and you never know where they might appear.

On top of all that, Sean and Kevin have also discovered some shoeboxes full of model cars that I had when I was a kid. I had all along been saving them for the boys to eventually play with. Together with their newer Hot Wheels racetracks and loops, they've got quite a lineup of cars stretching from room to room. And, every few days they even move them around and combine them with their other "set-ups." When my students call me on the phone, they often tell me that they're really calling to talk to Kevin or Sean, and not to me. They want to ask my sons questions about the cars mixing with the set-ups:

"Hey Sean, is that yak still driving the sports car?"

"Yeah, but we had to put the top down for his head." Or:

"Kevin, don't move that cow in the fire truck 'til I get there, OK?" Or:

"Can I fit that emu into the Volkswagen?"

Sometimes, however, these portable used car lots can cause a few problems during my lessons. These long lines of autos may stretch in front of the basement door, go across the top of the stairs, or even reach up and down the stairs. If you're not looking carefully, there's a chance that you might step on them or trip over them. We make our students take off their shoes when they come into our house, so that they don't track mud and snow all over. Over time, we've had a few students step on these cars, smashing the tiny vehicles and digging teeny steering wheels, tires, and headlights into their stocking feet.

Debbie is coming over in a few minutes for her trumpet lesson. She's in seventh grade, and she isn't very interested in the trumpet or in taking lessons. She's been playing for three years, but because she never practices, she's about a year behind the other kids. Her parents called me so that I could try and catch her up, but I haven't been able to improve her trumpet playing a whole lot so far. Not only does Debbie not practice, but she also forgets to bring her music to her lessons most of the time, too.

There's the doorbell:

"Hi Debbie. How ya doin'? Ready for another great lesson?"

"Uh."

That's her typical response to everything.

Debbie's not too keen on my son's set-ups and lines of cars, either. She turns up her nose as she steps around them:

"Those are *disgusting,* just like my little brother's, and he's *disgusting, too.* "

"Thanks, Debbie...I'll pass that along to Kevin and Sean. How 'bout getting your trumpet out now?"

"Uh."

I start to inspect her trumpet as she takes it out of the case. There are three piston valves that move up and down on a trumpet, and we use them to make some of the notes play higher and lower, like keys on a piano. They need regular oiling to keep them working properly.

"Uh-oh, Debbie. I think your valves are frozen again. They won't move at all...have you practiced this week?"

"Uh."

"Do you have your bottle of valve oil?"

"Uh."

"Do you remember how to oil them?"

"Uh."

I'm never sure if these grunts mean yes or no. I've tried to make her oil the valves herself at some of the lessons, but she procrastinates so much that I usually end up oiling them myself just to save time. Believe me, I know that Debbie is stalling, and I also know that she wants me to fritter away even more time oiling those valves. I guess I'll oil them myself again today.

"All right, Debbie, your valves are working again."

There's no response, so I add:

"You're welcome."

"Uh."

"OK, Debbie...now go ahead and get out your trumpet books."

"Uh, I left them at home."

"Uh."

That was me grunting this time.

Ten minutes have passed since the start of Debbie's wonderful lesson, although to me it seems like an hour. Since I'm tired of wasting time, I think I'll at least try and do something that's fun *for me* during her lesson today.

"Well then, Debbie, since you don't have your books, and it's obvious you haven't practiced this week because of your stuck valves, I've decided that we're going to listen to a recording of one of the greatest trumpeters of all time...*Maynard Ferguson!* You won't believe how high he can play...*it's amazing!"*

"Uh."

Maynard is a tremendous icon for trumpet players throughout the world. Hearing him play for the first time is like watching Babe Ruth hitting a home run, or Michael Jordan finishing a fabulous dunk. Even though you see it (or hear it), you just can't believe that some of these things are humanly possible! I often play recordings of famous trumpeters for my students, and Maynard is the person I start with, because he always leaves a great impression on the kids. He plays extremely high notes, and he has a terrific jazz band playing along with him.

I start the tape (remember, there are no CD's yet) of Maynard's version of the theme from the movie "Rocky." The kids all know this popular song already, and they get quite excited when they hear Maynard and his band. The band begins, then Maynard comes in after a few seconds, playing higher and higher into the trumpet stratosphere. I still enjoy it myself even after hearing it dozens of times.

"Debbie, how do you like that? Isn't he fantastic?"

"Uh."

"I'd sure like to play trumpet like that. What do you think...wouldn't you, Debbie?"

"Uh Uh."

At least I got two grunts from her this time. Maynard, you may be motivating yet another young trumpet student.

"Let's just listen for a while."

The song continues, but Debbie shows no reaction. However, I'm really getting into it until...

"What's *that!?* "

Debbie suddenly shouts out, as she peers about three feet ahead to a shelf in my basement. I can see that Kevin and Sean have strategically placed the head of a fierce looking toy dinosaur sticking out of a box, and it's staring right at Debbie. Maybe the boys knew she was coming over today?

"Oh, that's just one of my sons' toys."

"Well, it's *disgusting,* and it's scaring me. *Move it, now!* "

"Now, that's OK, Debbie, don't worry. Those dinosaurs just *love* music, too!"

"Uh. *Eewww*...what's *that!* "

"Where, Debbie?"

"On the floor, by my foot! It's biiittting mmmeee!!! AAAHHHH!!!"

As I look down, I have to suppress a laugh. Sean and Kevin have attached a rubber snake to the bottom of the music stand, and Debbie's foot must have touched it. I think the boys *had to* have known that today is her lesson day. Debbie's frightened...she gets up and starts running around:

"OOWWW!!!"

Oops, she's stepped on a toy car, and continues to hobble around:

"IIICCCKKK!!!"

Now she's gone over by a basement window, and a large, *real* toad is on the other side of the window, staring right at her through the glass! His big, buggy eyes are about three inches away from Debbie's face, and his feet are stuck on the window like suction cups. We have several window wells around our basement, and even though they have covers on them, toads somehow manage to occasionally hop down inside. Debbie's eyes begin to bug out to match the toad, as his amphibian stomach bellows in and out with every breath:

"YYIIICKKK!!!"

I'm trying my hardest not to laugh too loudly.

"OK, Debbie, sit down now. Nothin' to see here. Move along. C'mon, we can keep listening to Maynard."

She wasn't in the mood, though.

"Your whole house *stinks.* I wish I could go home *right now!"*

"Why, Debbie, do you want to go home so you can practice your trumpet?"

"Uhhh."

I turn off the tape of Maynard and look at the clock. Thankfully, almost thirty minutes have passed.

"OK, Debbie, I think we can grant your wish. Let's go upstairs and talk to your mom. Do you want me to write down the name of that album?"

"Uh-Uh."

I think that's a no from Debbie. Sorry Maynard, you've inspired more than one hundred of my students over the years, but you weren't able to get through to Debbie. As we head upstairs, Debbie and I dodge the line of cars and trucks on the side of each step. Uh-oh, I can see some little feet quickly scurrying by at the top of the stairs. I wonder what's about to happ---

"Oh—My---God. Eewww!!"

As Debbie reaches the top of the steps, her nose is right next to a bright red, foot long plastic lizard that my boys have placed next to the top step. Not only that, but this lizard is also standing in one of those fake vomits that you can buy. I guess Debbie is one of Sean and Kevin's favorite students, too, and they just wanted to leave her a nice greeting. Debbie continues:

"I'm leaving!"

Debbie starts to storm out the door to her mom's car. She's in such a hurry that she doesn't even bother to put her shoes on. She just picks them up and starts carrying them, but I can see that she's thundering right into the line of trucks that my sons have tactically placed in front of the do---

"Debbie, watch out for the…"

"Oowww!!"

Too late…with only socks on her feet, Debbie steps on a toy fire truck, smashing it into several pieces. She's now limping, and tries to hobble out the front door with a few tiny truck parts dangling from her foot. Kevin and Sean frantically begin gathering up the pieces, but they seem to be missing something. From the floor, Kevin calls out to Debbie in his three-year-old, piercing voice:

"Wait, big giwl! My watew hose is stuck undew youw giant toe!"

Debbie stumbles out towards her mom's car.

"UHHH!!"

*

Well, I just *cannot* believe it. This is it. Today is *the* day. After years and years, and still more years of driving from house to house to teach trumpet lessons, I'm now on my way to the last student's house that I'll ever teach in. *EVER!* At least I sure hope so.

For a long time, I drove to about thirty houses every week to teach trumpet students. But gradually, during the past few years, all of my lessons except one have been switched over to my own house. Several of my longtime students have graduated from high school, and they've gone off to college. There are many others of my trumpet "kids" that happen to live near us. I used to go to their houses for the lessons, but I've persuaded them all to come to my place now. And, whenever I get a call from a new student, I don't even give them a choice of location. I always tell them that the lessons will be at my house.

Some of my other students, of course, have quit taking lessons, quit playing the trumpet, and quit the band program entirely. I expect that they're now happy playing on their travelling tiddly-winks and curling teams. They get to have fun practicing at 5 am, or 11 pm, and for five or six days a week, too. But, they better not miss a practice, or the coach will keep them on the bench.

*Oh wait...how could I forget...*I've found out some interesting information through my other students over the years. Whenever I ask them what these quitters are up to now, they have told me that every single kid who has quit the trumpet for one of these never-ending teams has subsequently quit doing that, too! Here are some typical conversations I've had about this subject:

"Hey Ken, do you ever see Landon anymore? He should still be playing his trumpet, but he quit to be on that pickle-ball team."

"Yeah, Mr. B. I see him in gym class. He quit pickle-ball, too. It was too many hours every week, he said, and he got bored."

"Oh, really? What's he doing now?"

"Oh, he said he's not in anything anymore."

Here's another example:

"Hey Scott, have you run into Sydney recently? I wish she had kept playing the trumpet...she was good at it. But, she said she had to quit because the pig-Latin debate squad was taking up too much time."

"Oh, yeah, I see her just hanging out in the hall almost every day, talking on the phone. She isn't doing debate anymore, either. She said that the 'oach-cay' was an 'erk-jay.' "

What an 'aste-way.' I get so frustrated being a teacher sometimes. Too many kids start out just fine on the trumpet, and then the minute they have to put in a little extra effort to reach the next level, they quit. Worse yet, they're allowed to quit by their parents. Instead of trying a little harder, which will eventually make it even more fun for them, they just give up right away and move on to the next "flavor-of-the-month" activity. Of course I realize that very few of my students will ever become professional musicians. That's not why I teach. I just want my students to reach their potential in order to get the most out of playing the trumpet and being in the group.

But, by quitting the moment that the trumpet becomes slightly more difficult, these kids (and their parents) are giving up on an activity that could be enjoyable for many years, and they are letting down the entire school band, too. As I've mentioned, this quitting pattern tends to repeat itself over and over in lots of activities with the same students, not just with playing the trumpet. What kind of message are these parents sending their kids? Unfortunately, I know the answer to that already. I sure hope that all of these students who have quit are having a fulfilling high school experience, since now they're participating in...oh right...*absolutely NOTHING!*

Oh well, that's enough venting about them. It's their loss! As I drive, I'm getting closer to Andy's house now. Andy's home is the only one that I drive to anymore, and he's about to leave for college, too. It's hard for me to believe, but I've been coming here to teach for almost fifteen years now. I started with Andy's older brother Mark, back when Mark was in fifth grade. I think Andy was a toddler at the time. He used to stagger around wearing a diaper while I was teaching Mark.

After I taught Mark for a few years, I added Andy's sister Rachel as a student. Then, when Andy was about ten, I began to teach him, too. Before Mark graduated from high school, there were about two years when I would come over and teach the three of them all in a row! It's amazing for me to think that my own sons are now older than Andy was when I started driving to this house to teach Mark.

All three of these kids played their instruments through high school, and the older two kept playing into college as well. As a private teacher, I was extremely lucky to be able to give lessons to three siblings like that. Just imagine...I had ninety straight minutes where I didn't have to get back into the car and drive to another house. That was such a unique (and fortunate) situation for me, especially in the wintertime!

As I turn into Andy's neighborhood, I'm starting to feel sad that this will be the last time I get to go to his house. I'm actually getting a bit verklempt! Counting all of the family lessons during these years, I bet I've driven over here around 400 or 450 times...that is simply unheard of!

And now, just think, Andy's brother Mark is a lawyer with a big firm downtown. His sister Rachel is a teacher, and Andy is ready to start college. With this being my final house call, I can't help but recall the dozens and dozens of houses that I used to drive to, and about all of the students that I've taught in those homes, many of whom are now in their twenties or thirties.

It's always fun for me to reflect on the myriad of occupations that my former students are involved in now. Some became music majors in college, and they specialized in playing the trumpet. They've now become professional trumpet players and teachers, and a few of them are even competing with me for students and gigs...but that's OK, I guess. And, two of them went all the way on to get their doctorates in trumpet playing, if you can imagine that!

Many of these trumpet "kids" are now lawyers, investment counselors, doctors, and veterinarians. Several are involved in the numerous types of engineering, technology, and computer related fields. Plus, I can't even count how many are now teaching. Some teach music, but even more teach a variety of different subjects, ranging from elementary school, to high school English, to college tech courses, etc. On top of that, a previous student of ours is now the principal at a school where Ann and I used to teach!

I can recall with great fondness a former student who became a pastor. He was always very kind and encouraging towards children and adults, even when he was just a kid. His goal in life was simple: he really wanted to help people. *What a terrific outlook!*

Well, for the last time, I pull up to Andy's house now. He opens the door:

"Hi Mr. B. Last lesson, huh?"

"Right, Andy. I can't believe it."

Andy's now more than three feet taller than he was when I began coming over here.

"Oh, and Mr. B, my mom is home, too, and she wants to see you after the lesson."

"OK Andy, sounds good. Let's get started."

Somehow, I'll try and manage to get through Andy's lesson. I'm having trouble focusing, however, as my mind keeps drifting into the past. I keep thinking of Andy as a tiny tot, not as someone who is heading off to college in two weeks. And, I keep remembering how I sat in this same chair while I taught Rachel and Mark.

Since it is Andy's final session, I ask him what pieces he'd like to play. As usual, we end up having a really fun time, playing through some of his old solos, jazz duets, and we even toot a few pop songs to finish up.

Like so many of my old students, Andy plans to continue playing his instrument in college just for fun, although he's not going to be a music major. This is a fantastic way for a student to stay involved in music. Plus, when you are in a university band, you are already part of a terrific built-in social group as you begin your college life. The kids in these organizations have quite a lot in common, even in addition to the music. They are used to working together towards a group goal, and they have learned how to budget their time since they have the extra commitment of the band. Several dozen of my former students have done this over the years, and they've made friendships that can last for their entire lives.

After Andy and I finish the lesson, his mom comes into the living room, along with two visitors that I hadn't seen in quite a while:

"Hey, it's Mark and Rachel! How are you doing?" I exclaim.

"Hi, Mr. B." they reply.

Their mom adds:

"Mr. B, my older kids were coming over for dinner tonight anyway, and when I told them that this would be your last time at our house, they wanted to say hi to you."

"That's great...it's nice to see you!"

Their mom continues:

"Well, Mr. B, it seems as though this is it."

"Yes, I know. I really can't thank you enough." I reply. "All these years...I just can't believe it."

I turn towards Andy:

"Good luck to you, too, Andy. Let me know how things are going in college. And, Rachel and Mark, I'm glad you were here to say hello."

Their mom smiles broadly, and says:

"Mr. B, I just wanted to tell you one more thing. I guess you're finally going to have to find a different place to give lessons now. *After fifteen years, I have no more children for you!"*

AUTHOR BIOGRAPHY

Sam Bennett has taught more than 20,000 trumpet lessons over twenty years, which are the basis for the stories in *"Memoirs of a Trumpet Teacher."* He now teaches Band in public elementary schools, and also performs on the trumpet. He lives in the Chicago area with his wife (also a music teacher, and Sam's inspiration) and their two sons.

11939006R00148

Made in the USA
Charleston, SC
30 March 2012